Antique Lace

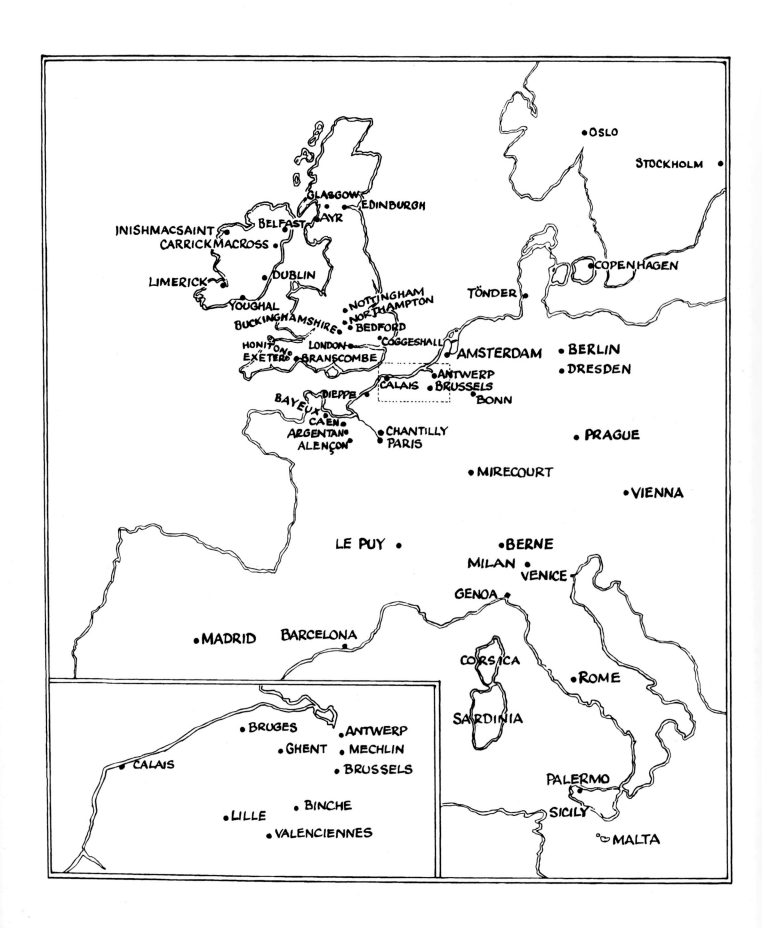

The Major Lace-making Centers of Europe

Antique Lace

Identifying Types and Techniques

Heather Toomer

Photographs by Heather Toomer and Cynthia Voysey
Line drawings by Graham Searle

4880 Lower Valley Road, Atglen, PA 19310 USA

Library of Congress Cataloging-in-Publication Data

Toomer, Heather.
    Antique lace, identifying types and techniques: with price
guide/Heather Toomer.
    p. cm.
    ISBN 0-7643-1384-3
    1. Lace and lace making--Collectors and collecting. I. Title:
Antique lace. II. Title.
    NK9404 .T66 2001
    746.2'2-dc21

2001003202

Designed by "Sue"
Type set in ShelleyAllegro BT/Aldine721 BT
ISBN: 0-7643-1384-3
Printed in China
1 2 3 4

Published by Schiffer Publishing Ltd.
4880 Lower Valley Road
Atglen, PA 19310
Phone: (610) 593-1777; Fax: (610) 593-2002
E-mail: Schifferbk@aol.com
Please visit our web site catalog at **www.schifferbooks.com**
We are always looking for people to write books on new and
related subjects. If you have an idea for a book please contact
us at the above address.

This book may be purchased from the publisher.
Include $3.95 for shipping.
Please try your bookstore first.
You may write for a free catalog.

In Europe, Schiffer books are distributed by
Bushwood Books
6 Marksbury Ave.
Kew Gardens
Surrey TW9 4JF England
Phone: 44 (0) 20 8392-8585; Fax: 44 (0) 20 8392-9876
E-mail: Bushwd@aol.com
Free postage in the U.K., Europe; air mail at cost.

Contents

Acknowledgments

All who have studied lace in recent years are indebted to Miss Santina Levey, formerly keeper of textiles at the Victoria and Albert Museum, London. Like many another, I have presented her with problem pieces of widely differing quality, technique and date over many years and have always benefited from her patient elucidation of their origins. Her book, 'Lace: A History', has been an invaluable reference source during the writing of this work. As far as possible, I have used it and Miss Levey's guidance in the dating and identification of the pieces I have illustrated but any errors are entirely my own.

I am also grateful to the late Kathleen Tipping and the late Valerie Cliffe for the generous loan of their lace for the photographs in **Plates** 12, 134 and 195; to Michèle Peloille for permission to reproduce the point de France flounce in **Plates** 36 and 38 and to Jacques Gaumé for the photographs themselves, and to Wilkins and Wilkins, London for permission to reproduce the portraits in **Plates** A-I and L.

Last, but not least, thanks are due to my husband for his advice and editing of the work in its early stages and to Richard Davin for his helpful comments on the finished text of the first edition which enabled some of the inevitable *faux pas* to be corrected.

Preface

It was an interest in antiques and craftsmanship that first brought me to lace; one of those happy chances in life when an advertisement in the local paper led me to buy the Brussels needlepoint illustrated in **Plate** 81. From that moment I was captivated. I started to look for the information I needed to identify my find but also to search out other laces in junk shops, market stalls and everywhere I happened to be.

Soon I found myself lecturing, exhibiting, and writing on my new-found enthusiasm and, in due course, the first edition of this book was published. It is with delight that I now find myself working on the second edition. This not only enables me to correct the few errors that crept into the first edition, to update information, and to share a number of new finds with readers but also allows justice to be done, at last, to Cynthia Voysey's photographs.

RD WENMAN KNIGHT, MARRIED.
ELDEST Dau.ᵗ of IOHN LORD
Of THAME OBIIT MAR. 9.ᵗʰ 1572.

Introduction

We all know what we mean by 'lace.' It is a decorative, openwork fabric; and, indeed, this was all it meant to me 25 years ago. Terms like 'Honiton,' 'guipure,' 'needlepoint,' and 'Chantilly' were as meaningless to me as to most people, yet only a century ago they were part of our common general knowledge.

Why was there a change? Fashion is partly to blame: fashion and technology. The struggle between hand and machine industries lasted throughout the 19th century but the economics of industrialized Europe allowed few people to earn a living by lace making in the 20th century. Our knowledge of a great industry and its beautiful hand-made products all but vanished.

Anyone who has tried to identify lace from the conflicting information in older books on the subject will appreciate the difficulty I faced in my early years of collecting. Fortunately for new collectors, the awakening of interest in the subject within the last twenty years has brought a number of new books on to the market, including the first edition of my own. Since then I have continued to collect and am still finding new pieces to intrigue, fill gaps and occasionally mystify.

My husband likens lace to cheese: a surprising analogy perhaps, but an apt one. Cheeses come in a variety of flavors and textures but, among them, there are a few types that have become renowned while a host of others are scarcely known outside their regions of manufacture. The same is true of lace and, just as the most desirable cheeses have been copied elsewhere in the world but the copies are sold under the name of their region of origin, the finest laces were likewise plagiarized. We thus recognize a few specific lace types by their technical characteristics but we can rarely know where surviving examples were actually made.

Of course cheese should not be too old nor too young, but the same cannot be said of lace: surviving examples may be up to a few hundred years old. How has anything as fragile as lace survived that long? Sadly, only a small proportion has but, when we do find an exciting example, most of us would like to know how old it is and, if possible, who made it and who wore it.

These facts are not easy to determine. Unlike silver and porcelain, laces bear no manufacturer's marks, rarely any date and few have come down to us with a believable provenance. It is only the technical features and style of design of the lace itself which can provide answers and these are among the factors that I shall try to elucidate in the following pages.

To this end I have treated each lace type in a separate chapter, listing the technical features which characterize it and illustrating classic examples. Laces which are similar or which might be confused are kept together where possible but, failing this, a direction is given as to where they may be found. In particular, the needlepoint laces are all grouped in the initial chapters, the bobbin laces at the end, and alternative techniques, such as crochet and embroidered nets, in the center.

I do not pretend to give all the answers as there is no room here for many of the less fashionable or prestigious laces made for home markets throughout Europe. Yet once the major types and techniques have been appreciated, it is these more unusual laces that intrigue and give added impetus to collecting.

Changes in lace designs cannot be treated here in a coherent manner, since periods in which different lace types were made overlapped. As far as possible, however, within the needlepoint and bobbin sections, the laces are discussed in the order in which they developed historically and the illustrations for each major lace type are given in chronological order. The portraits illustrated also give some idea of how lace was worn in different periods as the shapes and uses of lace articles are also important indicators of age.

Opposite page:
Plate A: Inscribed "…Wenman Knight,…married 1572," and of about that date.
The sitter is wearing a closed neck ruff of fine woven fabric edged with bobbin lace, with smaller versions of the ruff around the wrists.
Ruffs were made up from pleated lengths of fabric, usually lawn, often adorned with reticella embroidery and finished with a lace edging either of punto in aria (**Plate** 21) or, as here, of bobbin lace (**Plates** 127, 128). They were worn equally by men and women although women sometimes favored an open version that left the neckline bare.
The wrist ruffs of the 16th century were largely superseded by turned-back cuffs in the early 17th century but returned to women's fashion briefly in the 1620s-30s, though at this time sleeves were generally shorter so that they were worn just below the elbow.

How to Identify a Lace

Determining the basic technique

Lace is a decorative openwork fabric; but are all decorative openwork fabrics lace? The purist would say not. A true lace is one in which the pattern, and any ground which links the pattern parts, are built up gradually by the interworking of free threads. This excludes textiles such as embroidered nets in which decoration is added to a premade fabric.

To make true laces, a variety of techniques is used, each of which creates stitches which are peculiar to that technique and can be discerned in the finished work. The two main techniques are those of needlepoint laces and bobbin laces which are explained in general terms on pages 14 to 17 and 17 to 21 respectively. Minor techniques, such as tatting and knitting, are dealt with more briefly in the central chapters of the book. These also include details of other openwork fabrics which may not be true laces but are easily confused with them.

Machine laces are not within the scope of this book but a few examples are shown on pages 48 , 158, and 233-238 together with the hand-made laces which they imitate. Some distinguishing features are given but, since the range of machine laces is in itself vast, it is easier to pick out the hand-made laces by their own characteristics and to leave a study of machine laces for another occasion.

The initial step, then, when attempting to identify a lace, is to study its stitches and decide, with the aid of the introductory chapters, whether it is a needlepoint or a bobbin lace, or perhaps a mixture of both. If it is none of these, then the central chapters on alternative techniques may give an answer. But beware: machines also create fabrics with many of the characteristics of hand-made laces, so, before reaching a conclusion, look at the machine laces, as indicated above, and check that it is not one of these.

Classifying the type or region of origin

The basic techniques of bobbin and needlepoint laces were used in centers scattered throughout Europe and occasionally on other continents. The workers in each region tended to specialize in one technique: thus Venice became famed for her needlepoints, Devon for bobbin laces. Brussels was an exception; here both techniques developed side by side. Thus, once the basic technique of a lace has been determined, a step has already been taken in determining its type and it is the fine detail of its structure that must be considered.

In the early years of lace-making, laces had relatively simple structures and designs but too few documented examples survive for us to identify their country of origin with any certainty. Gradually, differences in technical detail or design were introduced in the work of various lace-making towns or regions and gave rise to the names by which lace types are still recognized.

The technical features which distinguish laces fall largely into three categories: the way the pattern is worked; the way the pattern is outlined; and the nature of the ground which connects the pattern parts.

The nature of the ground is particularly useful. The guipure laces (laces with open structures in which the pattern areas are connected by bars rather than a mesh, or net, ground) are to be found in the early chapters of the needlepoint section and in the early and later chapters of the bobbin section. The more common net grounds and the laces in which they occur are collated on pages 230-232.

Once a search has been narrowed to a few lace types with similar grounds, consideration must then be given to other features before a final classification can be determined. If the answer is still not clear, the reader must not be disappointed; even the most expert cannot always give a categorical answer.

Dating

Once a lace type has been identified, the date limits for most laces will already have been narrowed but, when finer dating is desired, what matters is the design and the style of an article. Lace was a highly fashionable accessory and, whether it was made in France, Italy or elsewhere in Europe, it had to be worked in the most up-to-date style if it was to sell in a competitive market.

To date a lace, whether it be bobbin or needle-made or of any other type, a search may be made through the whole of this book or through other reference works for a closely-similar design or style of article. Rarely will an exact match be found but illustrations with features of a similar character to those of the lace being examined may indicate a range of say 10 to 50 years. Before a conclusion is reached, however, one must bear in mind that many 17th- and 18th-century designs were revived in the 19th century or continued in peasant communities long after they had been discarded by fashionable society.

In very general terms, pointed edgings and geometric designs predominated in the late 16th and early 17th centuries but, as the new century progressed, stylized floral designs appeared and the points broadened into rounded scallops. By the 1650s, straight-edged flounces were being made in the Italian baroque style, with sweeping curves and scrolls of exotic flowers but, by 1700, designs had degenerated into narrow, trailing lines and curling tendrils.

In the late 17th century a new French fashion was introduced alongside the Italian baroque. This was essentially a classical style with ornamentation arranged about axes of symmetry but, in the early 18th century, this gave way to a new baroque form with densely packed, richly patterned designs and strong movement. By the mid 18th century, these designs had opened out into the light-hearted rococo style which in turn degenerated by the end of the century into minimalist floral patterns ranged along the edges of wide expanses of net powdered with dots and sprigs; alternatively it again gave way to narrow trailing lines, this time in neoclassical or branching forms.

In the early 19th century tiny flowerhead motifs grew into curving flower sprays until, in the 1830s, rococo designs reappeared. These were soon followed by more opulent styles, with massed bunches of naturalistically drawn flowers but, as these all-over patterns reappeared, heavy guipure laces also returned to fashion.

Laces in all the earlier styles, mixed or copied directly, were current in the late 19th and early 20th centuries.

A note on threads

Silk and metal threads were used for lace-making from its early years but few laces in these threads have survived from before the 19th century.

Linen thread was used from the 16th century onwards but was largely superseded by cotton in the 19th century, save in better quality laces, as cotton was cheaper and easier to use.

In this book I have used the word 'fine' to describe the gauge of the thread as well as its quality but I hope the context makes the meaning clear.

Opposite page:
Plate C: Unknown Gentleman by Cornelius Johnson, 1593-1661; late 1620s-30s
The falling collar (or band) seen here gradually replaced the stiff ruffs and standing collars of the early 17th century. The wide border of needlepoint lace edges a linen center (just visible) attached to a band which fastens high around the neck by means of strings; the tasselled ends of the strings are seen hanging.
 The lace includes a central panel with two bands of a scrolling design and an outer deeply scalloped edge with alternating floral motifs. The lace is designed to be made up into a collar; often edgings worked as straight lengths of lace were gathered to go round the corner.
The embroidered sash worn over the right shoulder is edged with a silver bobbin lace decorated with silver spangles (now more commonly called sequins).

General Characteristics

Needlepoint Laces

It may be difficult to appreciate that an entire fabric can be built up with a single needle and thread but this is how needlepoint lace is made. It is created on a design which would formerly have been drawn on parchment but is now more usually drawn on card or oiled cloth. This was often called a 'pricking' because stiff parchments were pricked with holes around outlines of the design but, to avoid confusion with bobbin-lace prickings, I shall follow current usage and call it the pattern.

To start the lace, the pattern is tacked on to two layers of fabric and foundation threads are laid over the surface, along the lines of the design (**Plate** 2). These foundation threads are couched down with additional threads which pass over the foundation threads and through the pattern and underlying fabric to hold them in place. The couching threads are the only threads which pass through the pattern: all other work is carried out on the surface. Eventually, when the work has been completed, the foundation threads remain within the lace while the couching threads are cut between the two layers of fabric to release the lace from the pattern, and are then removed.

Once the foundation threads have been secured, the spaces within and around the design motifs are filled with needlework, mainly in variations on the buttonhole stitch. Often the ground, or background part of a lace holding the motifs together, is worked first, and then the motifs are completed.

In 'guipure' laces (**Plates** 1-3), the motifs are closely spaced and joined both where they touch and by short 'bars' or 'brides' which cross the spaces between them. In their simplest form, these bars comprise a thread sewn to the outline of one motif, taken across the space to a neighbouring motif and returned to the first motif. More

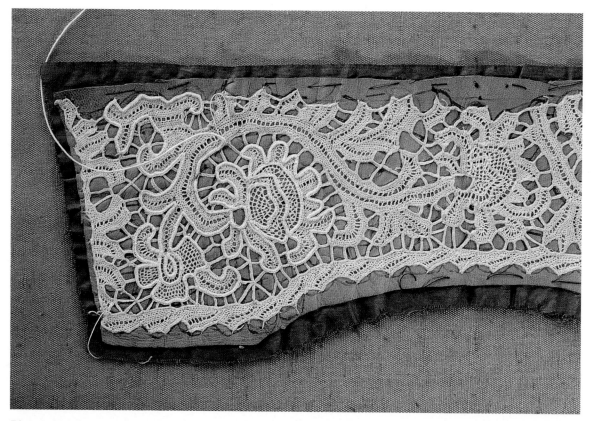

Plate 1: Needlepoint collar being made on a pattern drawn in black ink on green leather backed by darker green cloth. Green is favored as a support for needlework as it is less tiring for the eyes than other colors.
This type of lace, in which the motifs are linked by *bars*, or *brides*, is called a *guipure*; an alternative method of linking motifs is by means of a *net* ground, as seen in **Plate** 5.

usually, this simple bar is strengthened by buttonhole stitches worked tightly together along it and projecting points or loops, called 'picots', are often added as decoration. Where space permits, several bars may meet or cross to form coarse meshes.

In other laces, the ground consists of a network of fine meshes which may be created by loosely worked buttonhole stitches formed in rows and linked into the foundation threads (**Plate** 5). Most needlepoint laces have a needle-made ground but, in some Brussels laces, the needlepoint motifs are connected by a bobbin-made ground or are applied to a machine-made net.

Once a needle-made ground has been completed, the motifs are filled in with areas of close stitching worked over threads stretched across the pattern and linked to the foundation threads. When tightly worked, the stretched threads are completely hidden and the resulting structure resembles woven fabric (**Plate** 2). In looser work, (**Plate** 3), the loops of the buttonhole stitches and underlying stretched threads can still be seen, at least with a magnifying glass. The uniform, close work is often termed 'clothwork' although this term is more applicable to bobbin laces.

The motifs can also be enlivened with more open work created by different groupings of buttonhole stitches, some worked on stretched threads, others looped into previous stitches or formed into rings or stars. All these fancy variations are known as 'filling stitches', 'modes', or 'à jours'.

Once the design has been completed, the lace may be released immediately from the pattern. The result is a flat lace, an essentially two-dimensional structure. Alternatively, before being released from the pattern, the lace may be embellished with raised work. This involves further threads being attached to the surface of the lace, usually around its outlines (**Plates** 2 and 3).

The surface threads, loosely attached, may themselves constitute the raised work but often

they are covered with closely worked buttonhole stitches which form a smooth surface with a ridged edge: frills of picots may also be added. A clear result of this process is that the top, or right, side of a raised needlepoint lace is very different from the reverse, or wrong, side.

Some appreciation may now have been gained of the work that goes into a needlepoint lace, but the story is not yet finished. The completed lace with its design, ground and raised work, now released from its pattern, is often only a small part of a collar or flounce and must be joined to other parts of a design to make a finished, usable article. For this purpose, all the fragments of a design must be assembled, tacked on to a master pattern and sewn together invisibly.

In amateur work today, all these stages in a needlepoint lace will be completed by the same person but this was not always so. Lace could be made more quickly, more expertly and with greater uniformity by a group of workers each of whom specialized in a particular stitch or task. This was particularly true of the French industry in which more than a dozen workers might be employed on any one article, from the initial drawing of the design to the lifting of the lace from the pattern, the removal of the couching threads and the packing for sale.

Plate 2: Needlepoint lace motif in the making showing outlining threads couched down on to a pattern with areas of the design filled in with different stitches. The outlining threads are also taken into the centers of the motifs and show as thicker lines in the finished work. Part of the outline is being raised by the addition of surface threads covered with closely spaced buttonhole stitching.

Plate 3: Detail of the collar in **Plate** 1. The looser working of this piece compared with that of the motif in **Plate** 2 allows the looped structure of the buttonhole stitching to be seen; the more solid areas of pattern, termed '*clothwork*' are created by interlinked rows of stitches worked over supporting threads while the brides, or bars, linking the pattern motifs are formed by threads crossing the spaces between the motifs and covered with buttonhole stitches. A raised outline is in process of being worked; this comprises a single thick thread covered with buttonhole stitching, giving a simpler outline than the varied padding of the motif in **Plate** 2. This is termed the '*brode*' in French laces in which it is commonly used.

Plate 4: Detail of a modern needlepoint lace worked in a variety of threads and showing the looped needle-made structure.

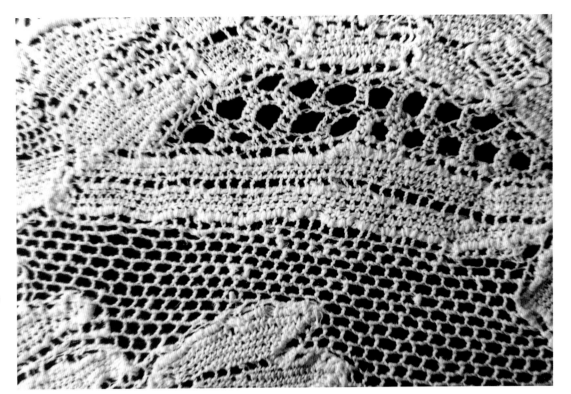

Plate 5: Detail of a needlepoint lace with a needle-made net ground. This lace would be made on a pattern in exactly the same way as the guipure collar in **Plates** 1 and 3 except for the working of the net between the motifs to link them together instead of the bars. The motifs have not, in this case, been embellished with a raised outline.

Bobbin Laces

While needlepoint laces are made with a single needle and thread, bobbin laces are made with a multitude of threads each carried on a small rod, or bobbin. The bobbins, which are 3-6in (8-16cm) long and usually made of bone or wood, have a neck at one end on which the thread is wound and are manipulated by their other ends to weave, cross and plait the threads together. The bobbins are in fact worked in pairs, one thread being carried between two bobbins. This simplifies the starting of a lace as the pair of bobbins can be hung from a pin fixed into a pattern to be worked and avoids the need for knots or loose ends.

In bobbin-lace making, the pattern is always called a 'pricking' since its pinholes are essential for locating the pins which keep the threads in place as work progresses. The pins are pushed through the pricking into a hard, straw-stuffed pillow which gives the lace its other name of 'pillow lace'. This, however, is somewhat misleading as needlepoints may also be supported on a pillow during working.

Bobbin laces, like needlepoints, comprise a design of motifs interconnected by a ground of bars or net which holds the lace together. The motifs are usually worked in a stitch called 'whole', or 'cloth', stitch since it forms a structure like a woven cloth although 'half' stitch, which gives a grille-like effect, is sometimes used (**Plate** 7). Areas of fancy, or filling, stitches often enliven the design as they do in needlepoint laces.

Although all bobbin laces contain the same basic stitches, they can be subdivided into three main groups: 'straight laces', also called 'continuous' laces; 'part laces', also called 'free laces'; and a third group of 'bobbin-tape laces' which combine features of the other two and are sometimes called 'semi-straight' laces.

Straight Bobbin Laces

A straight lace is one in which the entirety of the pattern and the ground of net or brides which joins the pattern motifs together is made in one continuous process. The result is usually a straight length of lace in which the design is repeated although curved and corner pieces and individual articles can also be made. The pattern is often outlined with a thick, or 'gimp', thread which is incorporated during the working of the lace itself.

Such 'straight' laces are distinguished from part and bobbin-tape laces in that threads continue from the ground into the pattern areas and out into the ground again. Also, in the clothwork pattern areas, the threads lie roughly at right angles to each other and parallel and perpendicular to the length of the lace whereas, in part and tape laces, threads follow the twists and turns in the design ignoring the general direction of extent of the pattern. Furthermore, the two sides of a straight lace are usually almost indistinguishable although, occasionally, tallies (see **Plate** 268) are worked over the surface on the right side. This type of 'raised' work is very different from the raised outlines common in part laces (**Plate** 10) and in needlepoints.

Although only a few bobbins (usually between 20 and 40) are needed for simple straight laces, several hundred may be used for complex patterns. The maximum workable width of a straight lace is limited to about 20 cm (8 in) and wider items must be made in strips or sections which are subsequently joined together.

Part Bobbin Laces

In part-lace making, individual motifs, such as flower sprigs or small areas of a design, are worked on separate prickings. When all the parts have been completed, they

17

are arranged upside down on a master pattern to be joined together. This method imposes no limit on the size and shape of articles that can be made and gives rise to the alternative name of 'free' lace. It also allows articles to be made by a number of different workers which quickens manufacture.

To facilitate the joining of the parts, the motifs are often made with an openwork surround to which the ground threads can be linked. As in needlepoint laces, the ground may consist of 'bars' or 'brides' to form a 'guipure' (**Plate** 10), or a network of meshes. It may be made with bobbins, in which case the ground threads are linked to the openwork edges of the motifs by bobbin-made stitches termed 'sewings' (see **Plate** 11 for further details), but in the 19th century the ground was quite commonly needle-made. Alternatively, the motifs may be sewn to a net made by hand or machine. The threads forming the ground do not, therefore, continue into the motifs as they do in straight laces.

The motifs themselves require comparatively few bobbins (between 20 and 60). Also the technique allows raised edges and ribs to be created on the right side of the work; these may comprise simple bundles of threads or strips of bobbin-made clothwork (**Plate** 10). The wrong side of the work, on the other hand, may have loose threads passing from one area of working to another. The right and wrong sides of a part lace may thus differ considerably.

Bobbin-tape or Semi-straight Laces

Bobbin-tape laces, like straight laces, are made in continuous lengths but are worked in meandering tape designs with some threads following the twists and turns in the design: the threads in the tapes do not, therefore, lie parallel and perpendicular to the length of the lace as in straight laces. Also, where edges touch or lie close together, threads currently being worked are looped into the previously made edge to join them together. This technique is called 'taking a sewing' (see **Plate** 11) and is also used in part laces. It results in a slight raising of the surface of a lace which is otherwise flat: this may not be noticeable without magnification.

'Sewings' are also used to link additional threads into edges to form decorative fillings or to form a net or bar ground between widely-spaced edges.

In bobbin-tape laces the width of the tape may be varied by the addition or removal of threads during working; this is a common practice in part-lace making but rarer in straight laces. The tape, which is usually worked in cloth stitch, may also be enlivened with filling stitches.

Bobbin-tape laces are distinguished from laces made with machine tapes by the way the threads are worked smoothly round corners, with no puckering or folding of the material, by changes in the width of the tape and the incorporation of different filling stitches within it.

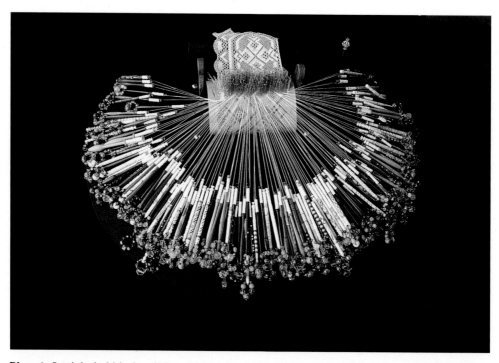

Plate 6: Straight bobbin lace being made on a pattern, or '*pricking*', fixed around a French roller pillow. The pattern is drawn in black ink on thick card in which pinholes are also pricked to receive the pins which keep the stitches in place as work progresses.

The highly decorated bobbins with their rings of glass beads, or '*spangles*', are typical English East Midlands bobbins.

The roller is seated in the pillow so that it can rotate and allows the pattern to be worked continuously. Lace pillows used traditionally in many regions of Europe are flat or slightly domed; on these, once the length of a pricking has been completed, the lace must be removed and repinned at the top of the pricking before the next length can be worked.

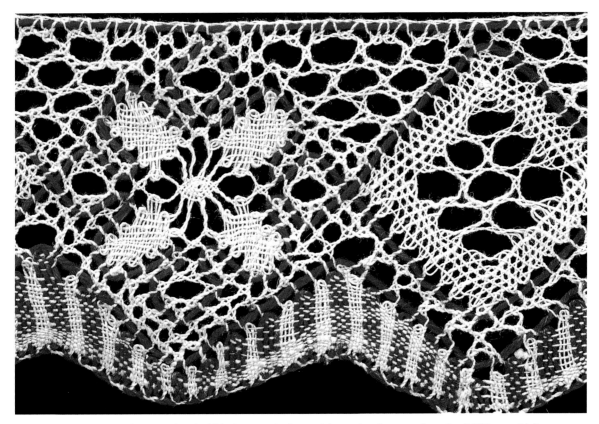

Plate 7: Detail of a straight torchon bobbin lace made from white and red cotton threads of different thicknesses, showing: a band of *'cloth'*, or *'whole'*, stitch of varying width along the bottom free edge, or *'headside'*; an open diamond formation in *'half'*, or *'grille'*, stitch; and other typical bobbin stitches formed by the crossing and twisting together of pairs of threads.

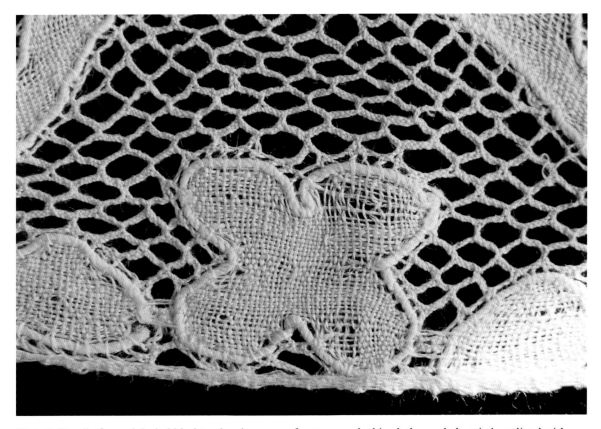

Plate 8: Detail of a straight bobbin lace showing areas of pattern worked in cloth, or whole, stitch outlined with a thick thread, called the *'gimp'*, and connected by a net ground. Note how the gimp is caught between the finer threads extending between the pattern areas and the ground.

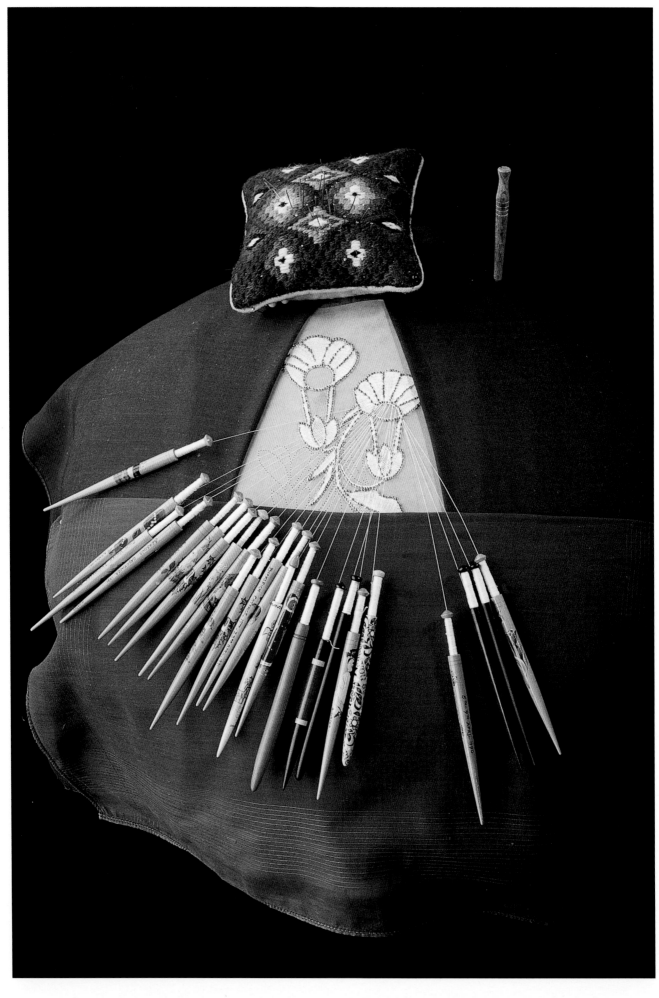

Opposite:
Plate 9: East Devon (Honiton) bobbin motif being made on a round Devon pillow. The bobbins, mostly modern, have pointed ends and no spangles as they are sometimes passed through a loop of thread to create a *'sewing'* (see caption to **Plate** 11) during the work. The motif is being worked by the part technique and, once completed, might be combined with other motifs to form a complete lace article.

Plate 10: Detail of a part bobbin lace showing pattern areas in cloth stitch with *'raised work'* formed mainly by bundles of threads caught loosely onto the surface; one surface braid on the right is formed in cloth stitch. The motifs are interconnected by plaited brides, or bars, each decorated with a point, or *'picot'*; the brides are worked with separate threads from the motifs and merely cross the spaces between them, being linked into the openwork edges of the motifs by a stitch known as a 'sewing' explained below.

Raised work is commonly, though not invariably, found in part bobbin laces; the right and wrong sides of part laces are thus frequently different whereas the right and wrong sides of straight laces are usually indistinguishable.

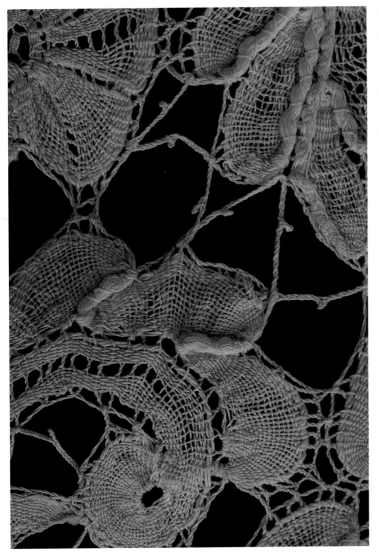

Plate 11: Detail of a bobbin tape lace: probably Russian (see also **Plate** 155c). In this example, the tape which creates the design is constituted by only three central pairs of threads, red, white and blue, and two outer white pairs. These threads follow a meandering path through the structure and are linked by white 'worker' threads which work backwards and forwards across them to form the very open clothwork of this example. Where parts of the tape lie side by side, the worker threads do NOT cross into the adjacent tape but form two-thread loops; during working, the lacemaker, working with two worker bobbins, hooks one worker thread from the current work into a previously made loop then passes the other bobbin through the loop to link all four threads together. This technique is called a *'taking a sewing'* and is also used in part-lace making.

Nine Worked Examples

Detail photographs are used to show the fine structure of a lace, which enables its type to be determined. To study actual examples, the reader must procure a strong magnifying glass. In many cases, 10x magnification will suffice, but 20x magnification will sometimes be useful.

Here, nine various pieces of lace are examined to determine their type, their date, and if possible their place of origin; they have not been illustrated elsewhere.

a   b

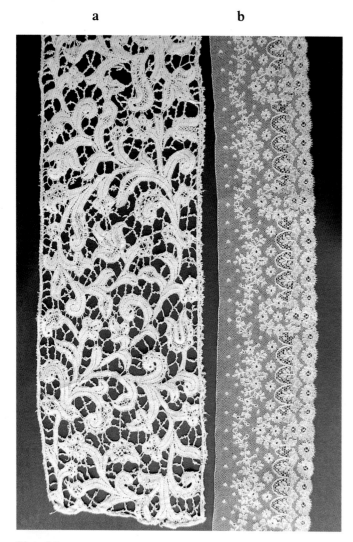

Plate I.1
a. EXAMPLE 1. Flounce. Depth 15cm (6in); pattern repeat 32cm (13in).
b. EXAMPLE 2. Edging. Depth 10cm (4in); pattern repeat 11.5cm (4.5in).

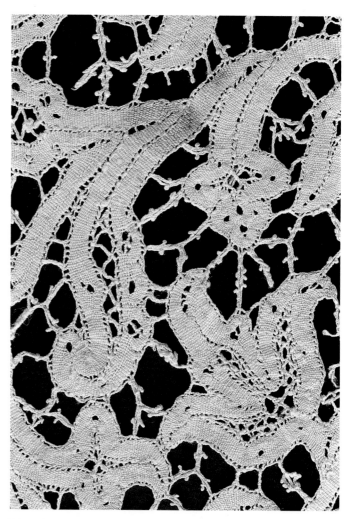

Plate I.2: Detail of EXAMPLE 1. **Plate I.1a**

Example 1

How was it made - with bobbins, a needle...?
Looking for obvious features, we see a pattern including woven clothwork: this suggests a bobbin lace. Looking more closely we see that the threads of the net ground continue into the pattern, suggesting a bobbin-made straight lace, but this feature also occurs in some machine laces.

The clothwork is unridged, the path of the threads in the net is clear and there is a gimp thread which is caught between pairs of the finer threads: it is cut at only one end of the motifs it surrounds.

This is a true straight BOBBIN lace.

What type of lace is it?

It has a net ground (- *is it illustrated on pages 230-232*)

The fine hexagonal meshes have two thicker sides which may be plaited: this is confirmed under strong magnification. This may be the Mechlin eis ground or the vrai drochel used in Brussels and Honiton laces. In the respective chapters we find that the straight technique and gimp thread are characteristic of MECHLIN laces: the Brussels and Honiton are both part laces.

Date and Origin?

Looking at the Mechlin chapter we see no design similar to Example 1, but what of the Alençon lace in **Plate** 58a? This has a similarly compartmented design along the headside and a trailing floral design nearer the footside; it dates from about 1850-75.

We also learn from the Mechlin chapter that the half stitch seen in Example 1 was introduced into Mechlin patterns in the later 19th century. This tends to confirm the date.

In the 19th century, particularly, not all Mechlin laces were made in Mechlin but the fine quality of this example suggests it is the product of a highly organized industry, such as that of Belgium.

Conclusion

A Mechlin-type lace of about 1850-75, probably Belgian.

Example 2

How was it made?

The pattern of woven clothwork again indicates a BOBBIN lace. This is confirmed by plaited brides linked into the edges of the pattern, unridged clothwork with threads smoothly following its twists and turns, and variations in its width and fillings - it is neither completely machine-made nor worked with a machine-made tape.

What type?

The threads of the bar ground do not continue into the pattern. This is a part or bobbin-tape guipure lace. Breaks in the design show it to be a part lace.

To identify a guipure we can start with the early bobbin chapters. We can rule out the geometric laces; but look at the Milanese work. On checking characteristics we find similarities - a part or bobbin-tape lace; flowing baroque designs formed by a varied tape with no gimp or raised work. 'Points to watch', however, directs us to Flemish laces (pages 132-139) and here we find similar characteristics. So: is it Italian or Flemish?

Looking more carefully at the ground we find many double brides. These meet in a manner not shown in the Milanese laces but there are similarities with Venetian needlepoints: a North Italian origin is suggested.

What date?

We can look at the designs in the Milanese and Flemish chapters and in the needlepoints. The flow and scale of the motifs are perhaps closest to those of the Flemish lace in **Plate** 148a, but the Flemish lace has a net ground. A quick check confirms that net and bar grounds coexisted, so 1670-90 is also possible for this example.

Before a positive conclusion is reached, however, could it be a later copy? Here only experience can help. The whole feel of the piece, its thread, its design, its technique, are right for a 17th-century lace.

Conclusion

A bobbin lace in the Italianate baroque style: probably North Italian, about 1670-90.

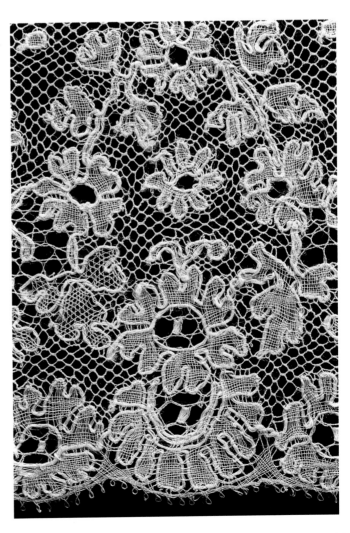

Plate I.3: Detail of EXAMPLE 2. **Plate** I.1b

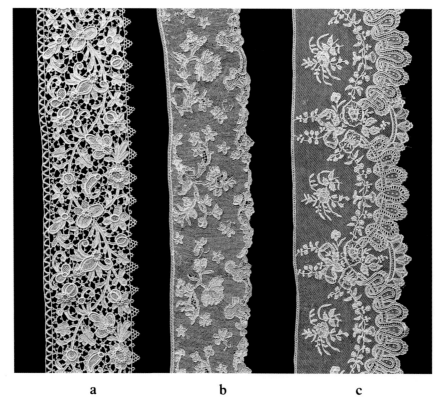

Plate I.4
a. EXAMPLE 3. Edging: Depth 9.5cm (3.5in); pattern repeat 16.5cm (6.5in).
b. EXAMPLE 4. Edging: Depth 8cm (3.3in); pattern repeat 42cm (16.5in).
c. EXAMPLE 5. Edging: Depth 13cm (5in); pattern repeat 15cm (6in).

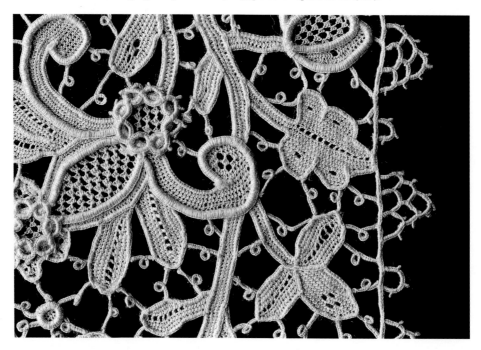

Plate I.5: Detail of EXAMPLE 3, **Plate** I.4a.

Example 3

How was it made?

The obvious features are the tightly buttonholed bars and raised work. This indicates a NEEDLEPOINT lace but one must check that there are no bobbin lace areas nor chain stitches of crochet — there are none in this case.

What type?

This is a guipure and a quick look through the book shows that most of these are dealt with in the early needlepoint chapters. It does not have the simple, symmetrical designs of reticella and punto in aria but a flowing, Italian baroque style. This, and the elaborate surface work, suggest a Venetian rose point.

What date?

The design is of a similar scale to that of Example 2 but it does not have the same vigor. The flowing lines of the stems are broken by flowers and leaves which curl back over them. The filling stitches are far more open, the thread and texture of the work far coarser than one would expect of a 17th-century Venetian work.

Conclusion

This is probably one of the copies of a late 17th century Venetian needlepoint lace. It may have been made in Burano, Brussels, or elsewhere in about 1900.

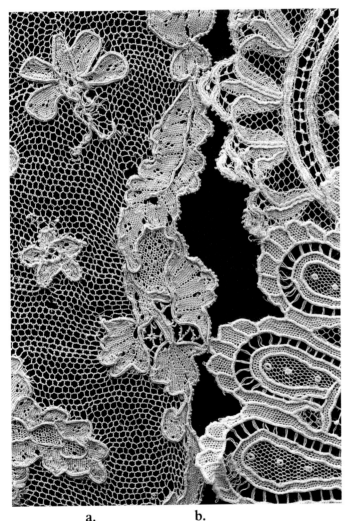

a.   **b.**

Plate I.6
a. Detail of EXAMPLE 4, **Plate** I.4b.
b. Detail of EXAMPLE 5, **Plate** I.4c.

Example 4

How was it made?

The close buttonholing of the raised outline again immediately indicates a NEEDLEPOINT lace. This is confirmed by close inspection of the ground and pattern.

What type?

The net ground has fine meshes with two threads twisted on each side; this is the French Alençon or the Burano ground. The hexagonal shape suggests ALENÇON and if we check the characteristics of French and Burano needlepoints we find that the FRENCH needlepoints have the tightly buttonholed outline; the Burano outlines are less well defined.

What date?

A search for a closely similar design in this book is fruitless but we do note that sparse designs were popular from the 1760s to 1840s. This example does not have the simple, repetitive design of about 1800; the freedom of drawing of its sprigs and its scattering of insects are closer to the styles of **Plates** 162c and 215c than of **Plate** 57d or 218a and b.

Conclusion

A French needlepoint with the Alençon ground, probably of about 1770-85, from the Alençon/Argentan region of Normandy.

Example 5

How was it made?

Pattern areas of woven clothwork indicate a bobbin lace but a closer look at the more open areas shows the looped structures of a needlepoint lace. The raised outlines also differ in different parts of the lace and a look at the back shows that the motifs are applied to the net ground. This is a MIXED lace.

What type?

Only one place is famous for mixed laces - BRUSSELS. Comparisons of the structure of the bobbin work and of the needlework with the Brussels chapters confirm this probability but what of the net ground? This is neither the Brussels point de gaze nor the vrai drochel but a simple twist net - its uniformity suggests machine manufacture.

Date and origin?

The twist net says '19th century'. The strapwork and ribbons in the design suggest post-1840 and fairly similar designs are seen in **Plates** 57e and 167e. The text indicates that manufacture tended to be outside Brussels at this time.

Conclusion

A Brussels mixed lace applied to a machine net: about 1850-75; probably Belgian, possibly Brussels work.

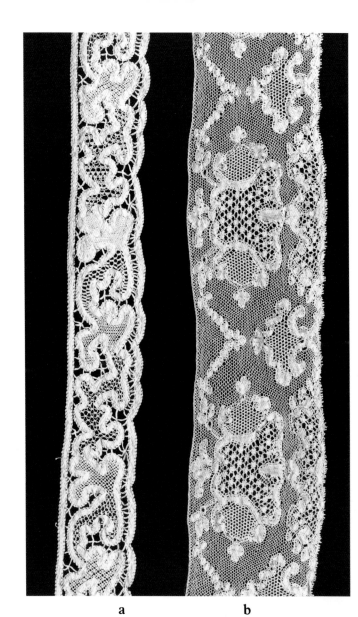

Plate I.7
a. EXAMPLE 6. Edging: depth 4.5cm (1.9in); pattern repeat 14.5cm (5.8in)
b. EXAMPLE 7. Edging: depth 8.5cm (3.5in); pattern repeat 15cm (6in)

a   b

Example 6

How was it made?

The obvious feature here is the meandering tape. This is folded over to turn corners. If we look at the chapter on tape laces we find that this is a sign of a machine-made tape. Also, if we look at the spaces between the tape, we see rows of looped stitches and brides covered with buttonhole stitches; this is a sign of needlework.

What type?

We already have our answer to this: it is a machine-tape lace.

Date and origin?

From the tape-lace chapter we find that tape laces were made from the 17th century onwards but were particularly fashionable from the mid 19th century and were made in many antique styles. This has an extremely simple stylized design, a little like those seen in **Plate** 107. The tape itself is rather different but **Plate** 104 shows that a wide variety of tapes were available.

Conclusion

This is a machine tape lace with needlepoint fillings, probably made in the late 19th century.

Plate I.8: Detail of EXAMPLE 6, **Plate** I.7a.

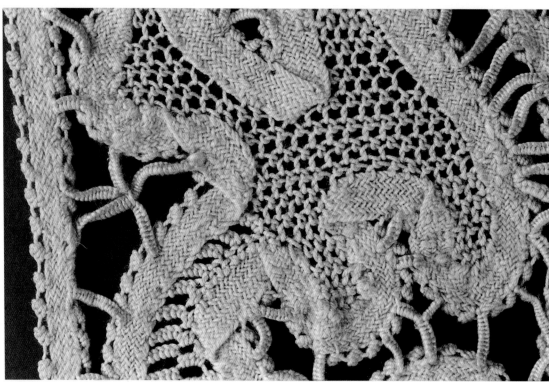

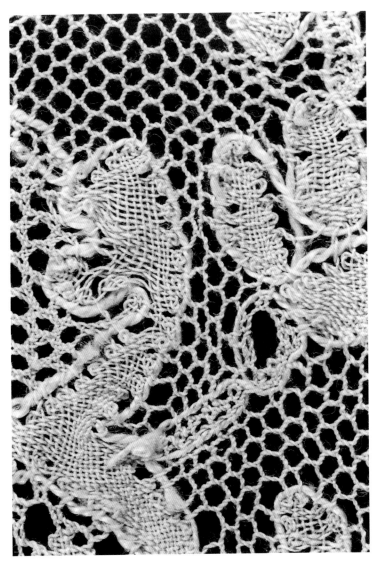

Plate I.9: Detail of EXAMPLE 7, **Plate** I.7b. Point ground

Example 7

How was it made?

The pattern areas look like woven cloth indicating a bobbin or machine lace, NOT a needlepoint. The pattern is outlined by a thick thread but threads pass across this from the clothwork into the areas of net and filling stitches; this would seem to be a straight bobbin lace but it might still be machine made. If we look more carefully at the outline we see that the thick thread is trapped between pairs of the finer threads where they cross: it is not run in with a needle. Moreover, the thick thread completely encircles some parts of the motifs and is cut at only one side of others: we read that, if it were a machine lace, we might expect there to be cut ends at both sides of a motif encircled by the outline. This is a STRAIGHT BOBBIN lace.

What type?

This example has a net ground so we can look at the summary of hand-made nets. It has a simple hexagonal mesh with twisted and crossed threads; this is the 'Lille' or 'point' ground found in Lille, Buckinghamshire point, blonde laces, etc. If we look at the relevant chapters we can immediately rule out blonde and Chantilly; this is not made in silk, nor does it have a half stitch pattern. It must be Lille or Bucks but if we read the chapters we find that laces of these types were made throughout Europe.

Date and origin?

If we look at the design we see similar cartouche shapes in the mid-18th century Mechlin laces in **Plates** 214 and 215 but, on reading the Lille and Bucks chapters, we find that these laces date to the late 18th century onwards: we also find cartouche shapes in the Bucks laces in **Plates** 238 and 240, although we read that designs were common throughout Europe and were revived at the end of the century.

Conclusion

This is a mid or late 19th-early 20th century Lille or Bucks type lace but there is not sufficient information to say exactly where it was made. Experience tells me this is an English lace.

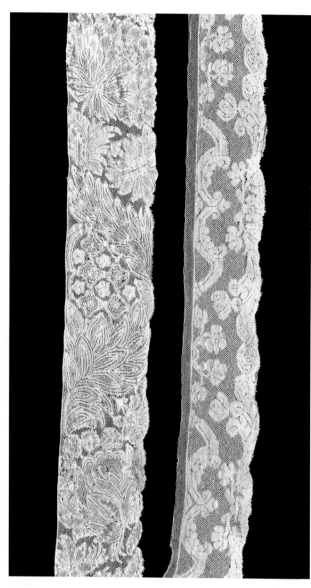

Plate I.10
a. EXAMPLE 8. Edging: depth 5.5cm (2.25in); pattern repeat 49cm (19.5in)
b. EXAMPLE 9. Edging: depth 4.3cm (1.75in); pattern repeat 18.5cm (7.3in)

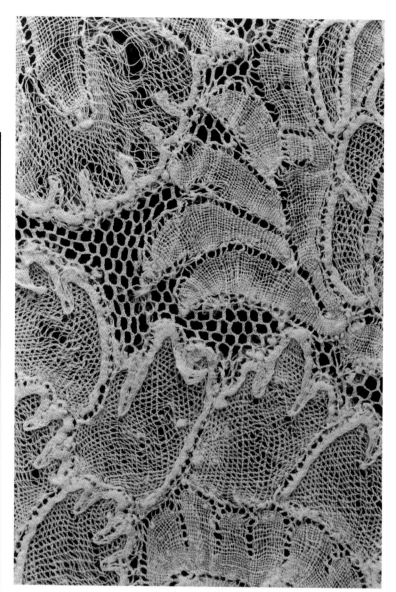

Plate I.11: Detail of the right side of EXAMPLE 8, **Plate** I.10a

Example 8

How was it made?

Looking at the details we see pattern areas in clothwork and in the more open grille stitch with raised rib outlines on the surface. Also the wrong side has loose threads from the ground crossing over the backs of the motifs. This appears to be a bobbin lace made by the part technique. Looking carefully at the ground we see a network of hexagonal meshes with long plaited sides. This also indicates bobbin work.

What type?

From the summary of net grounds we find two bobbin nets with hexagonal meshes with two plaited sides, the vrai drochel and Mechlin eis ground, but it is the drochel ground that is used in part laces; Mechlin lace is a straight lace. The drochel ground is used in Brussels and Devon (Honiton) laces. Looking at the two chapters we find that Brussels and Honiton made very similar laces which can be very difficult to tell apart but Brussels was noted for finer, more sophisticated designs. The design here is very fine – perhaps this is Brussels.

Date and origin?

Looking at the density of the design (the relatively large scale of the motifs with little net between them), we find something similar in the central Valenciennes lappet in **Plate** 198 which dates from about 1725-35. Looking at the Brussels lappets in **Plate** 163, the design of the central lappet is more dense than that of this edging while the left hand lappet is perhaps less dense but both have features in common with this edging: large feathery leaves; flowing movement; and areas of filling stitches. The central one is dated 1720-30 and the other about 1730-35; clearly we are looking at a date of about 1725-35 for this edging.

Before coming to a final conclusion one should think again about Honiton; none of the early 18th century Honiton laces illustrated is quite as fine as this example.

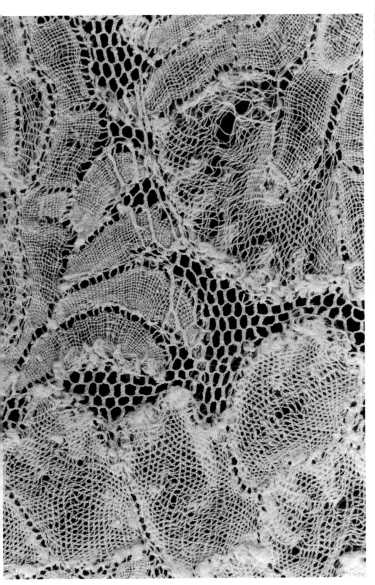

Plate I.12: Detail of the wrong side of EXAMPLE 8, **Plate** I.10a

Conclusion

This is probably a Brussels bobbin lace of about the late 1720s-30s.

Plate I.13: Detail of EXAMPLE 9, **Plate** I.10b.

Example 9

How was it made?

Again we see a clothwork pattern here which is very dense and flat; there is no gimp or raised work. The ground is a net with plaited sides to the meshes. All this indicates a bobbin lace and, indeed, there is no sign of the looped stitches of a needlepoint. The pattern is surrounded by a row of holes but, as far as one can see, the threads seem to pass from the ground into the clothwork. This looks like a straight bobbin lace but could it be machine-made? There is no outline, which often gives a clue, but the clothwork is very even; there are no ribs running through it, no strong directional bias. This does not look machine-made but, before coming to a final conclusion, what type of lace is it?

What type?

Looking at the net ground, some meshes look hexagonal and others diamond-shaped but they have plaited sides; the closest nets in the summary are the Flemish round ground and Valenciennes diamond ground: a fine version of the round ground was used in Valenciennes laces. This net is, indeed, fine and, on checking the Valenciennes chapter, we find that this is a straight bobbin lace. Checking the machine imitations we are told that the machine net may have a confused structure, not the clear plaits we see here.

Date and origin?

The fineness of this example, and the use of the round ground, suggest an 18th century date. In the Valenciennes chapter, the closest designs are examples d and e in **Plate** 204, dating between 1745 and 1780; the Mechlin chapter has a related design in **Plate** 214c dated 1745-60, although the motifs are perhaps slightly more elaborate than in this edging. **Plate** 56d, in the French needlepoint chapter, also shows an edging which is quite similar in its scale, openness and symmetry, if one ignores the bows; this is dated 1760-70. This is clearly the right date range for our example.

Reading the chapter, we find that the best Valenciennes laces were made in the town itself, but copies were made elsewhere.

Conclusion

A Valenciennes bobbin lace of about the 1750s-70s, but of unknown region of manufacture.

30

Plate D: Unknown Lady attributed to Paul van Somer, 1577/78-1621/22, but more in keeping with the late1620s-30s.
The sitter is here shown wearing a feminine version of the falling collar together with a whisk. The deep neckline of the bodice is edged with a broad, falling band of Flemish bobbin lace with a scalloped edge while an almost transparent collar edged with a similar lace falls over the shoulders. An additional narrow lace edging extends up into the neckline but is probably sewn to the edge of the chemise.

In addition, the sitter wears a whisk: this is a square of the same transparent fabric as that used for the collar, edged with the same bobbin lace, folded approximately in half and draped round the neck to cover the décolletage. More usually whisks are seen folded into a triangle but are worn in roughly the same way.

Plate E: British School; 1670-80.
The sitter is wearing the bib-fronted, or rabat, collar which replaced the falling bands of previous decades.
By the mid-17th century men's hair styles were so long that they concealed any lace at the back of the collar and so interest was focused at the front. The two rectangular panels of this collar are in an Italian-baroque style bobbin lace; this may be Italian or Flemish. The panels are joined by a very narrow band which passes round the back of the neck and is tied at the front.

Needlepoint Laces

Reticella needlework

Characteristics

1. Openwork embroidery in rectangular areas surrounded by bands of woven fabric with threads extending from the fabric into the embroidery.
2. Grids of needlewoven lines cross the openings parallel to and perpendicular to the edges.
3. Repeated patterns of geometric designs, stylized flowers or other motifs with angular outlines created by buttonholed, needle-woven and overcast bars with small areas filled with buttonhole stitches.
4. Cut edges of woven fabric neatened by overcasting.

Points to watch

Reticella needlework, braid-based reticella (pages 36-37) and the early style of free needlepoint lace called punto in aria (pages 38-40) were made in very similar designs and only the technical basis of the work distinguishes them. Look for the woven fabric with threads continuing into the design for reticella; the plaited braids of braid-based reticella; and absence of these features in punto in aria.

A variation on reticella needlework used a knotted buttonhole stitch in very densely-worked areas and was sometimes known as 'punto groppo' or 'punto avorio.'

Plate 12: Sampler of reticella needlework: English: 1650-1700. Width 15-16cm (6in); length 47.5cm (18.7in).
The woven linen fabric can be seen around the edges of the sampler and in the horizontal bands between the strips of reticella embroidery. All reticella patterns include distinct horizontal and vertical lines where the foundation threads of the linen fabric are strengthened with needleweaving but the rosettes also have distinct diagonal lines due to needleweaving on added foundation threads thrown across the open squares.
Collection of the late Mrs. Kathleen Tipping

Plate 13: Detail of **Plate** 14b showing: horizontal bands of woven linen with cut edges neatened by overcasting; horizontal and vertical needlewoven bars worked on threads of the woven linen remaining in the pattern; overcast and buttonhole-stitched bars; and picots.

a

b

c

d

Plate 14:
a. Linen band with pierced and embroidered whitework decoration and cutwork embroidery along the long edges: late 16th century-early 17th century. Depth 11.5cm (4.5in). This is a coarse example for furnishing use.
b. Linen band with reticella embroidery: late 16th century. Overall depth 5.5cm(2.2in).
This piece is of fine quality and could have been made for dress or for household use. (See **Plate** 13 for detail.)
c. Linen flounce with reticella needlework and a scalloped lower edging of bobbin lace: 17th century. Depth of reticella 17cm (7in); depth of lower bobbin lace edging 3cm (1.2in).
This is a coarse work of a type made and used as a furnishing lace, particularly for church linen, throughout the 17th century.
d. Linen band with reticella needlework: about 1600. Depth 6cm (2.5in).
The very closely worked triangles in this piece are particularly associated with Italian work.

Plate 15

(top: see **Plate** 21 for detail). Linen band with reticella embroidery and a pointed edging of punto in aria (pp. 38-40): about 1600. Depth of linen with reticella work: 5.5cm (2.2in); depth of punto in aria 2.5cm (1in).

Note the figures in the reticella and punto in aria.

(bottom right). Linen or cotton band with reticella embroidery and a pointed edging of punto in aria: late 19th century-20th century. Depth of reticella 5cm (2in); depth of punto in aria 4.5cm (1.7in).

There is little, other than the thread which can be judged only by experience, to distinguish this piece from the 17th-century work which it copies.

(bottom left). Square of reticella needlework: 20th century. Width 8cm (3.2in)

The frayed edges show that this has been cut out of a piece of fabric. The large scale of the design as well as the feel of the thread indicate that it is a late example.

Plate 16: Detail of **Plate** 12

34

History

Openwork fabrics were made in Egyptian and other early civilizations but the story of modern European-style laces begins in the 16th century. This, for the aristocracy, was a period of particular ostentation in dress, when rich fabrics, used in profusion, were further enriched with embroidery and couched braids of gold, silver and silk threads.

Linen undergarments, too, were decorated where they showed at the neck and wrists, often with blackwork embroidery, sometimes with insertions of knotted or filet lace (pages 104-107). Gradually, forms of whitework embroidery developed in which holes were pierced in the linen, threads withdrawn or small areas cut away to form various openwork fabrics.

By the second half of the century, large areas of fabric were being cut away and the spaces filled with needlework. Since the embroidery was based on the remaining threads of the linen which divided the areas into squares and rectangles and formed a foundation for the work, the natural tendency was to form repeated geometric designs. These continued, growing in elaboration, until well into the 17th century.

Much of this work was carried out by amateurs for whom pattern books, such as *Les Singuliers et Nouveaux Pourtraicts et Ouvrages de Lingerie* by Federico Vinciolo, Paris, 1587, were available. There were also considerable bodies of professional workers, particularly in Flanders and in Italy where this extreme form of cutwork came to be known as 'reticella', meaning a small grid or network.

It was these cutwork and reticella needleworks that came to decorate the wide ruffs, standing collars and associated cuffs fashionable particularly in Spain and northern Europe in the late 16th and early 17th centuries. Here the geometric patterns persisted even though more flowing designs, often with trailing plant forms, had started to creep into Italian work before the turn of the century. Such designs also incorporated animals, birds and people, often rather naively drawn and arranged at odd angles, with little concern for the relative scale of features portrayed.

As well as making a suitable costume lace, reticella was often combined with bands of drawn or pulled thread work, other forms of cutwork embroidery and with filet lace and used to decorate household linen. In Catholic Europe considerable quantities were made for church use and, in this conservative field, the geometric designs persisted long after fashion had turned to the flowing, exotic world of the baroque. The persistence in domestic work is shown particularly in English whitework samplers (**Plate** 12), many of which still exist and appear to date from the second half of the 17th century.

By the early 18th century, reticella was entirely outmoded in northern Europe but it continued to be made in peasant communities, particularly around the shores of the Mediterranean. Indeed, the persistence of this work in the Greek islands gave rise to the name 'Greek lace' when it returned to favor in the late 19th century.

The large scale of the designs and their clumsier workmanship often distinguish the peasant products from their fashionable predecessors but the dating of reticella is particularly difficult today; the elaboration of design and quality of workmanship in the early laces depended not only on their date but also on their country of manufacture, their intended use and on the personal taste and wealth of their owners. Added to this is a further complication. The lively interest in antiques in the late 19th century and the revolt of the Arts and Crafts movement against machine-made products led to a revival of interest in many forms of lace-making, including reticella.

In many countries this manifested itself in a wealth of amateur work, often in cotton thread on machine-woven cotton which is readily distinguishable from the early linen lace. Much finer work was, however, also done in various centers in Europe, sometimes in linen thread, in designs taken directly from the old pattern books. Particular exponents of this work were members of the Aemelia Ars Society in Bologna, Italy, who made extremely good reproductions of many antique lace types. Many of these later reticellas, now over a century old, are not easily distinguishable from their earlier counterparts; even the expert, with long experience, cannot always be sure.

In Great Britain an industry was based in the Lake District where cloth was again being woven on hand looms from hand-spun linen thread. The product was renamed 'Ruskin Work' after one of the leading members of the Arts and Crafts movement.

Braid-based reticella needlework

Characteristics

1. Foundation of plaited braids, some forming rectangular grids and with others along shaped edges.
2. Repeated patterns of geometric designs, stylized flowers or other motifs with angular outlines created by buttonholed, needlewoven and overcast bars with small areas filled with buttonhole stitches.
3. Free edges are often dentate (finished with a row of points), or scalloped, with a symmetrical motif filling each point or scallop.

Plate 17: Edging of braid-based reticella: probably Italian: about 1620-40. Depth 12cm (4.7in).
This edging is based on five plaited braids extending parallel to each other along the length of the edging and one braid which extends around the scallops. Note that the scallop motifs are wider than the rosette motifs in the main rectangular compartments. The design is typical of the rosette designs worked in reticella and punto in aria at the same period (See pages 32-35, 38-40).

Plate 18:
a. Edging of braid-based reticella: about 1640-50. Depth of scallop 6cm (2.4in).
The plaited foundation braids lie along the top edge and around the motifs in the scallops.
b. Edging of braid-based reticella: about 1640-60. Depth of scallop 10cm (4in). (See **Plate** 19 for detail)
The shallow scallops in both 18a and 18b date them to the mid-17th century. The tightness of working of the buttonhole stitches in 18a suggests that this is an Italian piece whereas the looser working of 18b and manner in which the design fills the space available suggest a Northern origin. The rather naive, sketchy drawing and retention of the strictly compartmentalized design at a late date suggest the latter is English.

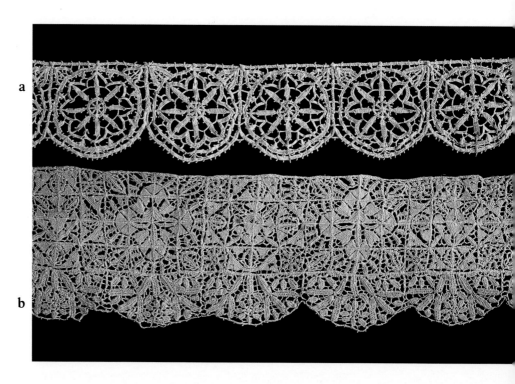

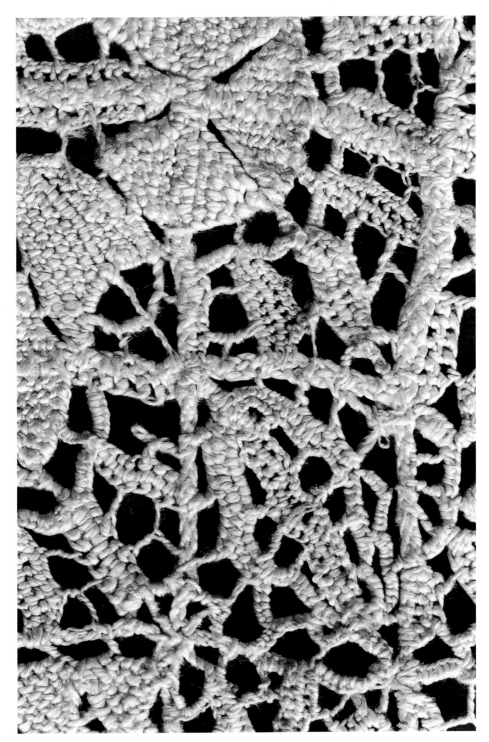

Plate 19: Detail of **Plate** 18b showing the foundation of plaited braids.

Points to watch
See under reticella needlework (pages 32-35) and punto in aria (pages 38-40).

History

At some time during the development of reticella needleworks it must have become apparent that a great deal of time, and hence money, was being wasted in spinning thread and weaving fabric which was to be cut out and thrown away. Why not forget the fabric altogether?

One alternative developed was a grid of plaited braids couched on to a pattern to provide the foundation for the embroidery which, in all other respects, was identical to true reticella needlework. This form of work did not oust the true reticella but was made alongside it, to the same designs and for the same uses and, like true reticella, was made in Italy, Flanders, England and other parts of Europe. Although more economical to make than true reticella, braid-based reticella was less firm and hard-wearing and therefore less highly prized.

Punto in aria and related needleworks

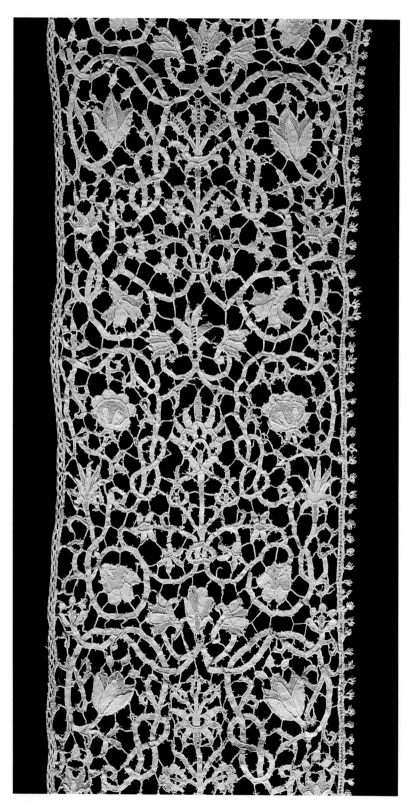

Characteristics (punto in aria)

1. Guipure needlepoint lace mainly in buttonhole stitch.
2. Designs:
    a. Geometric, like reticella (pages 32-35).
    b. Stylized flowerheads and other motifs connected by trailing stems and buttonholed brides.
3. Often found as pointed or scalloped edgings with a symmetrical design repeated in each point or scallop.
4. Lines in slight relief are fairly common: these are formed by needlewoven foundation threads within the design or closely buttonholed threads on the surface, around or within the design motifs.

Points to watch (punto in aria)

See under reticella needlework (page 32).

Punto in aria is often found as an edging to reticella needlework.

Many punto in aria laces differ from braid-based reticellas solely in the use of foundation *threads* rather than *braids* — the threads are usually hidden by overcasting, needle-weaving, or buttonhole stitches. I treat the two laces separately to stimulate close study of examples.

Punto in aria is, strictly speaking, an Italian needlepoint but similar laces were made throughout Europe. Italian work can sometimes be distinguished by the density and stiffness of its clothwork areas due to the extreme tightness of working of the buttonhole stitches. The looser, more supple Flemish and English work can be seen in **Plates** 23 and 18 respectively.

The type of trailing-stem design shown in **Plate** 20 was also carried out in the contemporary 'mezzo punto' technique (see tape laces - pages 98-103 and **Plate** 22). The closely woven tapes were embellished with needle-worked bars, fillings and raised outlines and the result is easily mistaken for punto in aria.

Plate 20: Flounce of punto in aria. Width 16.5cm (6.5in); length shown 38cm (15in).

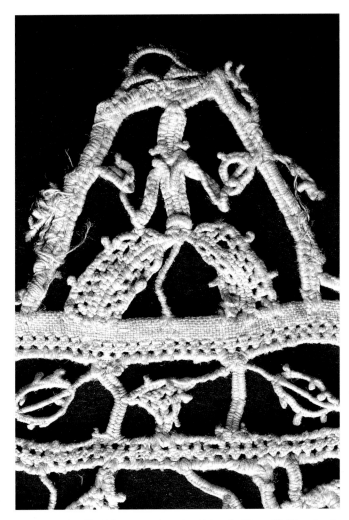

Plate 21: Detail of the punto in aria edging in **Plate** 15. Depth of point 2.5cm (1in.).
The foundation threads of the lacework are sewn directly into the straight edge of the woven linen fabric decorated with cutwork embroidery, or reticella. The man depicted in the design wears the typical full breeches of the period. The collar and belt details are worked in loose threads over the surface.

Plate 22: Point of gothic-arch shape from an edging of mezzo punto: Italian: 1620-40. Depth of point 12.5cm (5in)
It was only when I came to examine this piece thoroughly during research on this book that I realized that it is a tape lace, made with a combination of closely woven tapes and very tightly worked buttonhole stitches. The design is typical of Italian punto in aria of the period.

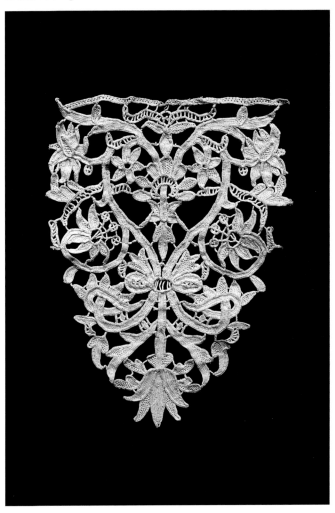

History (punto in aria)

Punto in aria, meaning 'stitch in the air', is the Italian name for the first true needlepoint lace which was made without a woven or plaited foundation. It began in the form of separate, decorative points around the neck and sleeve openings of the linen shirts and chemises worn by men and women in the 16th century. An example of this work is seen in **Plate** 15 and in the detail in **Plate** 21 which shows how the free needlepoint is linked into the edge of the linen band but is otherwise unsupported by it.

Gradually the points grew larger and more elaborate, as did the areas of cutwork and reticella needlework which they frequently edged, and it is this combination of work which is often seen in the portraiture of the late 16th and early 17th centuries. By 1600 the early, sharply triangular outline of the points had generally softened and broadened into the shape of a gothic arch, but this is not a fixed rule for identification. Vinciolo's Pattern Book of

1587 shows many designs for arched and scalloped edgings whereas a man's standing collar in the Rijksmuseum, Amsterdam has a pointed edging and is dated to about 1610. The constant feature throughout this period is the use of repeated or alternating designs within the points or scallops, always with a line of symmetry through the point, whether the design be geometric or floral.

As technical expertise increased in what was still a relatively new craft, the lace makers progressed from making separate points to continuous lengths of lace. These were used in the same way as reticella and, though lacking the constraints of a fabric foundation, were made in the same compartmentalized designs. Only gradually did stems of floral designs trail from one compartment to the next.

By 1620, designs of simple flowerheads borne on flowing, curving stems were common but the element of symmetry still remained. In Italy, the buttonholed clothwork

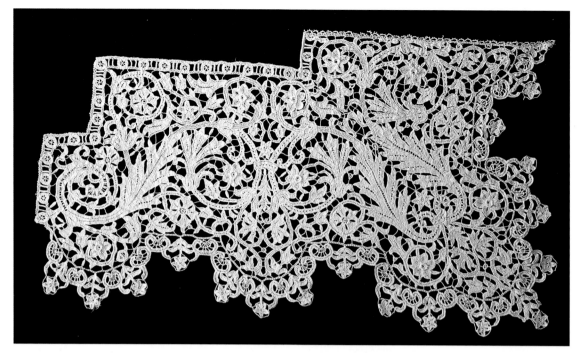

Plate 23: Corner fragment of Flemish needlepoint: 1625-50. Overall length 42cm (17in)
The broader scallop of this piece suggests that it is slightly later in date than the fragment shown in **Plate** 22. A Northern origin is suggested by the looser working of the stitches and absence of tight outlining which give it a suppleness not found in Italian work; the general quality of design and workmanship indicate a professional, Flemish origin. The motifs are joined by fine overcast bars instead of buttonholed bars and there is slight raised surface decoration around the flower centers.

was tightly worked, the stems narrow, of even width and often bounded by a raised outline leaving clearly defined spaces between the pattern motifs. The floral designs did, however, provide some broader pattern areas which could be enlivened with fancy filling stitches. These were few at first but presage the delights of the second half of the century.

Early Flemish Needlepoint

The development of free needlepoint laces was not confined to Italy. Flanders was also a center for the industry and designs followed much the same trends as in Italy in the early part of the 17th century.

It is not always possible, even for the expert, to distinguish work from the two areas but, in general: Flemish clothwork tends to be more loosely worked than the Italian; Flemish designs are not outlined with tightly-worked buttonhole stitches; the Flemish floral motifs tend to be more expansive and fill a greater proportion of the lace than Italian motifs; the overall feel of the Flemish work is one of suppleness compared with the firmness and crispness of Italian work.

In the mid to late 17th century, Flanders does not appear to have followed Venice's lead in the making of raised needlepoints (pages 44-47). Instead, flat points continued to be made but in the designs of the Flemish bobbin laces popular in the Low Countries (page 173).

English needlepoints of this period, as far as we can tell from the few surviving examples, tend to be closer in structure to their Flemish rather than Italian counterparts but are worked in a thicker, less even thread. Their designs tend to retain the compartmentalized form of reticella, including isolated motifs, rather than moving to more freely flowing plant forms.

Plate 24: Early 20th century flat needlepoint collar in a rosette design derived from early 17th century punto in aria designs; the collar shape and the graduation of the concentric rows of rosette motifs clearly indicate the late date of this piece.

40

Plate F: Unknown Man; Circle of Willem Wissing; about 1690

In the 1670s there was a radical simplification of men's dress with the introduction of the long, tight-fitting vest and coat, here disguised by the artist's use of drapery. The rabat collar was gradually ousted by the cravat, a long strip of linen which wrapped around the neck and tied at the front. Like the example seen here, it often had rectangular lace panels at the ends which fell in folds at the neck. These are of Venetian needlepoint.

Venetian needlepoints in the Italian baroque style

Venetian flat point

Characteristics

1. Guipure needlepoint lace.
2. Essentially a flat lace but thicker foundation threads within the work give rise to pronounced lines around and within the pattern areas.
3. Clothwork pattern areas of tightly-worked buttonhole stitches often enlivened with geometric arrangements of holes (see **Plate** 26).
4. Buttonholed brides, often decorated with rings and picots, interconnect the pattern areas.
5. Scrolling 17th-century baroque and branching coral-line designs.

Point to watch

Raised work (see pages 44-48) was often added to flat points in the 19th century.

History of Venetian needlepoints

By the mid-17th century Venice was already famed for her needlepoints. Her workers, many convent trained, made a good deal of the punto in aria exported to the rest of Europe and we have already seen how its style changed from the geometric to more freely-flowing forms. From these there was a natural progression to the continuous movement of the Italian baroque, a style already well established in other applied arts.

In Venice this style was interpreted in two ways: in the flat points seen in **Plates** 25 and 26 and in the more elaborate rose points (rose here meaning raised) seen in **Plates** 27 to 35. In bolder designs, not illustrated, large-scale exotic flowers and broad, scrolling leaves undulate continuously across the entire surface of the fabric, while backward-curling branches bring the motifs into close proximity and reduce the need for connecting brides. Heavy raised work incorporated in these designs gives the form sometimes known as 'gros point'.

In lighter forms the motifs are smaller, the connecting brides more numerous and often interlinked and decorated with picoted rings. The dense clothwork is enlivened with more varied filling stitches while frills of picots around the padded outlines add richness to the effect.

It has generally been assumed that the bolder gros point appeared first and decayed gradually through the lighter rose point into attenuated designs of curling tendrils and coral-like branches which were current at the end of the century. Certainly this is the underlying trend but portraiture of the period shows that the gros point coexisted with the lighter laces for most of the second half of the 17th century and it continued to be made, particularly for church and furnishing uses, into the 18th century.

By the end of the 17th century fashions had changed; clear designs which displayed well in flat expanses, as in the man's rabat collar of the 1650s to 1670s (see **Plate** E), were no longer needed for the cravats and gathered frills of the 1690s. Texture was more important than pattern and this trend reached its extreme in the raised needlepoint known as 'point de neige'. In this, what little form was left to the design was hidden beneath a froth of picoted rings and crescents scattered indiscriminately over the surface.

By 1700 the Venetian industry which only two or three decades earlier had produced the most expensive, prestigious and sought-after laces in Europe was in decline. The Italian baroque style was outmoded and was to remain so for the next 150 years.

The return came in the 1850s when guipures and heavier laces generally came back into fashion. Old needlepoints were rediscovered, unpicked and the techniques relearned in various centers. Although the modern copies were slow to catch on, by the late 1870s and 1880s these copies, together with antique originals whose motifs were cut and re-ordered to suit the current styles, formed a growing part of the needlepoint market. Innishmacsaint and New Ross in Ireland, Burano in the Venetian lagoon and various Belgian towns were only some of the centers which included 'Venetian' laces in their repertoires.

In many cases these late examples are easily distinguishable from the originals: the thread and workmanship are coarser, the designs are adapted to the shapes of 19th- and 20th-century costume items and are often inspired by, rather than copied from, the originals. But there are also direct copies, made with fine linen thread to a technical standard nearing perfection; only a certain stiffness of style and over-elaboration of detail distinguish these from the originals.

Plate 25: These four pieces show the general design trend in Venetian laces from the stronger baroque style of the mid-17th century to the decadent form of about 1700. Length shown 25cm (10in).

a. Flat point edging: 1660-90. Depth 10cm (4 in); pattern repeat 40cm (15.5in). The design flows almost continuously from one repeat to the next.

b. Flat point edging: 1670-90. Depth 10cm (4 in); pattern repeat 46.5cm (18.5in). The curving baroque lines are still visible but the pattern repeats are separated and on a smaller scale than in **Plate** 25a.

c. Flat point edging: 1680-1700. Depth 3cm (1.5in); pattern repeat 40cm (16in).

d. Fragment of flat point: about 1700. Size shown: depth 7.5cm (3in).

This lace has been cut and rejoined at a later date but the indeterminate design of tiny dissociated scrolls means that this is not readily apparent.

(See **Plate** 32c for a further example).

Plate 26: Detail of **Plate** 25a. Note the thick lines due to foundation threads within the work and the use of filling stitches to enliven the design; these are formed by patterns of holes in the clothwork and thus differ from the filling stitches worked in spaces between the motifs in many 18th- and 19th-century needlepoints.

Venetian rose (raised) point

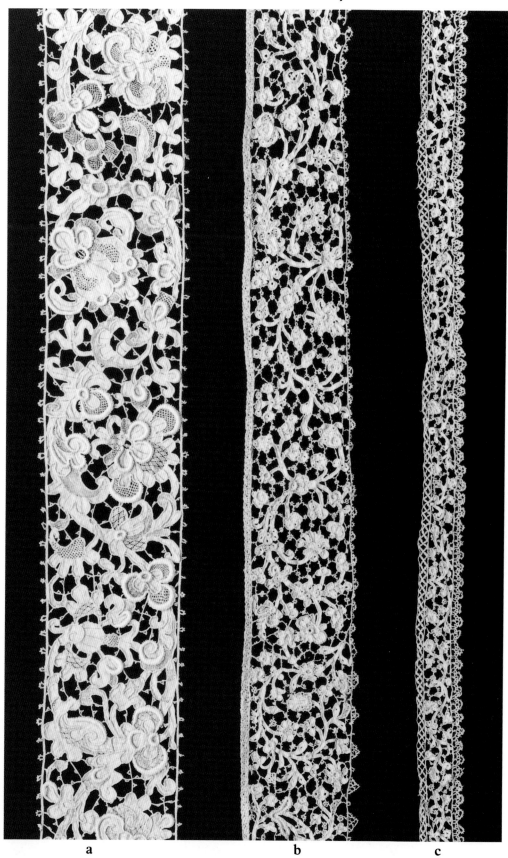

a   b   c

Plate 27: Group of Venetian rose points showing the same design trend as the flat point edgings in **Plate** 25.
a. 1660-90. Depth 9cm (3.5in); pattern repeat 47cm (18.5in).
b. 1670-90. Depth 6cm (2.5in); no clear repeat – altered?
c. 1680-1700. Depth 3cm (1.3in); no clear repeat.

Characteristics

Venetian rose point has the characteristics of Venetian flat point (pages 42-43) with the addition of raised work formed by buttonhole stitches over padding couched on to the surface. The varied nature of the padding gives different effects:

1. Raised ridges are formed by closely spaced buttonhole stitches worked over one or more surface threads and often outline features of the design.
2. A thick but almost uniform core of a multitude of threads can form snakelike convolutions which outline or complement the design underneath. Closely-worked buttonhole stitches form a smooth surface over this but may be decorated with picoted frills (**Plate** 28).
3. High quality examples in large-scale baroque designs include carefully graduated padding forming crescents which are thick in the center and narrow towards the ends. The surface is smooth and frills are sometimes added, as shown in **Plate** 29.
4. In smaller-scale designs, tiny padded rings and curves are scattered over the surface and overwhelmed by picoted frills (**Plate** 33).

Points to watch

Venetian rose point is essentially a 17th-century lace but close copies were made in needlepoint, in crochet and by machine in the 19th and 20th centuries.

The raised work in original Venetian needlepoints is worked into the lace during manufacture. In the 19th century, raised work was often added to earlier flat points but the threads sewing the new work to the old can often be distinguished on the back.

The snakelike form of raised work described in 2 (above) has often been ascribed to Spanish laces. Very probably it was a transitional form between the simple raised outline described in 1 and the beautifully modelled crescents described in 3 but it continued in use after the crescents had developed and was used by workers in other parts of Europe who copied the prestigious Venetian laces.

Many French needlepoints (pages 50-55) were made in the Italian baroque manner in the 1660s-1670s until a new French classical style was introduced, after which both centers copied each other's laces to some extent. It is often difficult to distinguish between them.

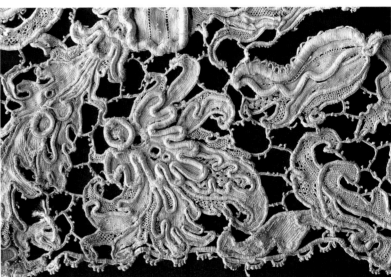

Plate 28: Detail of a rose point with convoluted, padded raised work: probably Venetian. The bundle of threads used to form the padding can best be seen in **Plate** 2 and in the tape-lace detail in **Plate** 106.

Plate 29: Detail of the flounce in **Plate** 31 showing the beautifully formed padded crescent with frills of picots, typical of Venetian work.

45

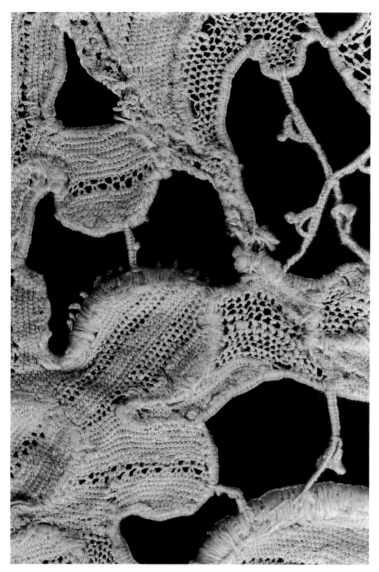

Plate 30: Detail of the wrong side of the flounce in **Plate** 31.

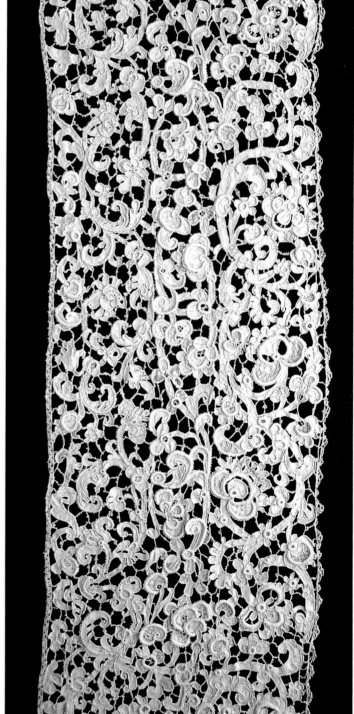

Plate 31: Flounce of Venetian rose point: 1660-90. Depth 23cm (9in);
Length shown 51cm (20in)
The flounce has been made up from three strips of rose point joined
edge to edge, probably in the late 19th century. A number of brides
have been remade but the flow of the design within each strip is still
visible; in many pieces altered in the 19th century the motifs are
completely rearranged so that the original design is lost.

46

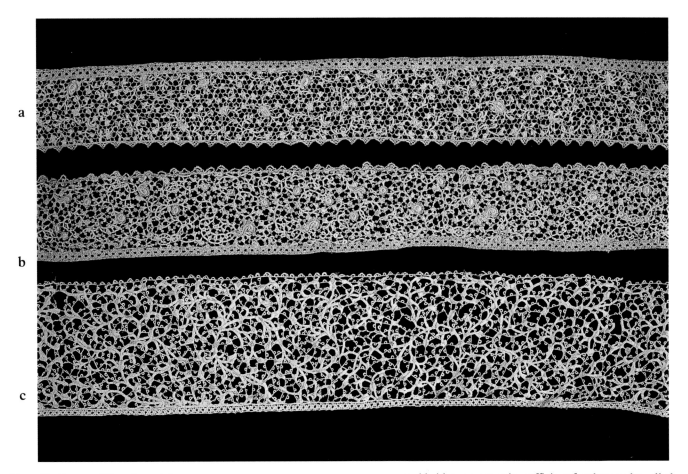

Plate 32: Group of Venetian edgings.
a. and b. Rose point edgings: 1690-1710. Depth 8cm (3in) including later bobbin-made footings.
Both have been cut down from their original depths as shown by the way the pattern is sliced through where the strips are joined to their later footing and heading. Both show the random patterning of the turn of the 17th century; the flurries of raised work and ornamented brides are not quite sufficient for these to be called 'point de neige'. Note the way the brides in edging a. form irregular meshes while those in b. are decorated with picoted rings.
c. Flat point edging in the random design commonly called 'coralline' from its branching, coral-like nature: 1690-1710. Depth 13cm (5in).

Plate 33: Detail of Plate 32b.

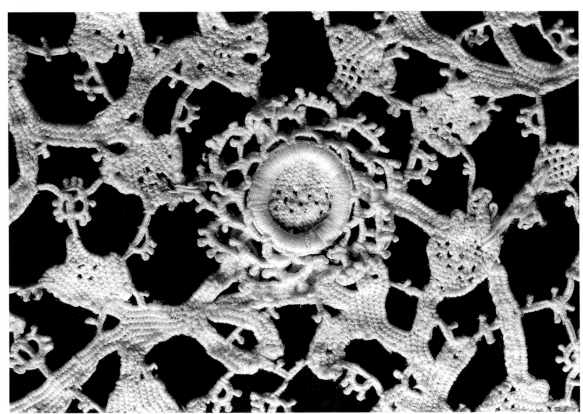

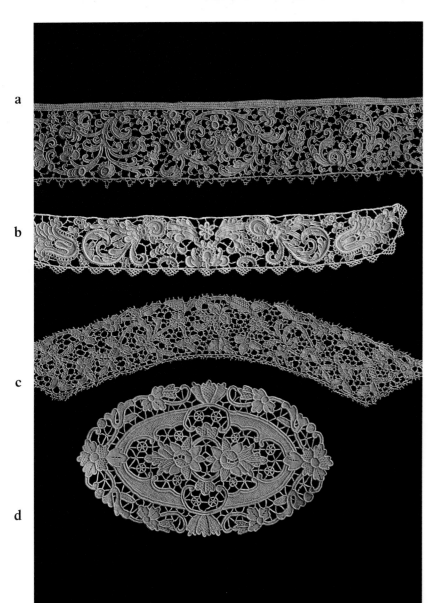

Plate 34

a. Edging: copy of Venetian rose point with a bobbin-made footing: late 19th century. Depth of needlepoint 6.5cm (2.7in); pattern repeat 33.5cm (13.5in); length shown 32cm (12.5in).

This piece is technically excellent, with an interesting but not excessive variety of fillings and a fairly long pattern repeat, but a certain stiffness in the design, regularity of the raised outlining, and comparative coarseness of the thread for the scale of design betray its 19th-century date.

b. Collar: late 19th-early 20th century. Depth 5.5cm (2.1in); overall length 39cm (15.5in).

Another technically excellent piece with fine, graduated raised work, but the effect is killed by its brilliant whiteness, produced by modern washing powders or bleach.

c. Collar: late 19th-20th century. Length of neck edge 30cm (12in); depth 5.5cm (2.2in).

This example is in very coarse thread and a hybrid 19th-century style, vaguely reminiscent of late 17th-century designs when pattern motifs were getting smaller and a coarse mesh ground was developing.

d. Table mat: about 1975. Length 24.5cm (9.7in); depth 14.5cm (5.7in).

This was bought new. The coarse brides, rigid outlining and formalization of design are typical of needlepoint lace made this century for household use. It is probably of Chinese manufacture.

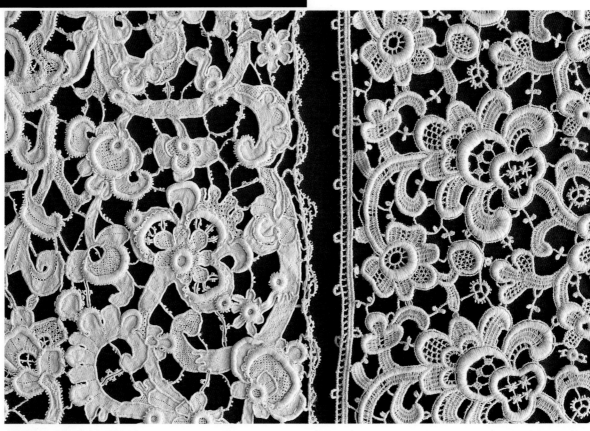

Opposite page:
Plate 35
a. Detail of a late 17th century Venetian rose point.
b. Detail of a late 19th century machine-made copy of Venetian rose point.
Note the open nature and woven appearance of the machine clothwork in
comparison with the dense stitching of the needlework. Also, the machine-made
connecting brides have a fuzzy appearance unlike that of the close buttonhole
stitching of the needle-made brides. Although not shown, the wrong side of the
machine copy is almost identical to the right side whereas the wrong side of the
needlepoint is very different, being almost flat (see **Plate** 30).
This machine copy was made on an embroidery machine; it is of a type known
as 'chemical' or 'burnt' lace as the embroidery is carried out on a fabric which is
subsequently dissolved away chemically (or burnt) to leave a lace-like fabric.

Above:
Plate G: Queen Mary II by Willem Wissing, 1656-
1687.
The falling collars of the second quarter of the 17th
century gave way to collars with a wide, almost
straight neckline, from shoulder to shoulder, in the
second half of the century but these are seen only in
formal portraiture. In this informal pose, Queen
Mary is seen wearing a loose-fitting robe over a
chemise which has a gathered frill of Venetian
needlepoint lace around the neckline and down the
front. Similar frills also adorn the cuffs which are
turned back and held in place with jewelled pins.

French needlepoints
Point de France

Plate 36: Part of a flounce of point de France: about 1680-1700. Depth shown 25cm (10in); pattern repeat 69cm (27in).

The flounce has been cut down along its footside but shows the arrangement of motifs about a vertical axis of symmetry typical of late 17th century French designs.

From the collection of Michèle Peloille; photograph by Jacques Gaumé.

Plate 37: Detail of a point de France flounce showing: narrow bands of clothwork surrounding areas of filling stitches; picoted brides connected into large-scale, irregular meshes; and a raised detail.

Characteristics

1. Mainly flat but with some pronounced foundation threads within the design and padded raised work on the surface (see points to watch).
2. Designs include narrow bands of clothwork which outline pattern areas worked in more open stitches or form branching patterns in late 17th-century examples.
3. Ground of interconnected, buttonholed brides with added picots forming irregular meshes.
4. Frequent use of bars or outlines based on a thick foundation thread with loosely worked buttonhole stitches forming a row of loops on one or each side.
5. Early designs are in the Italian baroque style of Venetian rose points but classical designs with baroque sub-features are more usual.

Plate 38: Detail of the flounce in **Plate 36**.

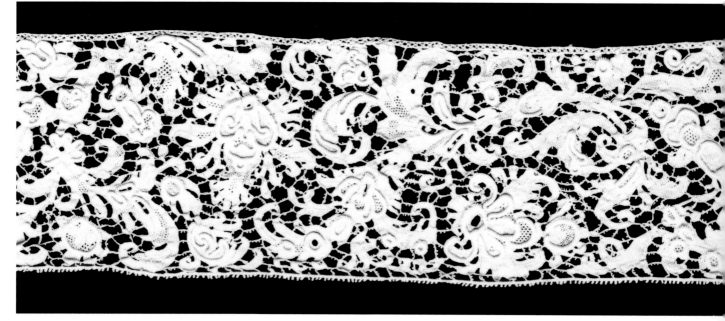

Plate 39: Edging of raised needlepoint: probably French: about 1670-90. Depth 9.5cm (3.7in); pattern repeat 45cm (18in).
This example is thought to typify early point de France: its motifs do not have raised outlines but they do have some graduated raised work around their centers.

Points to watch

French workers learned the technique of making raised needlepoints from the Venetians and no doubt some French products are indistinguishable from their Italian predecessors. It is thought, however, that 17th century baroque needlepoints in which the padded raised work surrounds central regions of the motifs, leaving the outer edges flat, are distinctively French (see **Plate** 40) : Venetian work has padded crescents or raised ridges along most edges.

Italian working tends to be closer, with fillings often constituted by arrays of holes in the clothwork, whereas French work tends to be looser.

Brussels also made needlepoints in the French manner (**Plate** 72a) and it is now thought that many early 18th-century flounces which had been attributed to Sedan in Northern France were probably made in Brussels. In needlepoints more certainly attributable to Brussels, however, the treatment of the work is often even lighter than the French.

Plate 40: Detail of **Plate** 39.

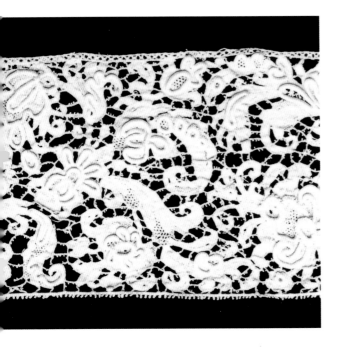

History

The French lace industry did not develop in commercial terms until the 1660s, the time of Colbert, Louis XIV's great finance minister. Realizing that imports of foreign luxury goods were damaging the economy, he persuaded lace makers from Venice and Flanders to settle in France to improve the quality of the local products. The Venetian workers were brought to Colbert's chateau at Alençon where, after a difficult beginning, successful imitations of the Venetian rose points were made. These were initially sold as 'Point de France', as were the bobbin laces, but later the term came to be applied solely to the needlepoints.

By the 1670s new styles were being sought and it was probably the influence of government-paid designers, firstly Le Brun and later Bérain, who caused the introduction of the lighter, classical designs usually associated with the French needlepoints of this period. In these, individual motifs still have a curving baroque appearance but are separated from each other and grouped about vertical axes. Human figures, classical ornaments and architectural features add a touch of life while the small scale of the motifs requires the use of a multitude of connecting brides, now organized into irregular meshes.

This light but all-over patterning suited the tastes of the late 17th century but fashion never stays still. In the

Plate 41: Detail of the wrong side of the lace in **Plate** 39.

early 18th century the trend was again towards fuller designs and the motifs, which had been small and slender, expanded to fill space previously occupied by the mesh ground. In the larger flounces, for furnishing and church use, many designs continued to be based on axes of symmetry but a new baroque influence was being felt. One example of the new style is seen in **Plate** 43 but it is seen more clearly in the bobbin-lace chapters.

By the 1730s, the guipure needlepoints were giving way to the mesh-grounded forms of 'Alençon' and 'Argentan' described in the next section.

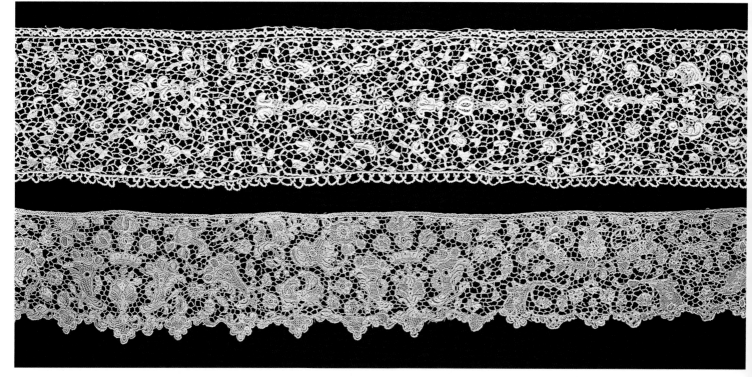

Plate 42
a. Edging: about 1700. Depth 10cm (4.0in).
This design, or rather lack of it, is more typical of Venetian work of the period but the looser working, use of bars with loops along each side (see point 5 above) and symmetry of the motifs, indicate a possible French origin.
b. Edging: about 1700. Depth 7.5cm (3.0in); length shown 32cm (12.5in); design incomplete.
The design of this piece, which has some later alteration, still shows a more definite arrangement of motifs about a larger motif defining an axis of symmetry, which is typical of the French style. This is not of the highest quality expected of point de France and could perhaps be Brussels work; **Plate 72a** shows an example more certainly attributable to Brussels.

Plate 43: shaped edging in the early 18th century baroque style: about 1720-35. Maximum depth 8.5cm (3.4in); pattern repeat 32cm (12.5in).
This piece has been cut down and altered slightly from a wider edging and therefore its original shape and purpose are uncertain. It displays the large-scale mesh ground formed from picoted bars typical of point de France but its raised work differs from earlier examples; it is not as heavily padded and it outlines the motifs rather than being worked over the centers. The outlining is not consistent, however, and is transitional to the form seen in the Alençon and Argentan laces described in the following pages.

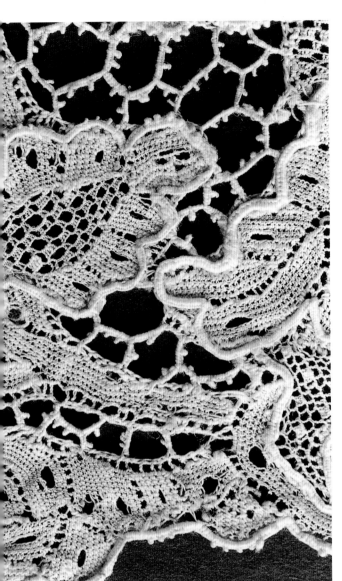

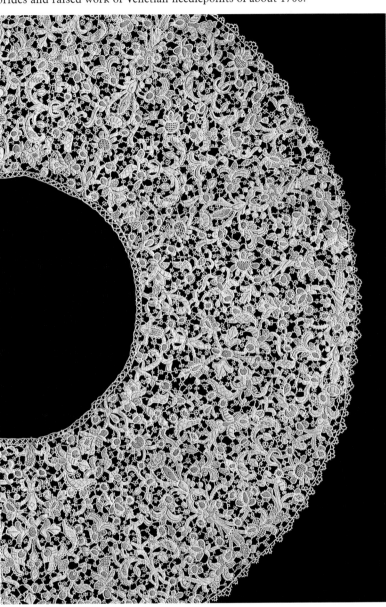

Plate 45: Part of a needlepoint bertha collar: about 1890-1900. Depth of lace 18.5cm (7.2in); diameter of neck opening 20cm (8in).
The complete bertha occupies one and a half circles. Circular bertha collars are typical of the late 19th to early 20th centuries and, in this case, would probably have been worn gathered over the full sleeves of the mid-1890s. The design is a hybrid of the repeated, symmetrical groups of point de France, here arranged around radii of the circle, and the decorated brides and raised work of Venetian needlepoints of about 1700.

Plate 44: Detail of **Plate** 43

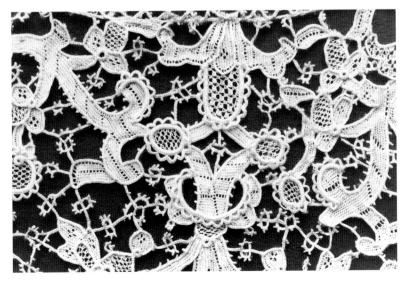

Plate 46: Detail of **Plate** 45

Plate 47: Sleeve ruffle and matching edging with the Alençon ground in the major area and the Argentan ground in the border: about 1760-75. Maximum depth of ruffle 14.5cm (5.6in); minimum depth of ruffle 7.0cm (2.7in); length of outer edge 106 cm (42in). Depth of edging 5.5cm (2.3in); pattern repeat 20cm (8in).

Until the middle of the 18th century, women's sleeve ruffles were attached to the chemise rather than to the dress and were worn above or below the elbow according to the decade. When shaped, as in the example shown, the wider part fell behind the elbow. Ruffles were often made in sets, in graduated sizes, together with a matching cap back, lappets and narrower and wider edgings for the cap frill and dress trimmings.

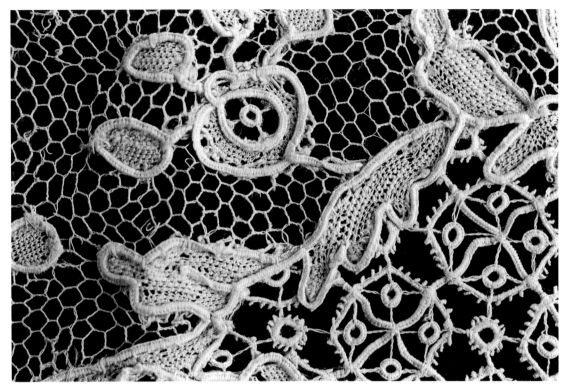

Plate 48: Detail of a French needlepoint showing the Alençon ground, the raised, closely buttonholed outline and filling stitches.

Characteristics

1. Needlepoint laces incorporating one or more of the grounds explained below.
2. Raised outline to the design formed by surface threads closely covered in buttonhole stitches and sometimes decorated with picots; called the 'cordonnet'.
3. Pattern areas filled with closely packed buttonhole stitches.
4. Areas of filling stitches common, particularly combinations of tightly buttonholed rings, stars and bars with open stitches along each side.
5. Grounds:

   a. Alençon (**Plate** 49) - roughly hexagonal mesh with two threads twisted together on each side. (This is formed by linked rows of loose buttonhole stitches usually worked at right angles to the length of the lace; each new row is looped into the previous row and a strengthening thread is run back through this row before the next is started. The strengthening thread is not tightened, allowing the meshes to retain a hexagonal shape.)

   b. Argentan (**Plate** 51) - hexagonal mesh of larger scale than the Alençon mesh, with buttonhole stitches worked closely together over the foundation threads on all six sides.

   c. Tortillée (**Plate** 52) - a hexagonal mesh with each side reinforced by an additional thread twisted or formed into widely spaced buttonhole stitches around it, giving an untidy appearance when magnified.

   d. Argentella (**Plate** 55) - complex, large-scale, hexagonal meshes enclosing clothworked hexagons - very rare.

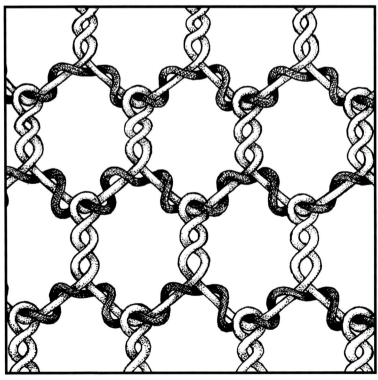

Plate 49: The Alençon ground.

57

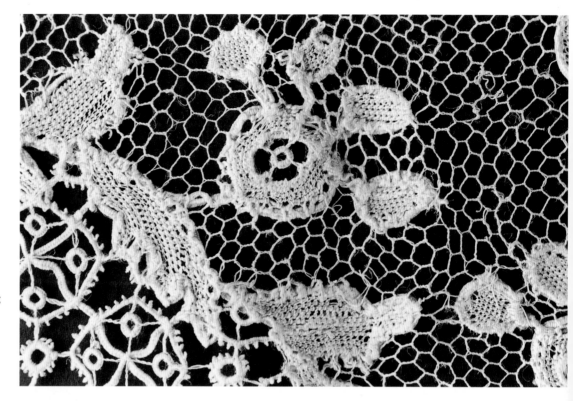

Plate 50: Detail of the wrong side of a French needlepoint with the Alençon ground.

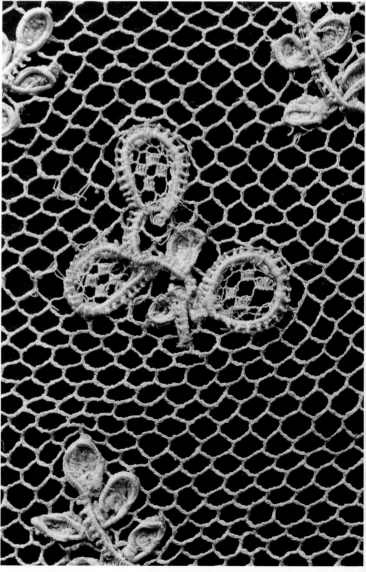

Plate 52: Detail of a French needlepoint showing the tortillée ground and plain and picoted raised work with a horsehair supporting the picots.

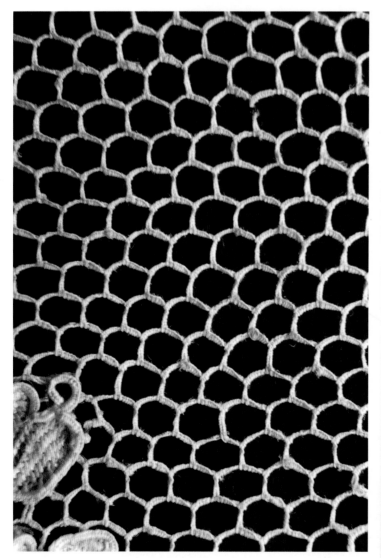

Plate 51: Detail of a French needlepoint with the Argentan ground.

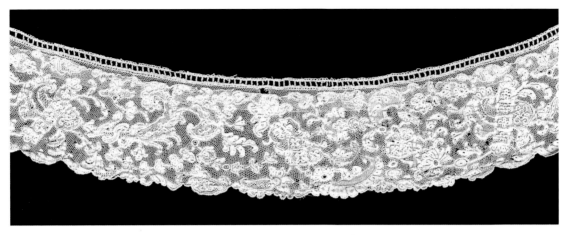

Plate 53: Transitional French needlepoint edging with the Alençon ground but with raised work in the style of point de France: 1700-20. Depth 6.5cm (2.5in); pattern repeat 28cm (11in).

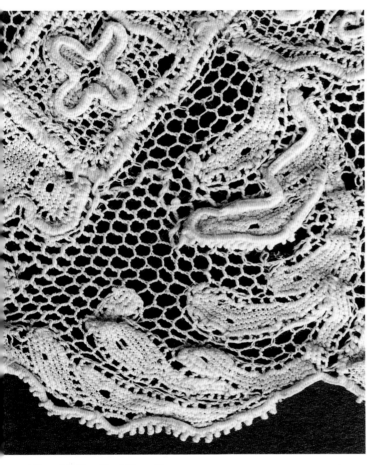

Plate 54: Detail of **Plate 53**.

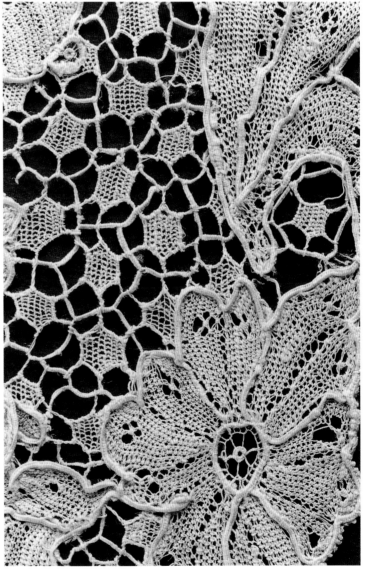

Plate 55: Detail from a fragment of French needlepoint with the argentella ground.

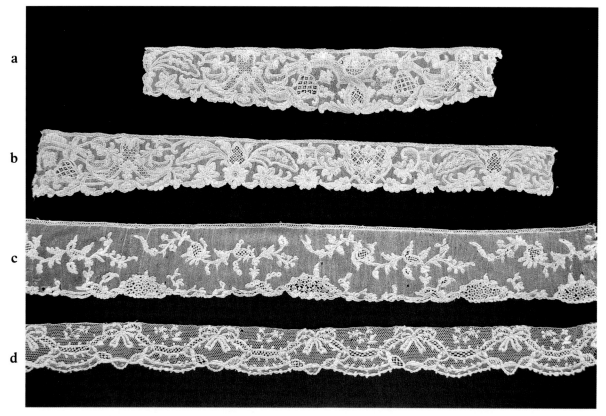

Plate 56: Group of French needlepoint edgings. Length shown 37cm (l4.5in)
a and b. Two fragments from the same design with the Alençon ground: about 1730-40. Design incomplete. Maximum depth 7cm (2.4in).
c. Alençon ground: about 1760-70; design altered. Depth 8cm (3in).
This is a typical example of a floral sprig springing from a border pattern and extending asymmetrically in two directions along the lace.
d. Argentan ground: about 1760-70. Depth 5cm (2in); pattern repeat 22.5cm (9in).
The symmetry of this design shows the influence of classical styles which gradually superseded the rococo in the late 18th century. The bow motif is also common in late 18th-century designs.

Points to watch

Burano laces (pages 66-67) use a ground very similar to the Alençon ground but the Burano ground often has a ladder-like appearance and the Burano raised work is not closely buttonholed.

French needlepoints with damaged grounds were often regrounded in Burano in the 19th century.

To the naked eye, well-made Alençon grounds look like the simplest of the bobbin-made nets, Lille, or East Midlands point, ground. A magnifying glass will show the looped buttonhole stitches.

The Alençon ground was sometimes used to ground part bobbin laces and tape laces in the 19th century.

History

In the early 18th century the French needlepoint industry, established around Alençon and neighbouring Argentan in Normandy, was in decline. Fashion preferred plain muslins and feather-light bobbin laces to the crisp, heavy texture of needlepoints. At this time, point de France was made largely in wide flounces for household and ecclesiastical purposes.

It was not until the 1730s that needlepoints were again made in any quantity for dress trimmings. By this time the coarse, picoted meshes of point de France had given way to much finer meshes of regular, buttonholed hexagons and an alternative, lighter mesh of open buttonhole stitches had developed: these grounds came to be known as the Argentan and Alençon grounds respectively although each was worked in both towns and they are often found in the same lace. The raised outline typical of French laces with the Alençon and Argentan grounds had also become common although it was not so stiff, nor so heavily decorated with picots as it later became.

These changes in technique were accompanied by changes in design. In the earlier years of the century, the more fashionable Flemish bobbin laces had been transformed by the introduction of the so-called 'bizarre' designs (see **Plates** 163 center, 184 center, and 198 center). These were also introduced into the French needlepoints but with less success. The movement of the design which should flow from edge to edge is often arrested by symmetrical groupings retained from the earlier French style; the odd lozenge and cartouche shapes filled with fancy stitches appear as clumsy insertions rather than integral parts of the design; and the leaf sprays, which should be light and feathery, are solid in outline and mixed with poorly drawn flowers.

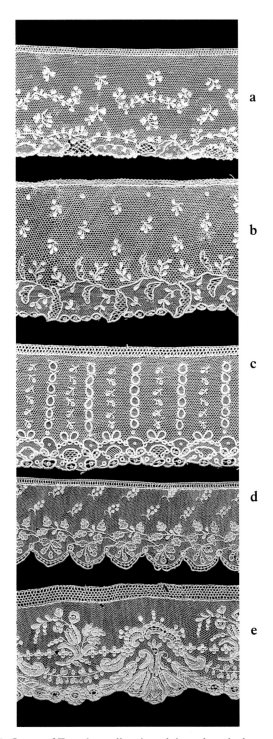

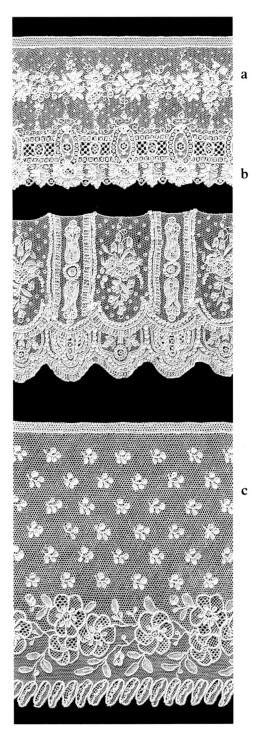

Plate 57: Group of French needlepoint edgings: length shown 14.5cm (5.7in).

a. With tortillée ground: about 1780-95. Depth 7cm (2.7in); pattern repeat 14.5cm (5.7in).

b. With tortillée ground: about 1780-1800. Depth 9cm (3.5in); pattern repeat 4cm (1.6in).

c. With tortillée ground: about 1785-1810. Depth 8cm (3in); pattern repeat 2.5cm (1in).

d. With Alençon ground: 1825-40. Depth 5cm (2in); pattern repeat 2cm (1in).

This shows a stage in the development of design in the 19th century from the straight-edged borders of about 1800, with simple, repeated flowerheads to slightly more elaborate floral patterns.

e. With Alençon ground: about 1845-60. Depth 7.5cm (3in); pattern repeat 10cm (4in).

All the edgings in this **Plate** have a later machine- or bobbin-made footing, which is included in the depth measurement.

Plate 58: In all of these 19th-century edgings the clothwork is much less closely worked than in the 18th-century examples. Length shown 15cm (6in).

a. With Alençon ground: 1850-75. Depth (including footing) 9cm (3.5in); pattern repeat 3.5cm (1.3in).

b. With Alençon ground: 1860-80. Maximum depth 10cm (4in); pattern repeat 2.3cm (1.3in).

c. With tortillée ground: 1880-1900, in early 19th century style. Depth 17cm (6.7in); pattern repeat 8.5cm (3.4in).

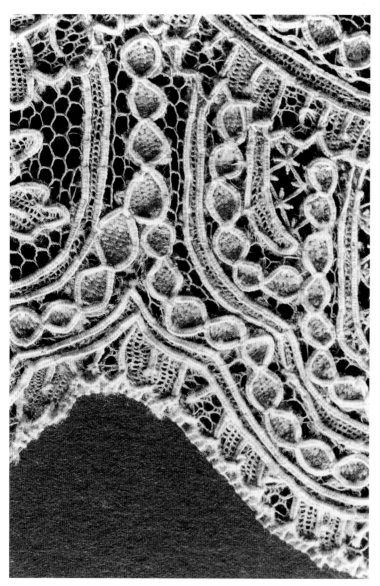

Plate 59: Detail of **Plate** 58b.

Plate 60: Detail of the wrong side of the lace in **Plate** 58b.

By the 1740s, designs had opened out from the dense patterning of the early French baroque to the lightheartedness of the rococo. Bands of foliage and cartouches still swept from edge to edge but were more finely drawn and crossed in the center to define open spaces. Into these burst asymmetric floral sprays, first from one side, then the other.

The trend towards lightness and openness of design continued. In the second half of the century, the bands of foliage and cartouches were largely confined to the edges of the lace. Floral sprays still burst from the borders but then spread along the length of the pattern as they were freed from confinement in enclosed spaces. Gradually they became thinner and weaker or broke entirely from the rest of the design. Occasionally in lace of the 1760s and 1770s, ribbons or narrow stems carrying tiny leaves and flowers meander along the center or edge of the design, or again cross from side to side.

As the 18th century drew to a close, the scale of the motifs grew smaller as it had in the late 17th century but the all-over patterning was not repeated. Instead, the sprigs and flowerheads were arranged along the edges of wide borders of net ground sprinkled with even tinier flowers and spots.

The general desire at this period for light laces which would gather into soft frills led to a discarding of the stiffer Argentan ground in favour of the tortillée which was quicker and easier to make, particularly in fine meshes. Surprisingly this was also the period when the buttonholed outlines of French needlepoints became stiffest and heaviest: both the outline itself and the picots which stand out from it like rows of bristles were often worked over horsehair and, although this should have been removed from the picots, it can still sometimes be seen.

Until the 1790s, the French needlepoint industry was fortunate in that, despite the underlying trend in fashion towards lighter fabrics which led to a decline in many areas of the lace industry, it supplied a product which was *de rigueur* at the French court in winter. With the

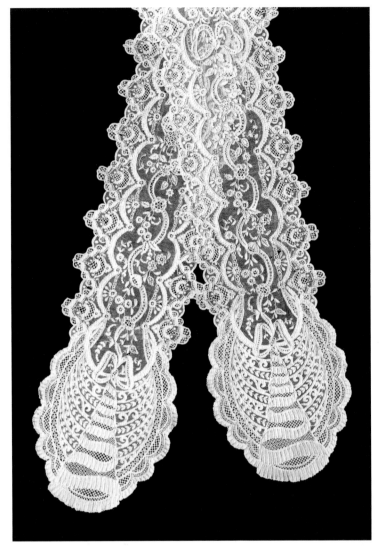

Plate 61: Scarf or pair of lappets made in one piece in the 19th century manner, with the Alençon ground: 1865-85. Width 16cm (6.3in); length 115cm (45.5in)

Revolution this came to an end. Many of the French lace makers are reputed to have fled the country or to have gone to the guillotine because their craft was associated with the aristocracy and even Napoleon's attempts to revive the industry in the early 19th century met with little success. Until fashions changed, the needle-lace makers were forced to turn their skills to embroidering muslins and machine-made nets. It was not until the mid-19th century that the rich, floral designs, to which French needlepoints were particularly suited, returned.

The later 19th century was a difficult period for the lace industry in general because of competition from machine-made products. The French needlepoint industry continued thanks to the vigour and enthusiasm of manufacturers like Lefébure at Bayeux who took great pains to supply good patterns to his workers and demand the highest standards of workmanship. The result was an extremely handsome and expensive product aimed largely at the top end of the market, with the most extravagant pieces being made for exhibition.

By the end of the century, the wheel of fashion had turned full circle and the designs of the late 18th century were being repeated, usually in a stiff mechanical manner. This was to be the end of the industry, as such. Small amounts of lace continued to be made at Argentan in the 20th century and the lace school at Alençon was re-opened but it is now too time-consuming and expensive a product to be truly commercial although some is still being made for special orders.

A note on technique

In France, each lace-maker specialized in her own task and a pattern piece was passed from hand to hand, one worker couching the outlining thread, another working the clothwork and others completing the ground and filling stitches. More than a dozen people might thus be employed from the start to the finish of a small piece. It is not certain when this practice developed but it was current by the late 18th century.

Mesh-grounded flat points

Characteristics

1. Flat needlepoint lace with a net ground.
2. Pattern areas of closely-packed button-hole stitches often enlivened with arrangements of holes.
3. The thick foundation thread outlining the pattern is barely noticeable.
4. Open filling stitches are used as well as arrays of holes in the clothwork.
5. Ground (see **Plate** 66, page 67): generally-rectangular meshes with two threads twisted on each side. The rows usually extend parallel to the length of the lace, not perpendicular to it as in French and Burano needlepoints.

a

b

c

Plate 62: Group of flat point edgings.
a. 1720-40; design incomplete and altered. Maximum depth 5.5cm (2.2in).
b. About 1740-50: depth 4cm (1.6in); pattern repeat 28cm (11in).
c. About 1760-75: design incomplete. Depth 4.7cm (1.8 in).
d. About 1775-90: depth 7cm (2.8in).
Edgings a, b and c all have the ground worked along the length of the edgings, as is expected in 18th century flat points, but edging d has it worked perpendicular to the length as is usual in the 'Burano' laces illustrated in the next chapter. The ground, thread and clothwork are the same as those of Burano laces; all that is lacking is the raised outline. Does this show the transition between earlier and later 18th century Burano needlepoints?

d

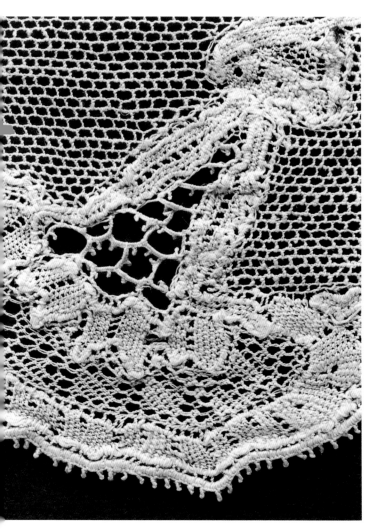

Plate 63: Detail of Plate 62c.

Points to watch

Flat needlepoints with mesh grounds were made in various parts of Europe in the 18th century and the origins of surviving examples are not easy to determine. Some were made in coarse thread, in scrolling tape designs derived from Italian bobbin and needle laces: these often have irregular grounds worked in different directions within the same lace and many may be attributable to Austria and Germany. Others, like the edgings in **Plate 62**, were worked in finer thread, in designs more acceptable to fashionable society. The finest of these were probably made in Brussels to judge from the very close similarity of their designs to those of contemporary Brussels bobbin laces. A superb example is illustrated in '*Lace: A History*', by S. Levey (Maney & Son, 1983).

In the past, laces of this type have been attributed to Venice and some, though not all, were probably made there. This origin is certainly supported by the similarity of their ground to that of later Burano laces (pages 66-67) and the fact that many of the filling stitches in the earlier examples are formed in the Venetian manner, by arrays of holes in the clothwork.

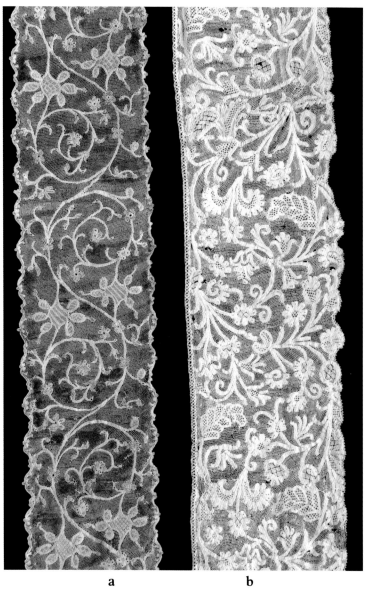

a   b

Plate 64
a. Flat point flounce with a shaped headside along both edges: probably first half of the 18th century. Depth 12.5cm (5in); pattern repeat 20cm (8in).
The clarity and flow of the scrolling design suggest that this is possibly an Italian needlepoint.
b. Flat point flounce: probably 18th century. Depth 14cm (5.5in); pattern repeat26cm (10in).
Here the design is much less sophisticated than in a, suggesting an origin in a less major, more northerly lace-making area, perhaps Germany.

65

Burano

Characteristics

1. Needlepoint lace with a net ground.
2. Raised outline to the design formed by surface threads sewn with overcast stitches.
3. Pattern areas often have a ribbed appearance.
4. A slightly fuzzy appearance is common, particularly in the ground, due to the poor-quality thread often used.
5. Ground (**Plate** 66): generally-rectangular meshes with two threads twisted on each side, arranged in rows perpendicular to the length of the lace giving a ladder-like appearance, unlike the Alençon ground.

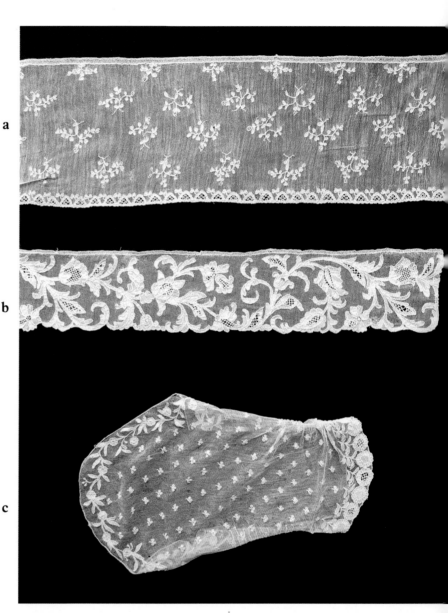

a

b

c

Plate 65:
a. Flounce: 1800-10. Depth 18cm (7in): depth shown 16cm (6.2in); pattern repeat 15cm (6in).
Note the cloudy, ladder-like appearance of the ground, typical of Burano work.
b. Edging: late 19th century. Depth 9.5cm (3.7in); pattern repeat 41cm (16in); length shown 50cm (19.5in).
This style of design, reminiscent of the late 17th century but with a distinctly later use of fillings and of the mesh ground, is characteristic of one type of Burano lace.
c. Sleeve: early 20th century: about 1910. Maximum length 38cm (15in).
The stiffness of the design and feel of this piece would betray its date if it had not been obvious from the sleeve shape. The row of flower heads along the edge is copied from early 19th-century designs.

Plate 66: The Burano ground.

Points to watch

See Alençon and Argentan laces. The rectangular Burano mesh distinguishes it from the structurally similar, but hexagonal, Alençon mesh. The ladder-like appearance of the Burano net is due to the fact that the rows of buttonhole stitches are worked over stretched threads whereas, in the French net, each row of stitches is worked first and then the strengthening thread is run back through them, a much more time-consuming process.

The tightly buttonholed French cordonnet is also distinct from the looser Burano outline.

History

Burano is one of the islands in the Venetian Lagoon and presumably its populace contributed to the extensive Venetian needlepoint industry in the 17th century. The collapse of this industry in the early 18th century was almost total but some lace continued to be made, possibly including the type illustrated on pages 64-65.

What is more certain is that, in the late 18th and early 19th centuries, lace with the characteristics listed above was being made in the simple designs then in fashion.

In the mid 19th century the industry almost died out but, in 1872, a particularly hard winter and famine brought about the establishment of a new lace school. At first, early 19th-century laces were copied but soon the industry was thriving again and lace was made in almost every style imaginable, from close copies of 17th-century Venetian rose points and fine mid 18th-century French laces to derivatives such as that shown in **Plate** 45.

Although demand for costume lace diminished in the 1910s, the Burano industry continued by making guipures for household linen. When increasing labor costs made this uneconomic, the market was left mainly to Far Eastern competitors.

The revival of interest in lace and lace making in the late 20th century led to the re-opening of the Burano school, as of other schools in Europe, but it is still largely the far-Eastern imports that continue to be sold as 'Venetian' or 'Renaissance' lace (**Plate** 34d).

Brussels needlepoints

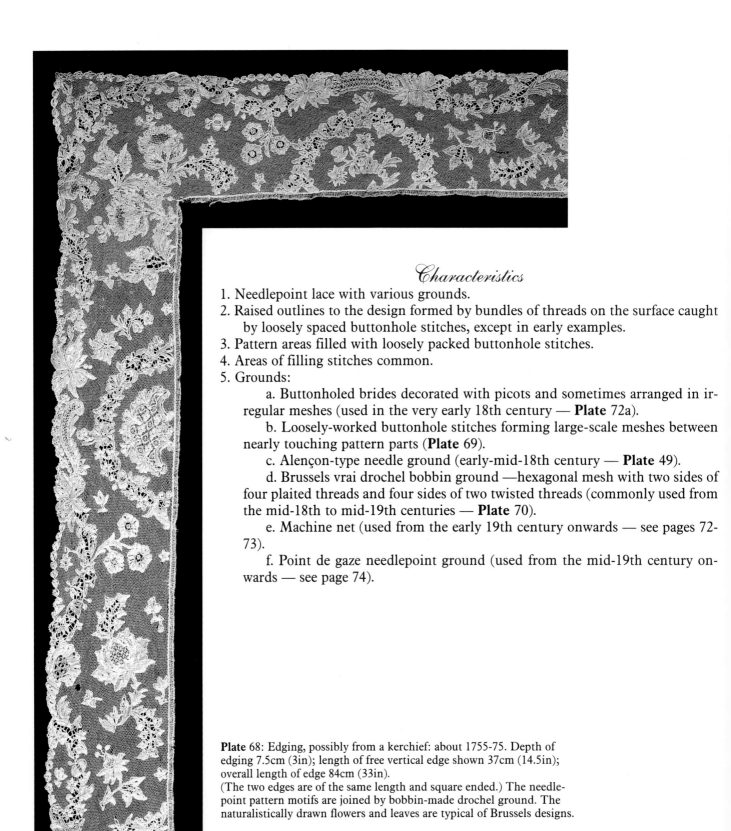

Characteristics

1. Needlepoint lace with various grounds.
2. Raised outlines to the design formed by bundles of threads on the surface caught by loosely spaced buttonhole stitches, except in early examples.
3. Pattern areas filled with loosely packed buttonhole stitches.
4. Areas of filling stitches common.
5. Grounds:

     a. Buttonholed brides decorated with picots and sometimes arranged in ir- regular meshes (used in the very early 18th century — **Plate** 72a).

     b. Loosely-worked buttonhole stitches forming large-scale meshes between nearly touching pattern parts (**Plate** 69).

     c. Alençon-type needle ground (early-mid-18th century — **Plate** 49).

     d. Brussels vrai drochel bobbin ground —hexagonal mesh with two sides of four plaited threads and four sides of two twisted threads (commonly used from the mid-18th to mid-19th centuries — **Plate** 70).

     e. Machine net (used from the early 19th century onwards — see pages 72-73).

     f. Point de gaze needlepoint ground (used from the mid-19th century on- wards — see page 74).

Plate 68: Edging, possibly from a kerchief: about 1755-75. Depth of edging 7.5cm (3in); length of free vertical edge shown 37cm (14.5in); overall length of edge 84cm (33in).
(The two edges are of the same length and square ended.) The needle- point pattern motifs are joined by bobbin-made drochel ground. The naturalistically drawn flowers and leaves are typical of Brussels designs.

Plate 69:
(top). Detail of **Plate** 68 showing the looped structure of the needlepoint motifs against the plaited and twisted meshes of the bobbin ground.
(bottom). Detail of the central edging in **Plate** 72 showing the closely spaced motifs joined by loose buttonhole stitches. Compare the raised outlines of these two examples with that of the French needlepoint in **Plate** 48.

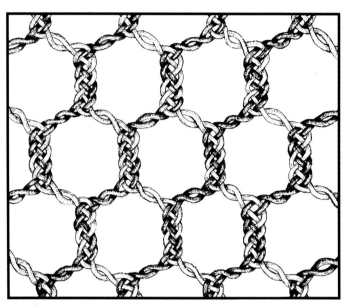

Plate 70: The Brussels vrai drochel bobbin ground.

Plate 71: Detail of the wrong side of the lace in **Plate** 68 showing strands of the bobbin-ground threads carried loosely over the backs of the more closely-worked areas of needle-made clothwork.

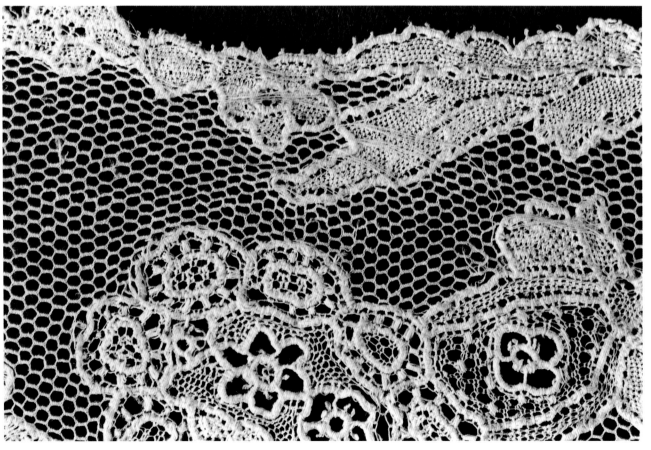

a   b   c

The early guipure needlepoint (**Plate** 72a) can be confused with point de France although its construction is generally looser than French work. A flat needle lace with a mesh ground similar to the Alençon ground was also made in Brussels in the 18th century - see pages 64-65.

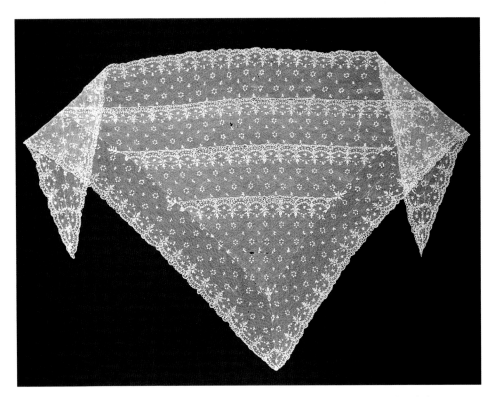

Opposite page:
Plate 72: Group of Brussels needlepoint edgings: length shown 35cm (13.7in).
a. With a ground of coarse irregular meshes: about 1700. Maximum depth 7cm (2.7in). This has a scattering of tiny motifs typical of Venetian laces of about 1700 (see **Plate** 32) but some are symmetrically grouped as in contemporary point de France lace (see **Plates** 36 and 42). The scalloped edge is also typical of point de France but the stitching is looser than in French needlepoints.
b. About 1720-30. (See **Plate** 69 for detail.) Depth 7.5cm (3in); pattern repeat 58cm (23 in).
c. Motifs joined by the bobbin drochel ground: about 1760-75. Depth 7.5cm (3in); pattern repeat 70cm (27.5in).

Plate 73: Fichu or half-kerchief of Brussels needlepoint applied to a bobbin drochel ground: about 1800. Maximum depth 51cm (20in); Maximum length (when flat) 109cm (43in).
The ground is made in three panels: a central triangle and two edging strips. Each of these is made up from narrower strips (about 1 cm wide) joined edge to edge. The design is in the classical style fashionable in the late 18th century and early 19th century.

History

Although Brussels lies in the province of Brabant, the history of its laces is so closely linked with that of neighbouring Flanders that we can no longer distinguish Brussels laces from those made in the Flemish towns in the 17th century. Only at the very end of the century did distinctions arise, both in the bobbin laces and in the needlepoints of these regions.

At this time France, under Louis XIV, was perhaps the most powerful country in Europe and dominated the fashionable scene. The classical style of point de France (**Plate** 36), with its underlay of baroque ornamentation, was adopted in Brussels and it is only the looser working of some Brussels needlepoints that enables us to distinguish them from their French counterparts.

As the lace trade picked up after the decline at the beginning of the 18th century, the styles of Brussels and French needlepoints diverged. The softer, more popular Brussels bobbin laces had developed feathery leaf patterns which were followed in some of her needlepoints while the rich texture of the 'bizarre' patterns introduced in the 1710s led to an increased use of fancy filling stitches.

Other changes were inevitable. The closely spaced motifs of the 'bizarre' period had little need for connecting brides and these were replaced by loose buttonhole stitches, sometimes forming large, open meshes. Where the larger scale of a design left wider spaces, and in the later less crowded laces of the rococo period, a net ground similar to that of Alençon (**Plate** 49) was adopted.

By the mid-18th century fashion preferred more open designs set off against clear spaces. Brussels was well placed to cater for this taste; its bobbin-lace makers had developed the gossamer-light drochel net and this was now used to ground its needlepoints. At first it was worked into the edges of the needle-made motifs which were arranged face down on a pattern; the threads of this bobbin ground can often be seen crossing loosely over the backs of the motifs from one area of working to the next (**Plate** 71). Later, as the size of the motifs diminished, it was quicker to make the ground in complete panels and then apply the motifs to it. This is the technique used in the fichu in **Plate** 73.

It is apparent from **Plate** 73 that Brussels could and did meet the demands of the late 18th century for fabrics lightly patterned with classical designs. These fashions were met equally well, however, and more cheaply, by fine muslins and gauzes, and by the lighter forms of bobbin lace. The resulting decline in the Brussels industry was aggravated by the loss of the French market due to the French Revolution and subsequent wars with France, but was not as drastic as in France itself. Even so, the volume of lace produced fell and was not to be restored fully until the mid-19th century.

In the early 19th century, the Brussels workers had one advantage over the French: they were accustomed to applying needlepoint motifs to bobbin-made net. This practice continued but they also transferred the technique to the machine-made nets which, by the 1820s, were widely available. They also quickened their rate of working by reducing the density of the clothwork areas and were thus able to produce fabrics which could compete with the less expensive embroidered nets, muslins and light blonde laces (pages 208-211) which were all the rage at the time.

By 1850 scarcely any bobbin net was being made but a new, lighter needlepoint net had been introduced. This was the 'point de gaze' ground, named for its light, gauzy appearance.

Fashions had again changed by this time. The patterns of tiny flowerheads along the headside of the lace in the early 1800s had developed into curved sprigs by the 1820s but, by 1840, the rococo style of the mid-18th century had returned. Many narrower edgings were made in patterns very similar to their earlier counterparts although wider flounces and bonnet veils, such as that in **Plate 74**, were often made in a lighter floral style. Here the weight of the design is still concentrated near the headside, as it had been for the last 60 to 70 years, but tendrils bearing stylized leaves and flowers stretch tentatively upwards. The scrolls, ribbons and strapwork which were to gain greater importance in the second half of the century are already seen in a narrow, trailing form. The overall feeling is one of lightness and asymmetry.

Plate 74: Bonnet veil of Brussels needlepoint applied to machine-made net: about 1840-50. Depth 49cm (19in); width shown 61cm (24in); full width 124cm (49in).
Veils became fashionable in the early 19th century and were particularly popular with the wide-brimmed bonnets of the 1820s and 1830s. During this period they were often a meter or more deep and just as wide. Veils for wear with the later close-fitting bonnets were correspondingly smaller.
Veils which were intended to be worn with a bonnet usually have a casing or a footing with a row of holes to take a drawstring along the upper edge. Most of the pattern is concentrated along the bottom edge but a narrow border usually continues up the two side edges as in this example.

The 1850s and 1860s saw a gradual development of this style with designs becoming fuller and more assured. The straight or slightly wavy headside of the 1840s gave way to deep scallops filled with massed flowerheads, cartouches or fanned strapwork. The footside, which had been substantially free of pattern, became filled with pendant sprays and garlands. These intertwined with richly-patterned strap-work, ribbons and floral swags stretching up from the footside to form frames for elaborate bouquets of flowers.

The whole effect is a fine combination of richness and balance. Individual sprays are rarely symmetrical and asymmetric scrolls often link one pattern repeat to the next but there is no sense of continuous movement; asymmetric flower arrangements are often confined within symmetrical frames and forwardly scrolling motifs in one part of a design are balanced by backward movement in another.

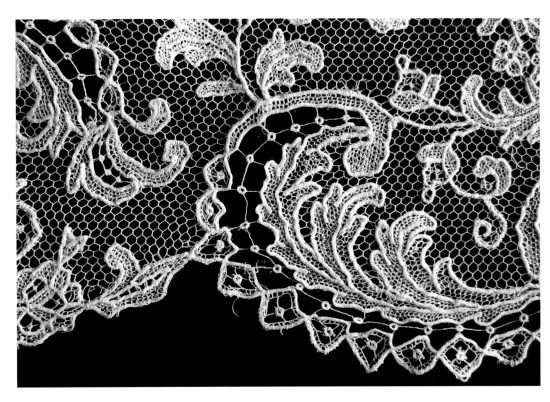

Plate 75: Detail of the right side of a Brussels needlepoint on machine net similar to the veil in **Plate** 74. Note the trailing lines or stems formed by bundles of threads like those used to outline the motifs and the extremely loose working of the buttonholed clothwork which makes the tenuous design even lighter. The clothwork becomes firmer again in the fuller, more opulent designs of the second half of the century.

Plate 76: Detail of the reverse side of the needlepoint in **Plate** 75. The diamond-shaped meshes of the machine net can be seen across the backs of the denser clothwork but are cut away behind the more open clothwork and filling stitches. This type of net was first introduced in about 1830.

73

Plate 77: Point de gaze fall cap: 1845-60. Depth of central piece 24cm (9.5in); overall length including lappets 109cm (43 in).

In the 19th century the separate lappets and cap of the 18th century were largely replaced by fall caps, comprising a pair of lappets joined by a central cap piece, or by pairs of lappets made in one piece to go over the head.

The early fall caps of the 1840s and 50s often had an asymmetric centerpiece, with a smaller lobe at the front and a larger lobe at the back. The centers of later fall caps, from the 1860s to 1880s, tend to be smaller and more symmetrical.

Note the symmetry in the design; the early, rather tentative use of strapwork; and the spots formed by buttonholed rings scattered over the ground. Spots are typical of 19th-century Brussels laces.

Plate 78: The point de gaze ground: roughly hexagonal mesh with a looped thread twisted on itself on two sides and a single thread on the other sides. It is formed by linked rows of loosely worked buttonhole stitches which are worked back and forth between the pattern areas. Alternate rows have slightly differing twists.

NOTE: The strengthening thread of the Alençon and Burano grounds is absent.

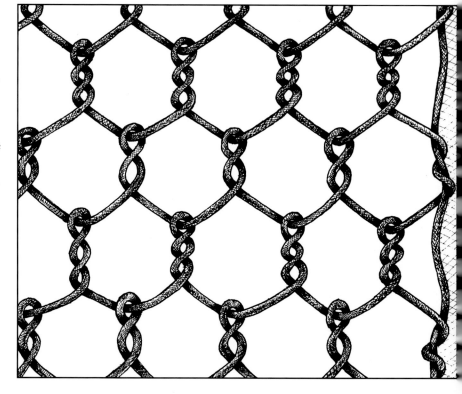

Plate 79: Detail of the right side of a piece of point de gaze showing: the very light gauzy net; the very open clothwork; the bundle of outlining threads caught down by well-spaced buttonhole stitches; and typical buttonholed rings.

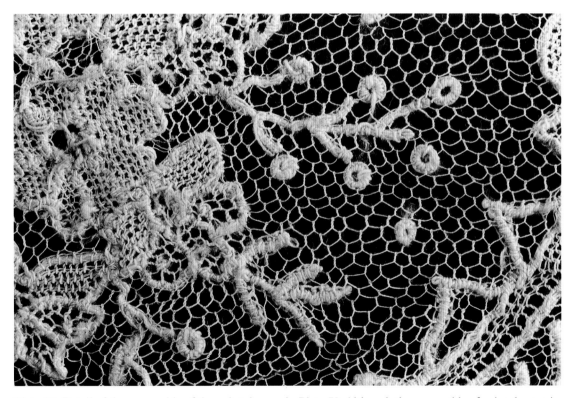

Plate 80: Detail of the wrong side of the point de gaze in **Plate** 79. Although the wrong side of point de gaze is flatter than the right side, the distinction is not so obvious as in French needlepoints because of the open nature of the Brussels work.

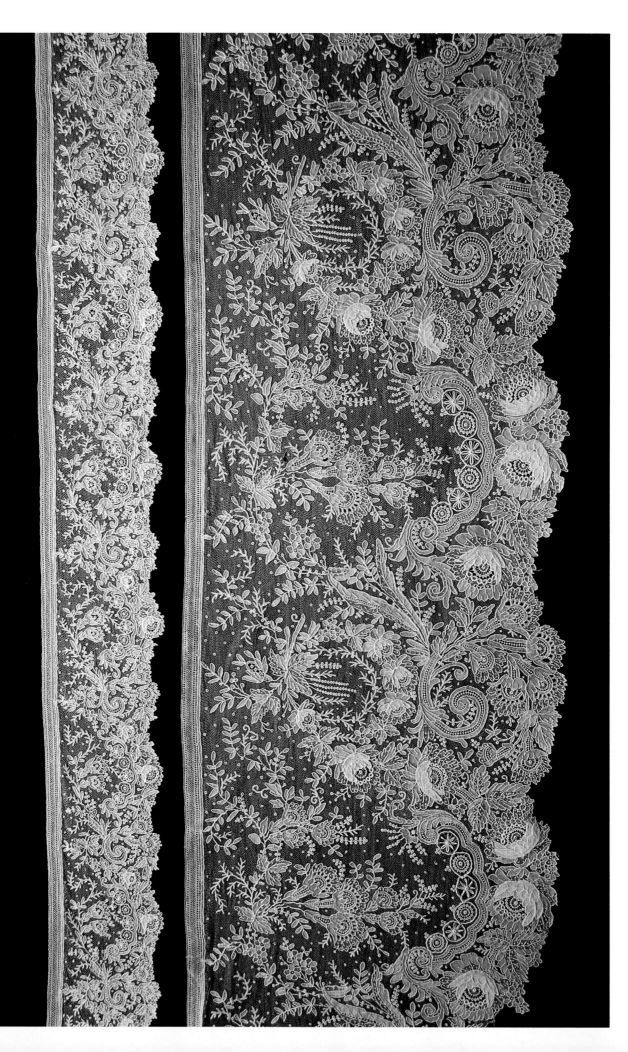

The 1870s saw little change in these designs apart from an increased interest in naturalism, in part achieved by the use of different densities of stitching in the clothwork pattern areas to give an effect of light and shade. More notably there was one technical innovation: the introduction of raised petals (**Plates** 81 and 82). These are worked separately from the rest of the design and sewn on to the surface along one edge to give a three-dimensional, tiered effect. Most commonly they are found on the roses which are almost ubiquitous in Brussels designs but occasionally they are found on other flowers or motifs.

As in other laces of the 1870s-80s, a certain stiffness and formality sometimes creeps into Brussels designs in this period but the point de gaze industry did not suffer the same decline as other lace industries as its rich flounces and matching trimmings retained considerable popularity for wedding trousseaux. It was no doubt this use that enabled its designs to continue through the 1880s into the 1900s, making the dating of point de gaze and associated Brussels bobbin laces extremely difficult.

The 1880s did, however, see the return of the rococo influence. Cartouches, scrolls and shell shapes patterned with filling stitches first became more prominent then, gradually, the flowers and strapwork became weaker and more insipid. By the late 1890s and 1900s the floral swags were often reduced to meandering tendrils and it is sometimes difficult to distinguish laces from this period from those of the 1840s. This is particularly true in the case of the long stoles which had been fashionable in the first half of the 19th century and now returned, having been ousted by shawls over the full-skirted dress of the 1850s-60s.

The 1900s brought a brief interest in Art Nouveau designs but the First World War sounded the knell of Brussels needlepoints. The fashions of the 1920s had little place for hand-made lace and the making of point de gaze almost died out.

Notes on point de gaze

The particular characterizing feature of point de gaze lace is its ground, the light, gauzy appearance of which gives the lace its name (see **Plate** 78). In other respects, point de gaze is technically similar to earlier Brussels needlepoints but its clothwork pattern areas are more loosely worked than in 18th-century laces and its raised outline is more pronounced. The addition of raised petals (see **Plates** 81 and 82) gives the form known as rose point de gaze, or simply Brussels rose point. Here 'rose' is used in the sense of 'raised' as in the earlier Venetian laces.

Point de gaze was made in huge quantities and in large pieces, such as flounces and shawls. To enable these to be worked, the designs were divided into small areas each of which was accomplished by a single lace-maker. The completed parts were then assembled on a master pattern and joined invisibly together. This way, only a small number of workers had access to the overall design which lessened the risk of pirating; lace designing was a very skilled and highly paid job in the major industrial centers of Europe. The Brussels practice thus differed in its organization from that of the French needlepoint industry in Normandy.

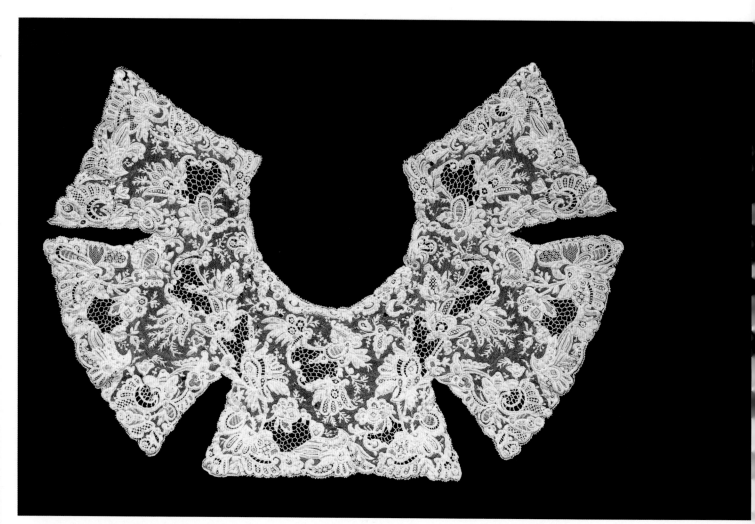

Plate 83: Brussels point de gaze needlepoint collar: about 1890-1900. Maximum width 60cm (23.5in); diameter of neck opening 18cm (7in).
The shape of this wide collar with its lobed edge harks back to early 17th century fashions while the rococo design, with its cartouches of filling stitches and asymmetric floral sprays, is derived from mid-18th century styles: this is typical of the eclectic mixing of antique styles current in the late 19th century.
The raised work is similar to that shown in the detail in **Plate** 84.

Plate 84: Detail from a flounce of Brussels point de gaze needlepoint: about 1880-1900.
This flounce has a rococo design similar to that of the collar in **Plate** 83: it also shows a similar treatment of the raised work which, in addition to the standard outlining, includes some graduated padding reminiscent of that used to highlight late 17th century needlepoints.

Plate H: Unknown Lady by Bartholomew Dandridge, 1691-1755; about 1750
Women continued to decorate the neckline of the chemise with a gathered frill of lace throughout the 18th
century. Ruffles were also worn beneath the dress sleeves: at first these were attached to the chemise, as in the
17th century, but the more flowing ruffles in fashion from the late 1750s onwards were often attached to the
inside of the dress sleeve. The sitter here is wearing sets of three ruffles, graduated in size. Her son has shirt
ruffles of plain lawn although lace might be used for formal occasions.

Hollie point

Characteristics

1. Flat needlepoint lace made with rows of knotted buttonhole stitches worked over stretched threads.
2. Simple designs created by holes left in the otherwise plain clothwork formed by the buttonhole stitches.
3. Found as insertions in babies' clothes from the early 18th to the early 19th centuries, particularly in caps, in the shoulder seams of shirts and in the bibs and detachable sleeves worn over babies' swaddling bands.

Plate 85: Baby's bonnet with hollie point insertion: 1800-25. Diameter of hollie point 4cm (1.5in)
The bonnet is of plain lawn gathered into the hollie point cap back and decorated with radiating lines of pulled-thread work. The buttonholed loops which stand proud of the surface are a common decorative feature in 18th-century bonnets; here they show how tradition preserves old design features. The bonnet is too large for a new-born baby and probably was not intended for a christening.

History

Hollie point is a peculiarly English lace. The knotted buttonhole stitch differentiates it from continental needlepoints and is found in English needleworks, such as samplers, stumpwork embroideries and tape laces, from the second half of the 17th century onwards. Its use in the form known as 'hollie point', with its distinctive delineation of design by means of holes in the clothwork, appears to date from the early 18th century.

The age of hollie point is difficult to determine because of its use of rather naive, unconnected design motifs, such as birds, flowers and coronets. Only a study of babies' wear can assist.

In general, early 18th-century bonnets tend to be plain apart from a circular or keyhole-shaped insertion of lace in the back and perhaps a lace frill around the brim. The second half of the century saw the introduction of a band of lace extending from the center front of the bonnet to the nape of the neck, sometimes with a circle in the back. This band was later accompanied by parallel lines of pulled-thread embroidery while, in the early 19th century, the circular cap back reappeared.

In trying to date babies' wear, it must be remembered that items decorated with hollie point were often made by the ladies of a household or the nanny rather than by professionals. They were often (but not always) made for christenings and were not subject to 'fashion' in the same way as adult dress so that older styles might persist for decades even after other styles had been introduced.

Plate 86: Plastron and collar of Youghal needlepoint: 1885-1900. Overall depth 55.5cm (22in); overall width 30cm (12in). The plastron was a decorative front sometimes worn over the high-necked bodices of the late 19th and early 20th centuries. This example has the long-waisted look of the 1880s and 1890s. The revived-rococo design of asymmetric floral sprays interlinked by cartouches of fancy fillings is also typical of the period. Unusually for an Irish lace, there are no shamrocks in the design.

Youghal (Ireland)

Characteristics

1. Mainly flat but with some pronounced foundation threads around and within motifs.
2. Pattern of buttonholed clothwork and open areas of linked rows of untwisted loops.
3. Motifs commonly surrounded by a narrow frill of open, asymmetric scallops.
4. Fancy fillings common.
5. Ground of irregular meshes formed by curved, interlinked, picoted brides. (Other large-scale mesh grounds occasionally used).
6. Sometimes made in cotton but usually in linen thread of good quality though coarse by continental standards.

History

Although some lace was made in Ireland in the 18th century, it was not truly a lace-making country until the mid-19th century when various crafts were introduced, or promoted, to provide the employment desperately needed after the failure of the potato harvests in the 1840s. The making of needlepoint lace was started in several centers. In Youghal, Mother Mary Ann Smith of the Presentation Convent is said to have unpicked a piece of antique Venetian lace to learn the technique, and, in 1852, a school was opened to teach local children the craft. The venture was so successful that copies of Venetian needlepoints were soon being made both there and in other centers.

In the 1870s, Youghal suffered the decline which occurred in many similarly situated industries. The initial impetus gave way to stagnation as the same designs were repeated and the lack of tight control over workmanship led to a drop in standards. In many places this was aggravated by the death or departure of the founder of what was, after all, a charitable movement, often reliant on the endeavors of a single person or group of persons to organize manufacture and promote sales.

The 1880s saw a drive throughout Ireland to improve the standards of design and technique in its craft industries and it was probably at this time that the distinctive type of Youghal lace described above developed. This was also a time of revival for rococo designs, with asymmetric scrolls and cartouches of fancy filling stitches: new designs from a particularly talented member of the convent community resulted in some especially delightful pieces, as seen in **Plate** 86, although whether this is from Youghal or from Kenmare, which also claims to have made the best of this type of lace, is impossible to say.

The Irish needlepoint industry survived into the early years of the 20th century.

Plate 87: Detail of **Plate** 86.
This shows the typical mesh and outlining of Youghal lace. It is interesting to note that the outline is similar to that of Branscombe tape lace (**Plates** 107-109), although there the likeness ends.

Embroideries & Minor Techniques

Tatting

Characteristics

1. A knotted lace made with a thread usually carried on, and worked with the aid of, a tatting shuttle (or two shuttles): the tatting shuttle comprises two boat-shaped plates with pointed ends joined by a bar on which the thread is wound so that it is housed between the plates.
2. Designs of knotted rings, often with circular loops of thread (picots) projecting from the rings; smaller rings are connected together to form larger circles, ovals and other geometric shapes.

History

The exact origin of tatting is unclear but it was probably derived from knotting, a popular pastime in the 18th century. This was carried out with the aid of a larger shuttle than the more commonly known tatting shuttle and resulted in a series of knots on a thread which could subsequently be applied to a fabric to form an attractive raised decoration.

Tatting, as such, was certainly known by the mid-19th century and was a common pastime in the second half of the century. Some tatting was also carried out professionally.

In early work, only one shuttle was used to produce a series of knots and picot loops on a thread which was then formed into rings but these had to be sewn together with a needle. Later a technique was developed which enabled adjacent picots to be joined with the aid of two shuttles without the knot created with the needle.

Plate 88
Tatted decoration for a sewing apron: late 19th century. Length of inner edge 71cm (28in); maximum depth of tatting 6cm (2.5in).
Three tatting shuttles, one of tortoiseshell and two of bone.

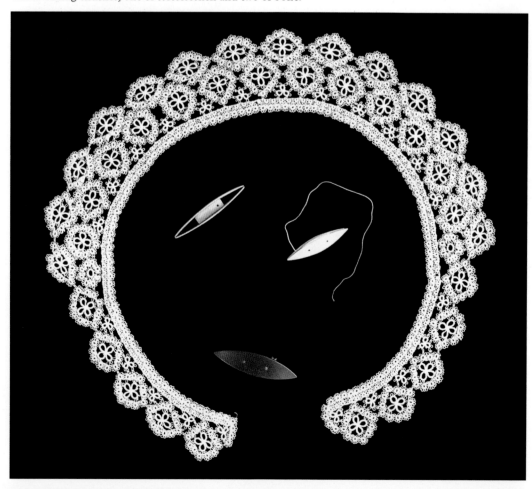

Macramé

Characteristics

1. A knotted work including a multitude of threads knotted together in various combinations to form mainly geometric designs.
2. Short lengths at the free ends of the threads often form a fringe.

Technique and history

In macramé work, the threads to be used are first supported so that they lie parallel to each other and then they are knotted together to form a decorative design. The technique was certainly known in the 16th century when the threads used were often the free warp threads at the end of a woven fabric: indeed the technique probably developed as a method of securing the warp ends in order to prevent fabrics from fraying. Once the decorative potential of the craft was recognized, of course, other ways were contrived of supporting the threads to be worked: usually they are knotted side by side onto a cord which remains in the completed work.

Macramé continued in use throughout the 17th century and into the 18th century. After a period of decline, it was revived as a domestic craft in the second half of the 19th century. Many examples in coarse string survive from this period while there was a further revival in the late 20th century.

Plate 89
a. End portion of domestic linen finished with a macramé insertion and a macramé edging: late 17th or 18th century. Depth of insertion 5cm (2in); maximum depth of macramé edging excluding fringe 9.5cm (3.7 in).
The macramé is worked separately and sewn on to the linen rather than being worked on the free ends of the warp threads of the linen as is sometimes the case.
b. Macramé sample worked in string: late 19th century. Overall depth including knotted fringe 25cm (10in); width 43cm (17in).

Irish crochet

Characteristics

1. Fabric of linked chain stitches.
2. Pattern motifs are often joined by picoted brides sometimes linked to form coarse, irregular meshes (see **Plate** 92).
3. Frequent use of 3-dimensional raised work either in the form of padded surface work or raised petals (see **Plate** 92).

Plate 90
a. Fall cap: 1850-70. Maximum depth 16cm(10in); length 66cm (26in).
The small-scale, random patterning of the fall cap is copied from Venetian needlepoints of about 1700 but the shape of the cap, with its integral lappets, is typical of the mid 19th century.
b. Collar: 1900-1915. Maximum width 48cm (19in); diameter of neck opening 15.5cm (6in).
The combination of two different textures within the same article, in this case very open patterning and dense patterning with different forms of raised work, is commonly found in laces from the late 19th-early 20th century.
The complexity of the raised work typifies Irish crochet; examples of the two types used in the collar are seen in **Plates** 92 and 96.

Plate 91: Detail of the fall cap in Plate 90a showing the lines of interlinked loop, or chain, stitches created by the crochet hook.

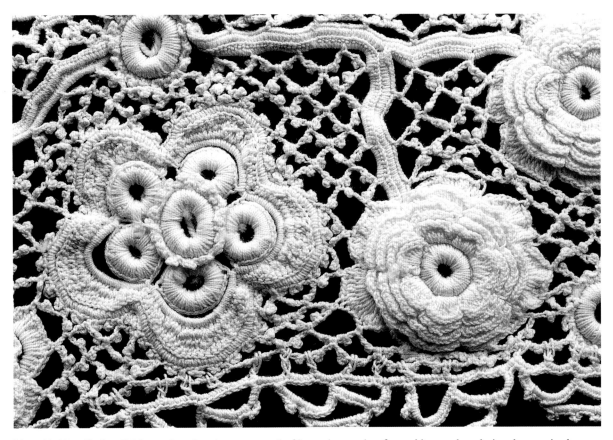

Plate 92: Detail of an Irish crochet showing: a ground of irregular meshes formed by crocheted picot bars; raised roses formed by concentric rings of overlapping raised petals; and padded rings, here covered with crochet stitches which create a chain-stitch outline which distinguishes crocheted work from needlepoint laces with their buttonholed outlines. The rings even have picoted frills in imitation of needlepoints.

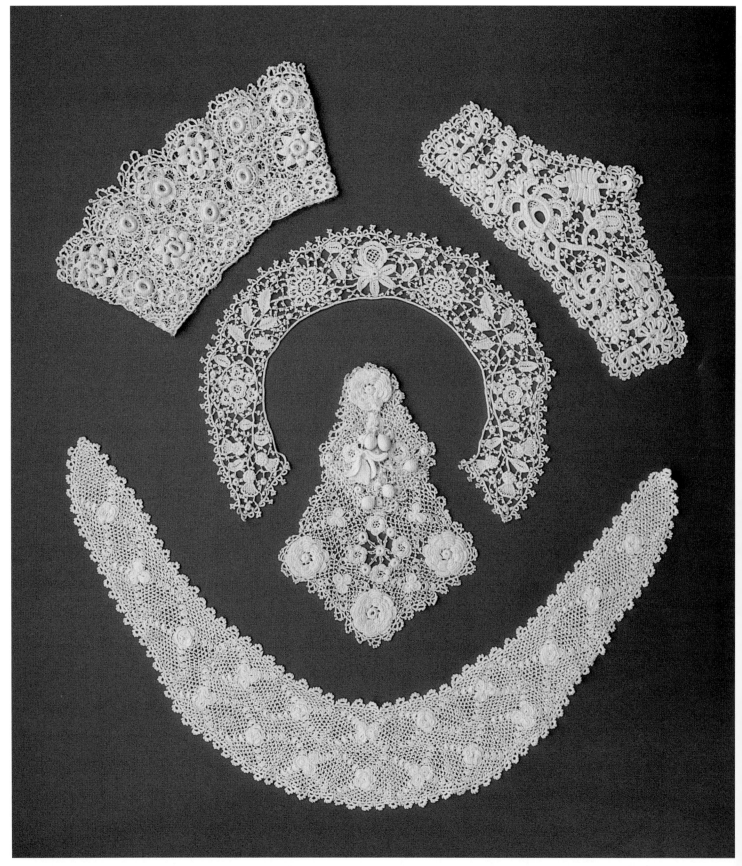

Plate 93
(top left) Cylindrical cuff: probably 1850s-60s. Cuffs of this type were often used to decorate the separate undersleeves, or engageantes, worn under wide dress sleeves in the 1850s-60s but were again used to finish dress sleeves in the 1900s.
(top right) Cuff: late 19th century.
(top center) Collar: mid-late 19th century. Diameter of neck opening 15cm (6in).
(center) Jabot: 1890-1910. Depth 22cm (8.5in).
(bottom) Collar: 1900-1915. Length of neck edge 36cm (14.5in). The diamond patterning of this collar is frequently seen in crochet designs in ladies' magazines and other sources from the 1900s to the 1930s.

Technique

Like knitting, crochet is worked in the hand, from a set of read or memorized instructions but the tool used is a hooked needle rather than knitting needles. Simple, flat, repetitive designs, of the type commonly used for household edgings, are worked in long lengths but more complex designs, and those including the raised work characterizing Irish crochet, are divided into small sections or motifs which are connected at a later stage.

Points to watch

In Ireland crochet was developed until almost any guipure needle lace could be copied, from the heaviest, most thickly padded to the finest of the Venetian needlepoints. Its looped chain stitch creates a closer imitation of needlework than any other technique and can easily fool the unwary, particularly when the motifs are joined by needle-made bars or decorated with buttonholed rings as is sometimes the case.

Lace superficially resembling Irish crochet was made on embroidery machines after about 1880.

Plate 94: Detail of the central collar in **Plate** 93 showing fine raised work on the thistle motif.

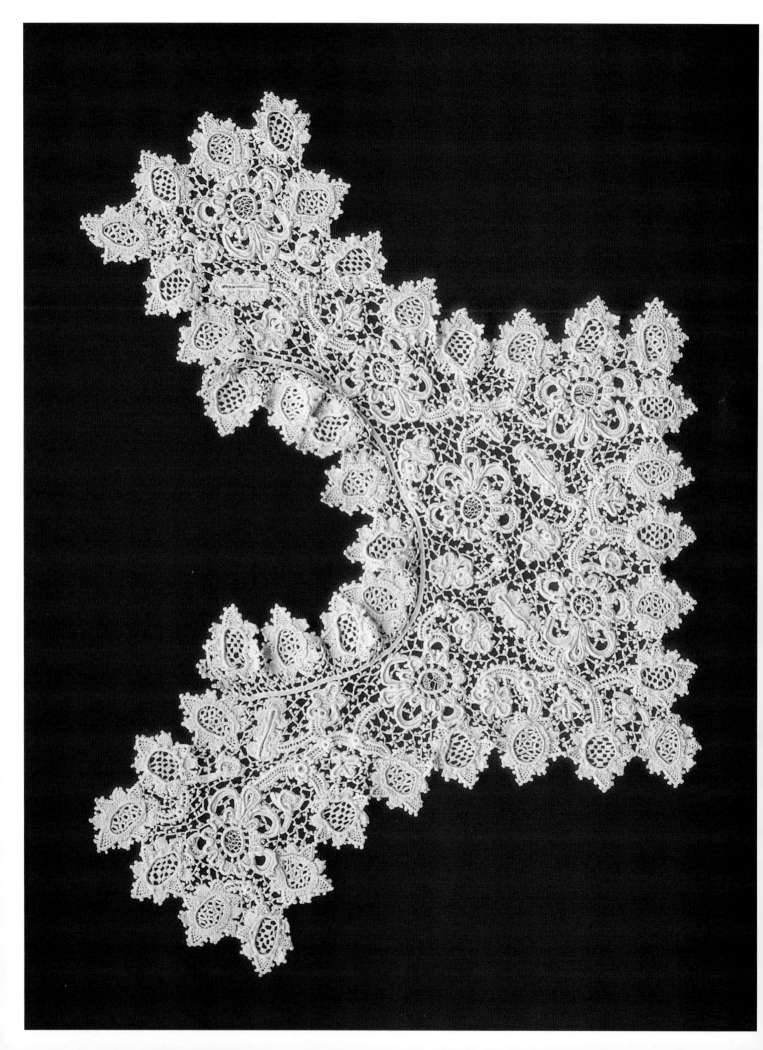

Opposite page:
Plate 95: Collar of Irish crochet in cream silk thread: about 1910. Maximum width 45cm (17.5in); diameter of neck opening 14cm (5.5in).
The collar has a central band intended to stand up around the neck and a shaped outer flounce which would fall over the back and shoulders.
The use of silk thread is supposed to have been introduced by Messrs. Hayward of Oxford Street, London, one of the many influential London shops which marketed lace from all parts of Europe. Although not a close copy, the design is inspired by 17th-century Venetian needlepoints and includes some padded raised work.

Above:
Plate 96: Detail of **Plate** 95. Many of the three-dimensional features of this example are created by the application of separately-worked motifs on top of a base design.

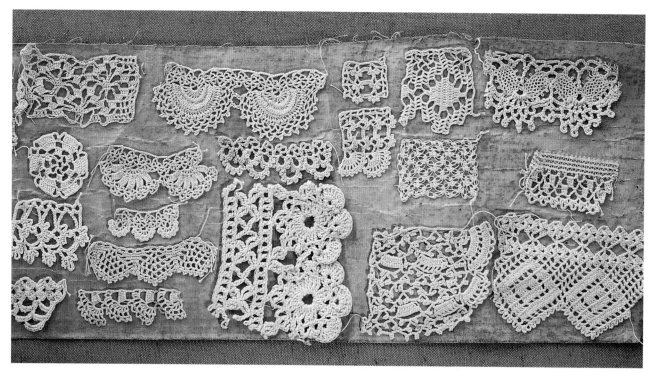

Plate 97: Samples of crochet work sewn onto glazed cloth.
Workers, traveling salesmen and shops alike all used to collate samples of designs and types of crochet (and, indeed, other laces) for selection by their customers; many such collections were sewn onto sturdy fabric, as in this case, and might be bound in a book with similar sheets or rolled for convenience of handling. I have seen similar examples, with many varieties of crochet, in several European countries so the provenance of any surviving article is uncertain without documentary evidence.

History

Crochet is an old craft, known in the 17th century and perhaps earlier but its popularity grew only in the mid-19th century. From then until the mid-20th century it was worked throughout Europe and America to form edgings in simple repetitive designs for household linen.

It was in Ireland that it developed its true potential. Here, in 1845, a school was established in Blackrock, County Cork, as one of the many famine-relief measures of the period. The craft quickly became popular and spread to other parts of Ireland as, unlike the net embroidery crafts (pages 108-115), it required little equipment and could easily be worked at home.

It is not clear how the crochet technique came to be adapted to copying needle-made laces but this must have been influenced by the contemporary growth of the Irish needlepoint industry (pages 83-84). Certainly, among the earliest crochet laces were copies of late 17th-century Venetian flat points in undistinguished designs of small crescents joined by irregular meshes (**Plate** 90a). Before long, padded rings were added and the heavier Venetian rose points were copied.

These new, complex designs could not be worked satisfactorily in continuous lengths and were split into small parts which were then joined together. A further innovation was the 'raised rose', a flower formed by concentric circles of raised petals which is found in almost all Irish crochets with floral designs.

Although the new raised crochet was well received in Europe, it was slow and difficult to make compared with household edgings for which there was also a ready market. Many workers therefore turned to these poorer-quality products and, in the 1870s, the Irish crochet industry shared the decline of so many European lace industries.

Fortunately, the revival of interest in lace in the 1880s favored the heavy guipures which could be copied effectively, and comparatively cheaply, by the crochet technique and by the 1900s even large costume items, such as jackets and fichus or shawl collars, were being made. The Irish industry recovered some of its prosperity and continued, if on a much reduced scale, through much of the 20th century.

Although Ireland was acknowledged as the home of raised crochet by the use of the term "Irish point" throughout Europe, it was widely copied both as a craft hobby and on a commercial scale. Only a few years ago I came across a town in Italy where 'punto d'Irlande' was still being made. It was a fascinating derivative: here was a craft inspired by 17th-century Venetian needlepoints, overlaid by Irish features and now again used in imitations of the earlier laces but with a decidedly 20th-century, Italianate flavor.

Plate I: Unknown Lady; Gainsborough's circle; mid-18th century.
The sitter's décolletage, showing the usual neck frill of the chemise, is covered by a fichu or cape of semi-transparent material, possibly fine muslin, edged with lace. She is also wearing an informal lace cap with lappets or strings which fasten under the chin. Her double sleeve ruffles can be seen to be made up from a lace edging sewn to a band of plain fabric: this was common practice although sleeve ruffles made completely of lace were also available (see **Plates** 47 and 185f).
The whisk seen in **Plate** D was still very much in use in the 18th century as an alternative to the shaped fichu but was generally called a kerchief or handkerchief. The ends were often tucked into the front of the bodice or under ribbons or cords across the stomacher, as shown here. The ends of larger examples might be fastened around the waist. A half-kerchief, comprising a square cut on the diagonal to form a triangle, was worn in the same way.

Sol or Ruedos
(sun or wheel) laces, including Tenerife (Teneriffe) and nanduti (nandutti)

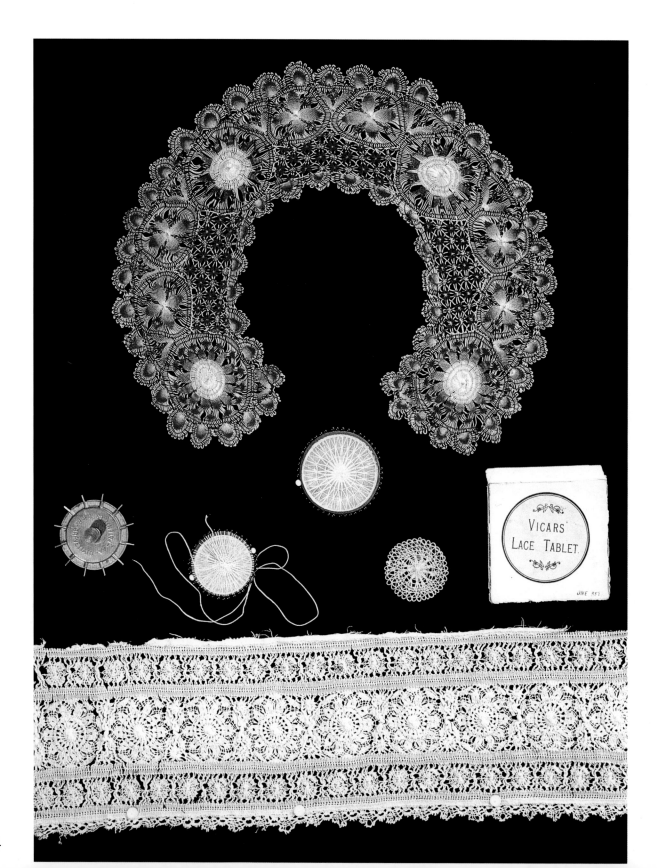

Plate 98:

(top) Collar in red and peach silk threads: late 19th-early 20 century; probably Paraguayan nandutti work. Maximum width 29.5cm (11.5in); diameter of neck opening 12cm(4.5in).
This shows only a few of the multitude of rosette or wheel patterns which can be made. The collar was probably worked as a complete item on a pattern, to facilitate the infilling of the spaces between the circular rosettes.

(center) A collection of tools available for the amateur sol worker including: a circular brass support with radial pins which can be retracted or extended (as shown) to support threads stretched diametrally across it for working; and two thick card supports with glass-headed pins in their peripheries and paper patterns on upper and lower surfaces. One pattern has threads stretched across it being worked. A completed wheel is also shown together with the box for the card patterns which also contained a set of instructions.

(bottom) Sol work fragment: 19th century or earlier. Width 23cm (9in); depth 12cm (4.5in). See **Plate** 99 for detail.
Horizontal bands of woven linen with simple pulled-thread work alternate with bands of the more complex 'sol' work; here, most of the horizontal fabric threads are removed and the remaining vertical threads are drawn into the sun, or wheel, patterns.

Characteristics

1. Needle-woven laces incorporating circular, rosette patterns in which foundation threads radiate from a center, like the spokes of a wheel, and are decorated with needle-weaving, i.e. a thread runs in and out of various combinations of the spokes, in ever widening circles, pulling different groups together to form an infinite variety of geometric designs.

2. The original sol work is based on a woven fabric: some threads are pulled out to leave others which are drawn together by the darning thread to form the spoked foundations before the decorative needle-weaving is carried out. The woven cloth is seen surrounding square or rectangular areas filled with the rosette designs; threads can be seen extending from the woven borders into the sol work (**Plates** 98c and 99).

The forms known as Tenerife or nanduti work have no fabric base. Instead the needle-weaving is worked on free threads stretched across a circular support or on threads stretched across a pattern. The first method creates individual rosettes which may then be inserted in openings cut in woven fabric or may be linked together to form an article. In articles worked on a pattern, areas between the circular rosettes are often crossed by additional threads also decorated with needle-weaving.

History

Sol work is a Spanish craft with a long history; examples are known from as early as the 17th century. It was used to decorate domestic linen, both for personal and for household use, and enjoyed a considerable revival in the 19th century when much of the professional work was carried out in the Spanish colonies.

The free form is known either as Tenerife lace (the spelling 'Teneriffe' is often used for the lace) or by its Paraguayan name of nanduti because of its particular association with these regions. Paraguay had a reputation for the finer work, sometimes in silk, but both regions produced high-quality goods, with complex and varied designs, and the products of the two industries are now often indistinguishable.

In addition to professional work, 'Tenerife' work was a popular amateur craft in the late 19th-early 20th centuries and various supports, such as those shown in **Plate** 98, were invented to assist ladies in this work.

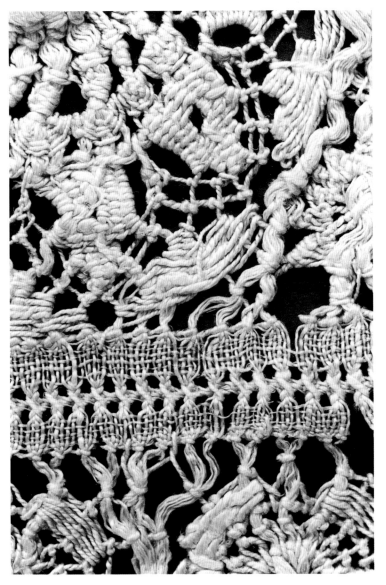

Plate 99: Detail of the sol fragment in **Plate** 98.

Bibila (Oya)

Characteristics

1. Lace worked in knotted stitches over stretched foundation threads.
2. Open pattern areas with tiny triangular holes between the stitches and the foundation threads.
3. Designs usually of floral sprays with angular outlines,

particularly with diamond-shaped leaves.

4. The floral sprays are often isolated in work for the domestic market but larger articles were made for export and often have a ground of curved, interlinked, picoted brides forming large-scale, irregular meshes.

Plate 100
(top) Padded tea cosy with an inner cover of green chiffon and an outer bibila cover in white cotton made for the Western European market: about 1910-30. Width 36cm (14in).
(center) String of individual floral motifs worked in artificial fibers on a cotton core: late 20th century Turkish. The motifs are sold in strings for the purchaser to sew to the edge of an article such as the headsquare on which it lies. Maroon silk headsquare or shawl with an edging of oya worked in silk threads: Turkish; late 19th-early 20th century. Silk square 70cm by 70cm (27.5in).

Opposite page:
Plate 101: Detail of a tray cloth edging of bibila work showing a flower with raised petals and a centre formed by a ball with a cotton wool core. The tray cloth is part of a set with the tea cosy in **Plate** 100.

History

Needle lace with the characteristics given above has long been made around the Eastern Mediterranean, particularly in Turkey, where it is known as 'oya,' and Greece, where it is called 'bibila' but also in Syria and as far east as Armenia. In its traditional form, as a decorative edging for scarves, kerchiefs etc., it was usually worked in colored silks but, when it became popular in Western Europe in the late 19th century, goods for export were more often made in white cotton to suit the Western taste.

The main centers of the export industry were Crete and Cyprus, where goods were made to Western require-ments well into the 20th century. Armenian refugees from Turkish oppression in the late 19th and early 20th centuries also earned a living from sales, particularly to the USA and Britain. The story is movingly told by Alice Odian Kasparian in her book *'Armenian Needlelace and Embroidery'* (EPM Publications, 1983) which also gives an excellent account of the technique of oya lace-making.

For a fuller account of Bibila lace and other Greek laces, reference may now be made to the recent publication *'Greek lace in the Victoria & Albert Museum'* by Lila de Chaves (Indiktos Publications,1999).

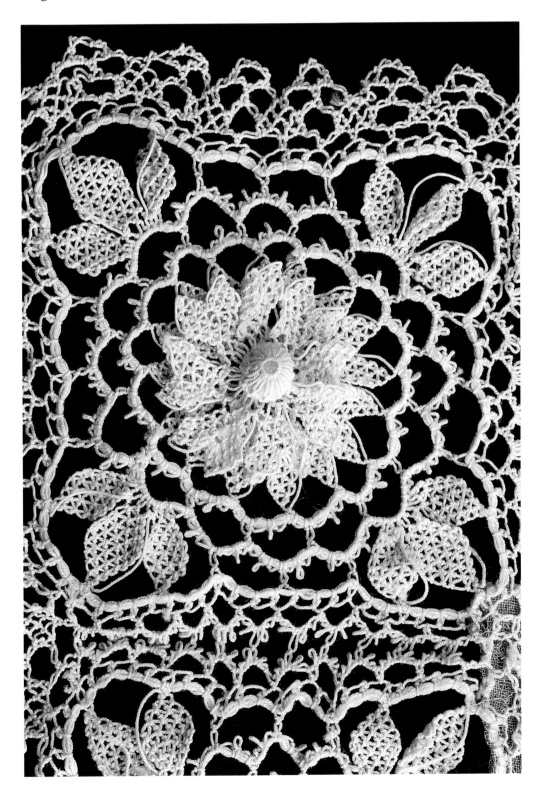

Tape or braid laces with needlepoint fillings

Characteristics

1. Pattern of pre-made tapes (or braids) completed with needlepoint clothwork, fillings and grounds.
2. The tape is puckered or folded around corners and curves in the design unless it is of very open structure.
3. Wide variety of tapes used (see **Plate** 104).
4. Grounds: Bride and net grounds are found as in true needlepoint laces.

Plate 102: Tape lace decoration for an apron being worked on a pattern drawn on glazed cotton: about 1860s.
The complete pattern includes a curved edging for the apron: the motif shown here was probably intended for a pocket. Patterns such as this were widely available for the amateur needlewoman in the late19th-early 20th centuries.

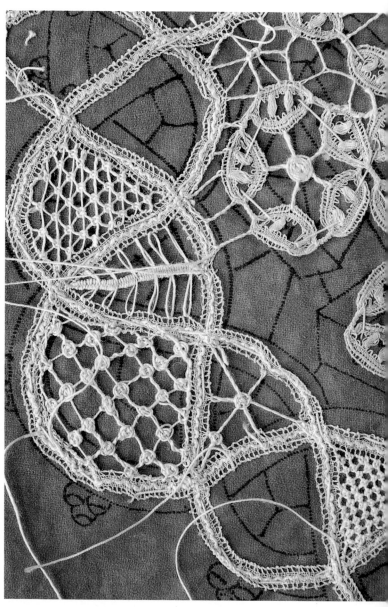

Plate 103: Detail of **Plate** 102 showing two different tapes tacked onto the pattern to provide the outline for the design and a variety of stitches worked to fill in the motifs.

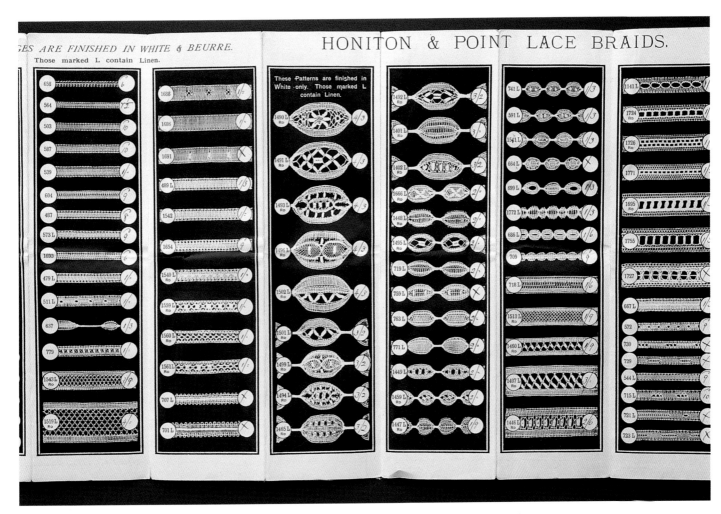

Plate 104: Detail from a trade leaflet showing a variety of machine-made tapes available for lace work.

Points to watch

This chapter is concerned with tape laces made with a tape (or braid) manufactured as a straight length, usually by machine although, particularly in early examples, it may have been hand-woven or braided. In all cases, the tape is either of uniform width or varies with very short pattern repeats. The puckering or folding of the tape around corners distinguishes this type of tape lace from bobbin tape laces (see **Plates** 11, 141, 146, and 154) in which the tape is worked with bobbins on the pattern so that the threads can be turned smoothly around corners.

The width and patterning of bobbin-made tapes can be varied although this is not always done. Bobbin tape laces are usually joined by bobbin-made brides or net but are sometimes connected by needlework.

Technique

Tape laces are made in a very similar manner to true needlepoints, the difference being that a prefabricated tape is tacked on to a pattern to provide the foundation for the work instead of a single thread or pair of threads.

The tape usually outlines the pattern motifs although it can pass through the centre as in the example in **Plate** 105. Once the tape is in place, the motifs are filled in with needlepoint stitches and the ground connecting the motifs is worked. When the lace is complete, the tacking stitches, which are the only stitches passing through the pattern, are cut to release the lace from the pattern.

Plate 105:
a. Alb cuff of tape lace: probably Italian: about 1690-1710 with later alteration. Minimum depth 13cm (5.3in)
Woven tapes pass through the center of some motifs rather than outlining them and are also used in the lower guipure edging.
b. Part of a shawl collar of tape lace: collar late 19th century: lace about 1675-1700: probably English. Width shown 32cm (12.5in); maximum depth 32cm (12.5in).
The original tape lace was remodelled as a collar in the late 19th century. The design and the use of raised work imitate the 17th-century Venetian needlepoints (**Plate** 27) but both the shapes of the motifs and the padded raised work are clumsy compared with true Venetian work.

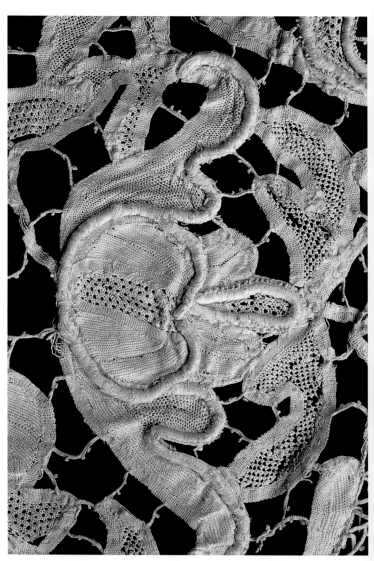

Plate 106: Detail of the shawl collar in **Plate** 105. The bundle of padding threads in the raised work is visible where the surface buttonhole stitches are worn and broken.

History

In the 16th century, prefabricated tapes and braids in colored silk and metal threads played an important role in the surface decoration of fabrics. With the growing interest in whitework embroidery and linen lace, the step of incorporating linen tapes in this new work must have been a natural one. Certainly, by the early 17th century, tape laces were being made in the designs of contemporary punto in aria, designs to which tapes were particularly well suited as will be seen from the example in **Plate** 22.

Much of the early tape lace was made in Italy, where it was called 'mezzo punto', but the technique spread into other parts of Europe and was found to provide a simple and comparatively quick method of imitating the elabo-
(text continued on page 103)

Plate 107:

a. Dress ornament of Branscombe tape lace: probably 1900-20. Depth 11.5cm (4.5in). A detail of Branscombe lace is shown in **Plate** 109.

b. Tape lace edging: late 19th-early 20th century. Depth 5cm (2in). The tape has a thick thread woven on to its surface.

c. Tape lace collar: 1870-90. Depth 5cm(2in); length shown 39cm (15.5in); actual length 48cm (19in).

d. Tape lace edging: late 19th century. Depth 10cm (4in); pattern repeat 39cm (15in).

Needle-made net grounds are less common than bride grounds in tape laces, partly for reasons of fashion but also because they were slower to make and tape work became popular as a quick and easy form of needlework.

e. A group of machine-made tapes which could be used in making a tape lace.

Plate 108
a. Flounce of tape lace worked with a wide variety of very fine filling stitches; late 19th-early 20th century. Maximum depth 21cm (8.3in);pattern repeat 23cm (9in).
The quality of workmanship in this example suggests that it may have been made at Arlanc in the French Auvergne which was renowned for such work but I have no specific provenance for it.
b. Collar worked in écru colored thread with white tapes: early 20th century. Length of neck edge 36cm(14in).

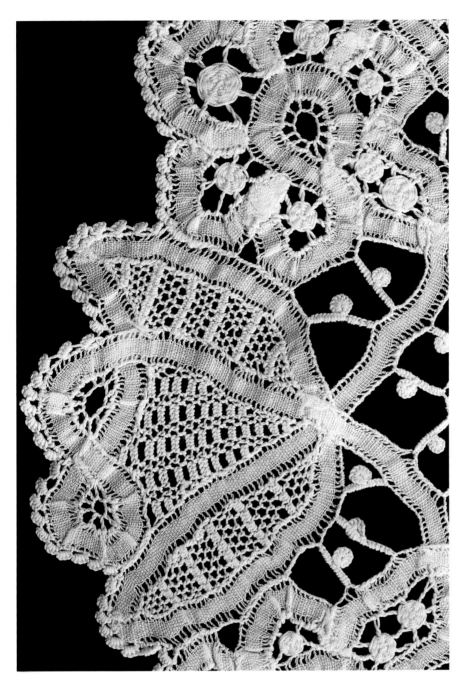

Plate 109: Detail of the back of a Branscombe
tape-lace mat: early 20th century.
The edging of tiny buttonholed scallops, the
brides decorated with picoted rings, and the
variety of fillings, including the needle-woven
wheels, are typical of Branscombe work.

rate Venetian needlepoints of the second half of the 17th
century. The lighter laces of the 18th and early 19th centuries did not lend themselves to copying in this way
but, when guipure laces returned to fashion in the mid-
19th century, tape laces returned with them.

In this later period, machine competition forced lace
makers in many areas to turn to this quicker and easier
form of work to earn a living. In England the craft is
associated with Branscombe, a small fishing village on
the South Devon coast, where Honiton lace had been
made until the slump in this trade in the late 1860s to
1870s. Surviving early examples include very narrow
tapes whereas later work incorporated wider tapes and
often the distinctive outline shown in **Plate** 109.

In continental Europe the work does not appear to
have become important industrially until the 1880s or
1890s. Although much very fine work was done in this
period, the craft survived in Belgium through the 20th
century in a very coarse form, known as 'Luxeuil'; in
this, wide, openwork tapes are linked by thick threads
with little, if any, elaboration by way of fancy fillings.
This form derives its name from the French town of
Luxeuil where much of this lace was manufactured: most
modern examples are made in the Far East.

In addition to professional work, much tape lace was
made as a craft hobby for which patterns were widely
available in shops and magazines. Many of the designs
were vaguely 17th-century in style and were known as
'Renaissance Lace'. Others were sold as 'Honiton point',
'Milan' lace or under various fanciful names intimating
that the finished product would be an acceptable substi-
tute for its more prestigious, fully hand-made counter-
part. In the USA, the work, particularly in its coarser
forms, is generally known as Battenburg lace.

Filet lace (lacis) and Burato (Buratto)

Characteristics of filet lace

1. Knotted net with regular square meshes and darned (needle-run) patterns
2. Each mesh has one thread along each side and a knot at each corner. The mesh threads usually lie parallel and perpendicular to the length of the lace so that the meshes look square but are sometimes at 45 degrees to the length giving diamond-shaped meshes
3. The darning threads run in and out of the meshes.
4. The darning threads are usually similar to the mesh threads and are worked in two mutually perpendicular directions, parallel to the sides of the meshes, so as to form pattern areas resembling woven fabric with angular outlines.
5. A heavier thread is sometimes used, particularly to outline designs, and may follow a curved path to soften the outline.

Plate 110: Filet lace being worked. A completed square of filet netting is stretched on a frame and the pattern is being darned in with a needle as seen more clearly in the detail in **Plate** 111. Square 18cm by 18cm (7in)

Plate 111: Detail of **Plate** 110 showing the filet meshes with knots at each corner and the pattern being darned in: the pattern threads are darned in parallel to the two directions of the net, at right angles to each other, giving a superficial likeness to woven fabric.

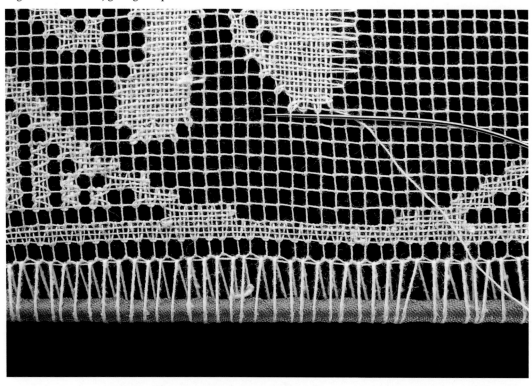

a

b

c

Plate 112

a. Typical filet lace edging with the pattern darned in the same thread as the net and in only two mutually perpendicular directions so that the patterned areas look like woven fabric: late 19th century. Depth 9cm (3.6in); pattern repeat 15cm (6in).

b. Filet lace edging: probably 18th century. Depth 7.5cm (3in): pattern repeat 14.5cm (5.7in).

Heavy darning threads are worked through the ground regardless of the direction of the meshes which are arranged to appear diamond shaped. The design is a derivative of the 17th-century Italianate baroque laces but is poorly drawn and coarse compared with the originals; this suggests a peasant origin, perhaps German from the use of thick darning threads.

c. Burato edging: late 16th-early 17th century. Depth 13.5cm (5.3in); pattern repeat 24cm (9.5in); The stylized plant forms arranged in alternate orientations are typical of late 16th-century filet, burato and drawn or pulled work but are not illustrated elsewhere in this book since they are not commonly found in true laces.

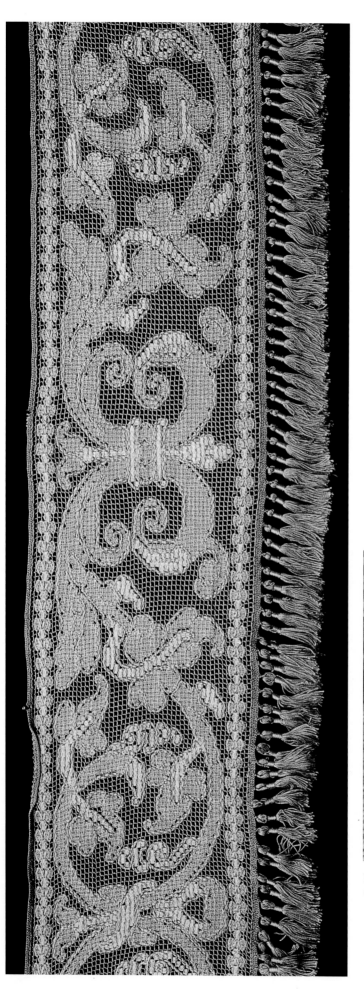

Plate 113: Filet lace flounce worked in white cotton and mustard-yellow silk thread on a base of filet net in olive-green silk thread, with silk tassels: second half 19th century. Depth including tassels 23cm (9in).

The white thread creates the body of the design, being worked parallel to the two directions of the net, while the thicker silk thread is worked in curving lines to soften the outlines of the design as a whole and to define features within it. In some areas the white thread is carried over two meshes of the net to conceal the net threads and vary the texture and color of the pattern.

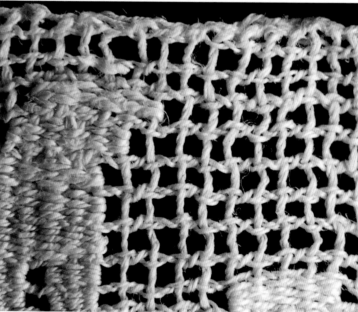

Plate 114: Detail of **Plate** 112c showing the woven burato ground and darned pattern.

Burato work (see below) looks superficially like filet lace but the latter is readily distinguished by the knots at the corners of the meshes.

Copies of filet lace were made in the 19th century on the net curtain machine but, again, the knots of true filet are distinctive.

History

The making of knotted nets is an old craft, used for centuries in the fishing industry, in agriculture and for household purposes. By the 16th century the net, called 'lacis' in Italian or 'filet' in French, was being decorated with embroidery and was in widespread use in Europe for household decoration. Here it was used in much the same way as cutwork embroidery with which it was often combined. Finer examples were also used in dress.

Filet lace was still popular in the early 17th century but later fell from favor except in peasant communities. In the last quarter of the 19th century it was revived both commercially and as a craft hobby. At this time, ladies unwilling to spend laborious hours handknotting the ground could buy the net ready-made and concentrate on the more pleasing task of decorating it with embroidery.

As filet lace was often made on a large scale for household fabrics such as coverlets, curtains and tablecloths, it provided one of the few opportunities in lace textiles for pictorial design. Legends from classical antiquity and fairy tales were particularly common sources of inspiration.

Characteristics of Burato

1. Square-meshed, open-weave fabric with darned, or needle-run, patterns usually with angular outlines.
2. Each mesh is bounded by one thread on two sides and by two threads crossed on the other two sides.
3. The darning is mainly worked parallel to the length of the fabric.
4. Colored threads, particularly silk, are found more often than in other lace-like fabrics.

Points to watch

See filet lace, above.

History

Whereas filet lace was made throughout Europe, Burato appears to be a product specifically of Italy. In the 16th and 17th centuries, the woven Burato mesh was decorated with needlework in exactly the same way as filet and often to the same designs. Like filet lace, it went out of fashion in the late 17th century but continued in the peasant tradition, the same de-

signs being repeated time and again in the 18th century so that dating surviving examples is nigh impossible.

Although some Burato was made in the craft revival of the late 19th century it never regained the popularity of filet lace.

Plate 115: Burato flounce: 18th or 19th century. Width including fringe 23cm (9in); pattern repeat 31cm (12in).
The two stylized figure motifs alternate throughout the length of the flounce.

Embroidered machine nets
Tamboured net

Characteristics

1. Chain-stitch embroidery carried out with a hooked needle on machine-made net.
2. Lines of linked chain loops are visible on the right side of the fabric and lines of straight stitches on the wrong side.
3. Areas of fancy filling stitches, often darned in, are common.
4. A hand- or machine-made picot edging is often sewn around the edge of an article.

Points to watch

Tamboured net can be impossible to distinguish from net embroidered by machine. Some of the earliest hand sewing machines used a single thread to create a chain stitch identical to that made with a tambour hook and,

Plate 116:
a.(outer) Handkerchief with edging of machine-made net decorated with tambour work and darned fillings; possibly Limerick: about 1840-60. Full width (not shown) 47cm (18.5in); Depth of net edging 7cm (2.5in).
b. (inner) Handkerchief with edging of machine-made net decorated with chain-stitch embroidery; probably tamboured: 1870-90. Full width (not shown) 34cm (13.5in); Depth of net edging 9.5cm (3.7in).

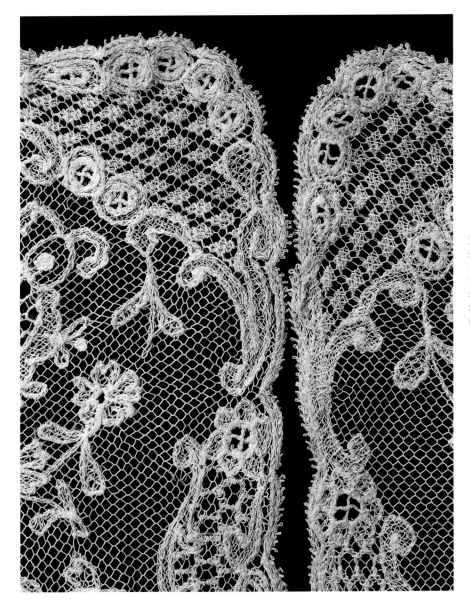

Plate 117: Detail of **Plate** 116 showing the right side of the work to the left and the wrong side of the work to the right. The net always makes the two sides difficult to distinguish but the chain stitches are visible on the surface on the right side while lines of straight stitches lie over the surface on the wrong side.

when they came into widespread use in Europe in the 1860s, they were sometimes used to decorate net. For this purpose, a pattern was drawn on the net and the machine's needle was guided along its lines by eye. Needless to say, similar deviations from the true pattern occurred as in tambour work in which a pattern is followed in the same way.

What, then, of regularity of stitch? The earliest machines did not always create regular stitches because of difficulties with their feed mechanisms and a good tambour worker would have prided herself on her ability to work into every mesh, or alternate mesh, of a net.

In the late 19th century multi-needle industrial machines were developed and used to embroider very repetitive designs in both chain and darning stitches. Here the regularity of the work is a true and obvious indication of origin.

History (see also pages 111-112)

Tambour work was probably introduced into Europe from the Near East in the early 18th century and derives its name from the tambour (drum)-like frame which sup-

ported and stretched the fabric to be embroidered during working. The embroidery itself is carried out with a hooked needle, like a crochet hook but sharper because of its initial use to embroider woven fabrics which needed to be pierced.

In the late 18th century, tamboured whitework on fine lawns and muslins was particularly popular and this no doubt contributed to the transfer of the technique on to machine nets as they became available. Certainly, by the 1810s, the tamboured net industry was well established alongside that of darning on net and from that time their histories are interlinked.

In the early years of their manufacture, the novelty of embroidered nets made them fashionable in even the highest circles of society and they were widely used for bonnet veils, stoles and many other dress accessories. To make the larger items the net was stretched on long frames, sometimes big enough for several workers to sit at together. Work on this scale was, of necessity, carried out in workshops as the frames could not be accommodated in small cottages.

By the middle of the century the novelty had worn off but embroidered nets were still in demand. Together with the patterned machine laces now available, they provided a cheap alternative to 'real lace' for many people who wished to be fashionable but could not afford the completely hand-made article. Lace was no longer the exclusive prerogative of a wealthy and aristocratic minority and this was its downfall.

For a brief period in the 1870s and 1880s, lace was out of fashion. By the 1890s, when it had regained favor, many of the hand-lace industries had declined to such an extent that they were unable to recover. In an age of machine lace, tamboured and needle-run nets had the advantage of being hand-embroidered and this gave them a cachet which maintained their popularity up till the First World War.

London Dresses for March.

Published March 1 1812. by Vernor Hood & Sharpe.

Sands. sc.

Plate J: Fashion Plate; about 1808-10.
In the early 1800s fashion had no great need of lace but veils which draped from the hair or from a bonnet were starting to come into vogue. These might be of embroidered machine net rather than true lace as patterning was minimal, being reserved to a narrow border along the headside and scatterings of spots or sprigs on the ground.

Needle-run or darned net

Characteristics

1. Embroidery on machine-made net made by darning with a needle.
2. Pattern threads pass in and out of the meshes of the net.
3. Cloth-like areas of close lines of running stitches are common.
4. Areas of fancy filling stitches are common; in some of these the embroidery threads are used to pull larger holes in the net.
5. A hand- or machine-made picot edging is often sewn around the edge of an article.

6. Often combined with tambour work (see pages 108-110).

Points to watch

Embroidery darned into a machine net can look deceptively like a true bobbin lace, especially when worked in simple designs with little clothwork and few filling stitches, or in floss silk in imitation of blonde laces. Look for the way the design threads run in and out of the net in an embroidered example but are caught between other threads in a bobbin lace. Also, check whether a picot edging is made integrally or added on.

Needle-run threads were used to outline designs in the early patterned machine laces to imitate the gimp threads of bobbin laces (see pages 284-286) and picot edgings were also added to these.

History
(see also tamboured net)

Hand-knotted nets had long been decorated with needle-run embroidery (see filet lace, pages 106-107) when machine-made nets were introduced in the second half of the 18th century and provided a new foundation for this type of work.

Plate 118: Stole of needle-run machine net: 1825-40. Width 41cm(16in); length 218cm (86in); length of patterned end 43cm (17in).
The curved sprig motifs used here are typical of designs of the late 1820s and 1830s. Unusually, the three sprigs are different but are repeated at the opposite end of the stole. Note the variety of filling stitches in the sprigs and in the border which surrounds the entire stole. The picot edging is bobbin-made.

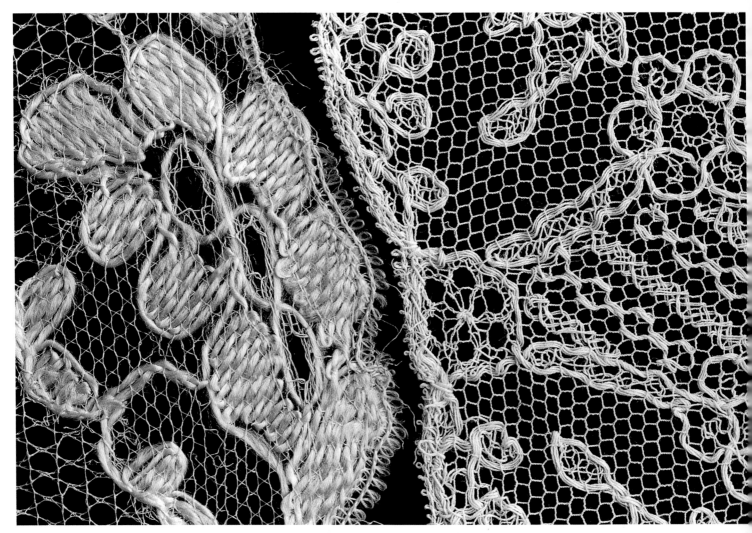

Plate 119:
a. Detail of a collar of needle-run net. The coarse thread used in this example can clearly be seen running in and out of the meshes of the net.
b. Detail of an edging of machine-made silk net copying a kat stitch ground darned with a floss silk in imitation of bobbin-made blonde laces. Compare the wavy appearance of the floss silk as it runs in and out of the net with the smooth surface of the blonde lace in **Plate** 243.

The earliest of these nets easily unravelled and little has survived but, by the 1790s, more stable nets were being made on the stocking frame (point net) and on the warp machine (warp net). Both the point and warp nets had a looped construction and were readily distinguishable from hand-made bobbin nets but, in 1809, John Heathcoat patented a machine which manufactured a net substantially identical to the East Midlands point (or Lille) bobbin net. This was to become the most popular ground for both needlework and appliqué laces (see Honiton and Brussels laces) until the advent of a much lighter net with a diamond-shaped mesh in the 1830s.

Much of the early development of the net- and lace-making machinery occurred in Nottingham and this became the main centre of the needle-run and tamboured-net industries in England. Coggeshall in Essex was also a noted centre in the first half of the 19th century while London produced goods of particularly high quality.

The famous Limerick industry in County Cork, Ireland, was established in 1829 by an Englishman, Charles Walker. It produced nets embroidered both by needle-running and tambouring, often in combination: the tambouring usually formed the outlines of the designs and the needle-running the fancy fillings. This industry thrived until the 1850s when a lack of new designs and a drop in the standard of workmanship caused its decline but it was revived in the 1880s and survived well into the 20th century.

Embroidery on net was not confined to the British Isles. France and Belgium, in particular, both had flourishing industries making not only the shawls, flounces, collars and trimmings required for fashionable dress but also household goods, such as tamboured net curtains. The advantage given by good designers working for the lace industry as a whole enabled the French and Belgian industries to continue even through the slump of the 1870s. As we have seen, this was in part caused by the embroidered net industry itself.

Carrickmacross

Plate 120
a. Collar of Carrickmacross work: about 1890-1900. Maximum width 56cm (22in).
The large size and lobed shape of this collar date it to about the 1890s. It is worked as a muslin appliqué on net with both the net and muslin cut away to form the guipure areas. The fancy fillings are of needle-run embroidery.
b. Scarf of Carrickmacross guipure: late 19th century.

Characteristics

1. Cutwork embroidery, in some cases applied to machine-made net.
2. Pattern areas of woven fabric.
3. Pattern outlined with a thick thread couched on to the surface.
4. Article often bordered by picots formed by loops of the outlining thread.
5. Grounds:

   a. Brides, or bars, usually covered with closely-spaced buttonhole stitches and often decorated with picots.

   b. Machine-made net.

6. Fillings:

   a. In guipure forms, needlepoint lace fillings are sometimes found.

   b. Forms with a net ground often include needle-run fillings (see pages 111-112) and areas of guipure work.

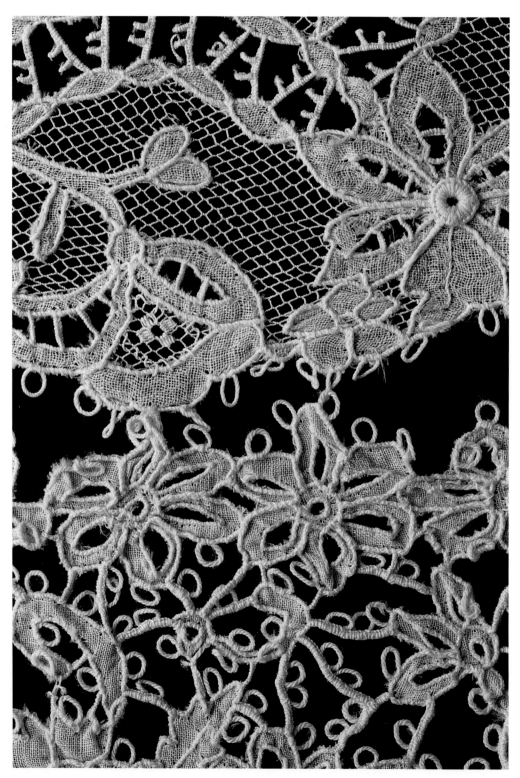

Plate 121:
a. Detail of **Plate** 120a. The machine-net foundation can be seen through the sheer muslin used for the pattern.
b. Detail of **Plate** 120b. The woven muslin and couched outlining thread of Carrickmacross work can be seen more clearly without the foundation net.

114

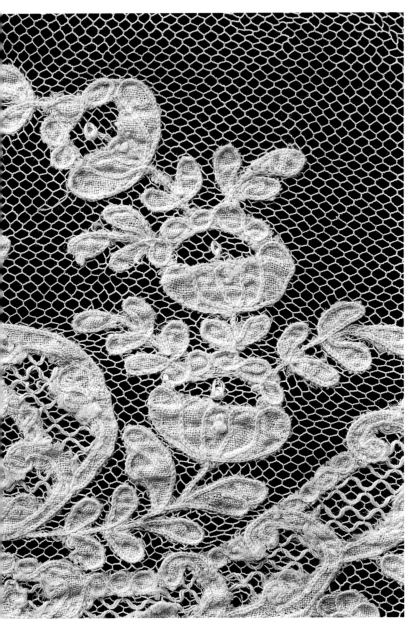

Plate 122: Detail of an appliqué work in which the muslin is applied to a machine-made net by means of a chain stitch. Work of this type is particularly associated with Brussels but was also carried out elsewhere in Europe, including Ireland.

The filling stitches are usually effected by the needle-running technique on remaining areas of net but parts where both net and muslin have been cut away may be filled with needlepoint stitches. Where wide areas of net and muslin are cut away, the spaces are crossed by needle-worked brides which are normally worked before the cutting stage to ensure that the work remains flat when lifted from the pattern.

In the guipure form of Carrickmacross lace, the net is omitted entirely. The outlining thread is couched on to the muslin and the brides which are to connect the various parts of the design are worked before the unwanted muslin is cut away.

Points to watch

The fabric areas of cutwork embroideries are easily distinguishable from bobbin clothwork since the fabric threads are all evenly spaced and run in the same two mutually-perpendicular directions over the entire area of the work, regardless of the design. In bobbin clothwork, the spacing and directions of the threads vary even in straight laces.

The technique of cutwork embroidery on net with a couched thread outline was introduced into Ireland from Italy and continued in use in continental Europe although an alternative form of work with a chain-stitched outline instead of the couched outline was also introduced. This could be produced either with a tambour hook or by machine (see **Plate** 122).

History

In the 1820s, Mrs. Porter of Donaghmoyne, who is said to have acquired a novel piece of applied muslin on machine-made net on her travels in Italy, taught the technique to local women in an attempt to provide a form of gainful employment in a period of depression. The scheme was dependent on private orders and was of limited success but, with the potato famines of the 1840s, a more businesslike approach was taken with the setting up of lace schools on the Bath and Shirley Estates at Carrickmacross.

Here the appliqué work, subsequently to be known as 'Carrickmacross lace', was taught and the guipure form developed. The products of this work had an initial period of success which was followed by a decline, as in the Limerick industry, due to a fall in the standards of workmanship and design. Revivals in the 1880s and, in particular, in the 1890s when great care was taken over design, led to the production of large quantities of fine quality goods which found ready markets abroad and also resulted in the survival of the industry in Ireland through the 20th century.

Technique

In Carrickmacross appliqué work, a layer of net and an upper layer of muslin or other fine, woven material are tacked on to a pattern and a thick outlining thread is couched on to lines within and around the design: the couching stitches pass through both the woven fabric and the net to sew them together. Unwanted muslin is then cut away, both around the outlines of the motifs and in spaces to be decorated with filling stitches; in some areas both the muslin and the net may be cut away to form a guipure. A pair of special scissors with a knob on one point is used for the task to prevent any accidental cutting of the fabrics.

Lace knitting

Characteristics

Fabric of looped stitches interlinked in various ways to create areas of differing density and texture, usually in simple geometric patterns.

Points to watch

Knitted laces worked by hand and by machine have very similar structures and not even an expert can always tell them apart by eye.

The looped structure of knitted textiles can sometimes be confused with needle lace but knitted loops are roughly Ω-shaped: the arms of the loop are often open and, although they may touch, they do not twist over or around each other like the loops of buttonhole stitches; the threads in knitted loops do, of course, loop into other stitches to build up the knitted fabric.

It is very difficult to date lace knitting as the general nature of its designs did not change: only the shape of the finished article or sometimes its thread can help.

Although only simple lace designs were, in general, created by hand knitting, warp-knitting machines were developed by the mid-19th century which could reproduce all the complex designs in vogue at the time.

Plate 123: Bonnet knitted in white cotton: probably about 1830-50. Diameter of circular back 7cm (3in)

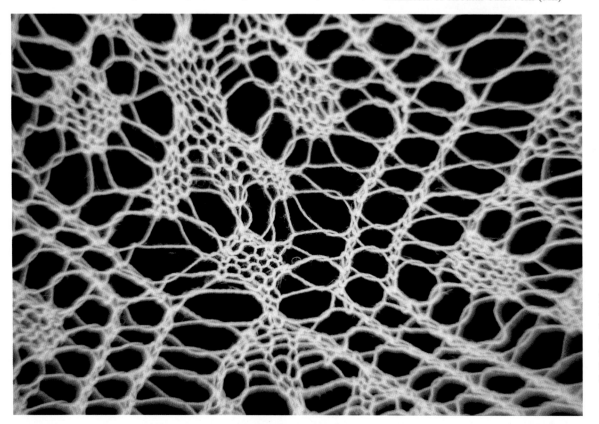

Plate 124: Detail of lace knitting showing characteristic omega (Ω) shaped loops which differentiate knitted structures from needlepoint laces.

History

Although hand knitting itself is an old craft and the stocking frame (the earliest knitting machine) was invented in the late 16th century, lace knitting seems to have developed in the second half of the 18th century when there was a vogue for lighter laces and for the geometric designs to which this craft is suited. During this period many innovations were made to the stocking frame to enable it to make plain net instead of the usual close-textured knitted fabrics and then, gradually, patterning was achieved. Hand knitting of laces developed contemporaneously.

Lace knitting remained popular in the 19th century and became a cottage industry in the Shetland Isles in the second half of the century when the fine wool from the Shetland sheep was found to be suitable for shawls and Scottish wedding veils; some of these, though perhaps six feet square, could be pulled through a wedding ring.

The Shetland industry continued into the 20th century, at times using imported cotton or other threads instead of local wool. Industries also developed elsewhere in Europe and in her colonies; a product still commonly found on the market is lace doyleys from the Azores knitted in the local aloe fibre.

The Bridesmaid.   *The Bride.*

Plate K: Fashion Plate from '*La Belle Assemblée*', Sept. 1832. Both the bride and bridesmaid in this fashion plate are shown wearing bonnet veils with their fashionable wide-brimmed bonnets. Such veils usually had a draw string along the upper edge by which they were attached to the bonnet.

The shape of bonnets varied enormously in the 19th century. In general the long narrow shape of the 1800s was transformed by the late 1820s and 1830s into a bonnet with a flaring brim which gradually shrank through the 1840s until, in the 1860s, it became simply a small cap worn on the back of the head; the size and shape of the veil varied with that of the bonnet.

Examples are seen in **Plates** 74, 166, 229, 248, 252, and 259.

117

Bobbin Laces

Torchon

Characteristics

1. Straight bobbin lace in a variety of threads.
2. Cloth stitch and half stitch pattern areas.
3. Largely geometric designs.
4. Usually made with uniform threads, with no raised work, but a gimp thread or raised tallies are sometimes incorporated.
5. Grounds: large-scale meshes with threads, unusually for bobbin laces, worked at 45 degrees to the edge:

    a. Torchon ground comprising diamond-shaped meshes with two threads crossed or twisted on each side.

    b. Other very open grounds including the five-hole ground comprising a checkered arrangement of roughly square openings alternating with squares of crossing threads defining five smaller holes.

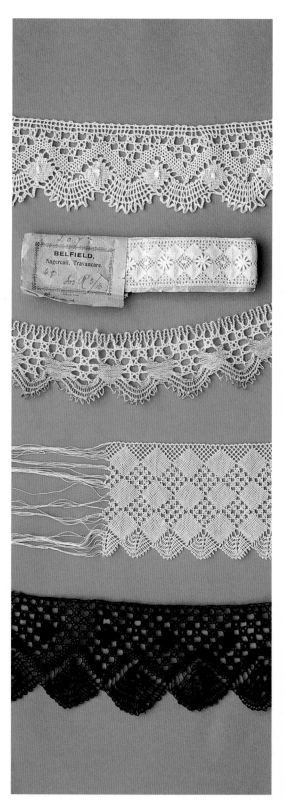

Plate 125: Group of torchon edgings.

a. In cream worsted wool; late 19th-20th century. Maximum depth 8.5cm (3.4in). The design consists of: triangles of five-hole ground along the footside; a half stitch zigzag trail; cloth stitch diamonds with a raised tally over each center; and fans along the scalloped headside.

b. Insertion in cotton thread made at Nagercoil in Travancore, India and still in its original wrapper. Depth 4.5cm (1.75in).

The Nagercoil industry was one of many started by European Christian missionaries in colonies throughout the world. It supplied local needs for European-style textiles and a surplus for export.

c. In a mixture of cream wool and gold wrapped threads (see **Plate** 126 for explanation). Depth 8cm (2.8in).

d. In cotton, still showing the free ends of the threads as it would be immediately on removal from the lace pillow. Late 19th-20th century: depth 11cm (4.4in).

e. In black worsted wool. Maximum depth 10cm (4in).

Laces in worsted wool were known as 'yak' laces and were worked in torchon and other simple designs. It is said they originated in the lace-making area around Le Puy when a shortage of cotton thread led manufacturers to seek an alternative working medium but were later made elsewhere as well.

Black yak laces were often used on mourning dress, particularly on outer garments.

Plate 126: Group of torchon laces in metal threads from a manufacturer's sample book: bought in Clermont Ferrand and most likely made in the Auvergne region of France which had a reputation for this type of lace, among others. Probably 19th century. Length shown 9cm (3.5in)

Metal threads used for lace making consist mostly of two types: narrow strips of metal foil, usually gold or silver but sometimes copper; and metal foil wrapped around a fiber core, commonly of silk. The stiffness of the resulting threads makes them unsuitable for complicated designs.

In these samples both types of thread are seen. Most are in gold but the second sample includes a mixture of gold and silver. The top sample is very tarnished compared to the others and is probably in lower carat gold: metal lace was priced by weight and depended on the quality of the metal.

The top sample is worked with the 'torchon' ground.

At times gold and silver thread laces were worn in such quantities that strict laws (sumptuary laws) were promulgated to restrict the quantity and quality worn by different ranks. The restrictions in the 16th and 17th centuries probably played a part in the development of more elaborate lace designs which could be achieved in the supple linen and silk threads.

History

Laces with the characteristic geometric designs of torchon laces have been known since at least the 17th century but in the mid-19th century they became particularly popular and acquired the name 'torchon'. Being the simplest of the bobbin laces, they could be made quickly and cheaply and became the mainstay of many lace-making areas in Europe as the competition from machine laces forced workers to turn away from the more difficult laces which were rapidly becoming uneconomic.

Early Bobbin Laces

in geometric and simple trail designs and later copies

Characteristics

1. Mixed bobbin techniques.
2. Uniform threads (no gimp or raised outlining).
3. Simple patterns formed by narrow trailing lines of clothwork or plaited braids connected by plaited and twisted bars and wheatears.
4. Little use of fancy filling stitches other than wheatears.
5. Found as straight-edged insertions and pointed and scalloped edgings with a symmetrical design repeated in each point or scallop.
6. A footing is often worked integrally with the lace in early examples.

Points to watch

It is difficult to distinguish early Flemish and other Northern examples from Italian ones but, as with needlepoints, the Italian work is often tighter: this can make the clothwork pucker. Also, Italian laces include more wheatears than Flemish laces whereas laces constituted simply by very fine plaited braids are particularly associated with Flanders.

Early laces are often made in continuous lengths, with the same threads throughout, but incorporate sewings (usually associated with part or bobbin tape laces) to join touching parts; 19th- and 20th-century examples are more usually made as pure straight laces.

History

Bobbin laces appear to have developed in the 16th century, probably from plaited and woven braids, and at first had very simple, essentially geometric designs. Many were worked in silk or metal thread and were applied as surface decoration to the rich fabrics of the period. Others, in linen thread, were used as insertions in domestic linen, both for furnishing fabrics and in garments. It may not have been until about the 1570s that bobbin laces were used as decorative edgings but many later portraits show ruffs bordered by spiky laces formed by very narrow, flowing lines which give an open, spidery effect, different from that of contemporary needlepoints.

It is uncertain whether Northern Italy or Flanders first produced these bobbin laces; as with the needle laces, early references occur in the records of both regions. In Italy the main centers were Genoa and Milan but Venice also made bobbin lace while many of the Flemish towns which later became famous for specific lace types had industries in this early period.

In the early 17th century the geometric style was still popular. If anything, designs for insertion laces became more rigidly organized into rectangular compartments filled with repeated, rosette-like motifs in imitation of the reticella needlepoints. These are perhaps most effective in the tightly worked Italian laces, particularly those with a proliferation of wheatears (**Plate** 127d) which may be Genoese.

At the same time, freer designs were developing. This was a natural trend in the bobbin laces which, unlike reticella needlework, did not have the constraint of a fabric foundation. The first signs are seen in the 16th-century edgings in which narrow tapes or plaits twist to and fro, working down one edge of a point and up the other.

As the early pointed edgings gradually gave way in the 17th century to tiny, rounded scallops or pointed arches, floral motifs became more common but designs formed by tapes which snaked from one scallop to the next, forming a symmetrical, geometric pattern in each scallop, continued into the 1640s. This was particularly true of Northern laces but, as the scallops became shallower, the designs, which had been very open in the 1620s

Opposite page:
Plate 127:
a. Edging: probably late 16th century: Flemish? Depth 3.2cm (1.3in) The lower geometric border is sewn to a later 17th century insertion.
b. (upper left). Insertion: 17th or18th century peasant lace in the late 16th century style. Depth 3cm (1.1in).
c. (lower left) Insertion: probably late 16th century in a style seen in pattern books from about 1560 onwards: probably Italian. Depth 3cm (1.1in).
d. (right) Insertion: probably early 17th century in a style of about 1610-40: Northern Italian. Depth 5.5cm (2.2in).
The design of rosettes in rectangular compartments is copied from reticella designs (pages 32-37). The pointed wheatears are particularly associated with Genoese work.
e. Edging: 17th century, in the pointed style of the last quarter of the 16th century: North Italian. Maximum depth 6cm (2.3in)
f. Edging: 17th century or later, in the style of the early 17th century: probably Italian. Maximum depth 3.5cm (1.3in).
g. Edging: about 1610-30: Italian or Flemish. Maximum depth 6cm (2.3in)
The thread and tightness of working of these pieces show them all to be of early date but b, d, e, and f are in coarser threads than would have been used on fashionable dress; they could have been made for household or church linen or for peasant dress at a later date than suggested by their designs. (See also **Plate** 14c and **Plate** 130c.)

121

and 1630s, became more crowded and the spaces between the tapes became filled with an early form of mesh ground.

By the mid-17th century, simple, geometric designs were no longer fashionable but they persisted in coarser, household laces and in peasant communities, in some regions even into the 19th century. Indeed, it is said that Genoa supplied the lace makers who gave impetus to the Maltese industry in the 1830s (pages 218-221) although the products of the 1840s and 1850s were generally more complex than the laces seen in **Plate** 127.

The mid-19th century was a period of massive expansion in the lace trade but also a time when the hand-lace industry was suffering greatly from competition from cheaper machine laces. In the 1860s, examples of the earlier, simpler bobbin laces were rediscovered in the Cluny Museum in Paris and were then reproduced at Mirecourt, the center of the French lace industry of Lorraine. Immediately, other makers of poorer-quality laces turned to these easier, more quickly made products, now known as 'Cluny' laces, to scrape a precarious living and they and their derivatives became the staple output of many areas of Europe. The laces made in these different regions are now often indistinguishable from each other but they were cheap products, made largely for the home market, and are likely to have been made where they are now found. They were worked in black and white cotton, cream and black silk and other threads.

The Cluny and related guipures are usually readily distinguishable from their 16th- and 17th-century counterparts by their thread and their workmanship but this is not always true. The interest in antique laces in the 1850s and again in the 1880s and 1890s led to some close copies of the old designs being made in fine linen thread. One noted producer of reproductions of antique bobbin laces of this type but also of other antique laces, was the Aemilia Ars Society referred to on page 35. When trying to date lace one must always be on one's guard.

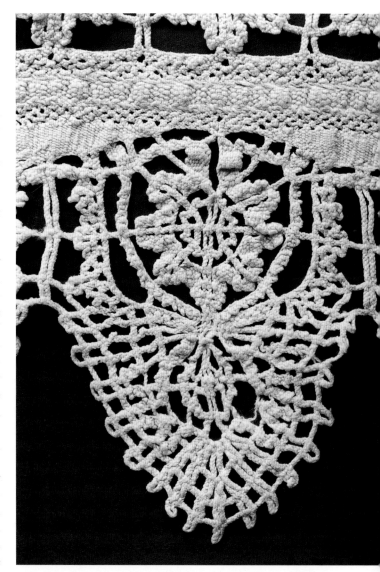

Plate 128: single point from a bobbin edging: about 1600-10 or perhaps late 16th century. North Italian or Flemish. The predominance of narrow trailing lines formed by twisted or plaited threads and the massing of these threads near the footside as they pass from one point to the next indicate the very early date for this piece. Depth of point 7cm (2.7in).

Plate 129: Scalloped bobbin edging: about 1620-40; probably North Italian. Depth of scallop 7.5cm (3in). The broad scallop, broader areas of clothwork and inclusion of wheatears suggest a later date for this edging than for that in **Plate** 128.

Plate 130

a. Edging: early 20th century in the style of the 1620s. Depth 8.5cm (3.3in).
The design of this example is copied exactly from a 1620s pattern; only the thread betrays its 20th-century origin. This has turned brown, which is typical of thread used by workers organized by the Aemelia Ars Society in Bologna in the early 20th century.

b. Collar: 1850-70: probably English, East Midlands. Maximum width 31cm (12.2 in): depth of lace scallops 5.5cm (2.2in)
The close similarity of the lace design to that of the edging in **Plate** 127g will be apparent, but this collar could have been made only in the 19th century, most probably in the middle years when fashion required neat, round collars, which fitted closely round the high necks of day dresses.

c. Insertion and edging joined.
Insertion: early 17th century in an alternating geometric design: Italian, possibly Genoese. Depth 2.2cm (0.8in)
Edging: late 19th century in the style of about 1630-50. Maximum depth 5.5cm (2.1in)
This combination demonstrates a further trap for the unwary: the edging and insertion could, stylistically, be of the same date. Only the difference in feel and quality of the threads points to their differing ages, and this can be judged only by experience.

d. Edging: late 19th century. Depth 8cm (3.2in)
This shows the type of design most usually referred to as 'Cluny' because of the inclusion of a divided trail of clothwork (the two clothwork tapes separated by a row of holes). This example is probably English East Midlands work.

123

Milanese and North Italian

Characteristics

1. Bobbin-tape or part bobbin lace.
2. Flat lace with uniform threads (very occasional surface work).
3. Pattern of scrolling clothwork.
4. Fillings formed by arrays of holes in the clothwork and areas of fancy stitches in spaces in the designs.
5. Right and wrong sides differ: the wrong side often has occasional groups of threads, usually plaited, passing loosely across the motifs from one area of working to another.
6. Grounds:

   a. Bobbin-made bars often arranged in pairs and decorated with picots (**Plates** 132 and 135) or more complex bars. In bolder forms the pattern motifs touch and only a few bars are needed.

   b. Round or diamond mesh ground (**Plate** 133). The round mesh has four threads plaited or crossed on six sides, enclosing an almost round hole. Clear pinholes are often visible at four corners. When very tightly worked, the meshes can appear diamond shaped.

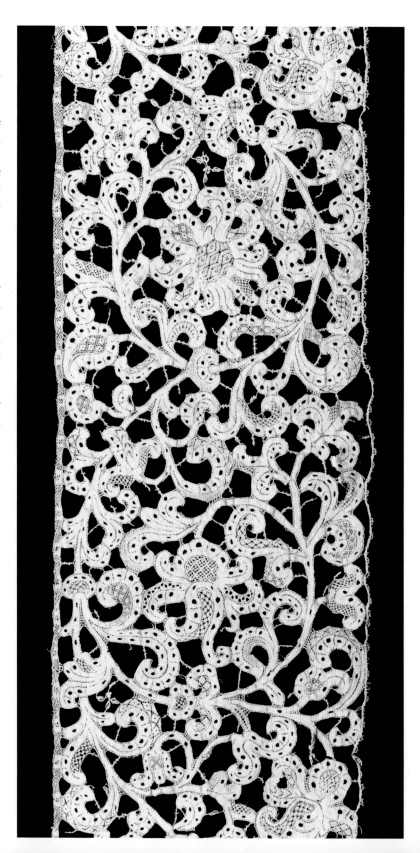

Plate 131: Milanese flounce: about 1650-75. Depth 20cm (8in): pattern repeat 46cm (18in).
The bold design with its scrolling motifs and rich patterning is typical of the Italian baroque style. Note, in particular, the way the stems scroll in alternating directions to terminate in large, stylized exotic flowerheads almost surrounded by the stems. The motifs are arranged to touch each other so that they can be joined to form a fabric without the need for a multitude of brides which would clutter the otherwise clear spaces between them.

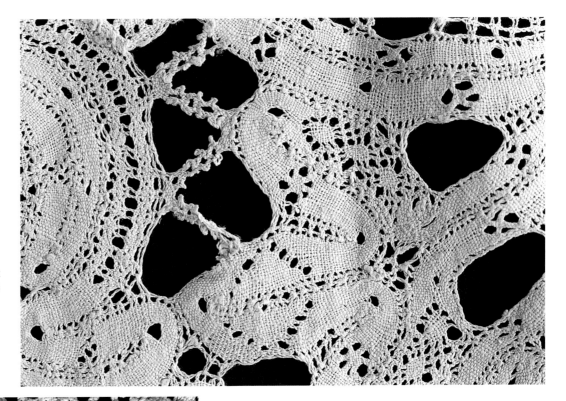

Plate 132: Detail of the Milanese flounce in **Plate** 136 showing: typical patterning of the dense clothwork with filling stitches; lines of openwork along the edges of motifs for linking with adjacent motifs either by connecting brides or where they touch by means of bobbin-made 'sewings'.

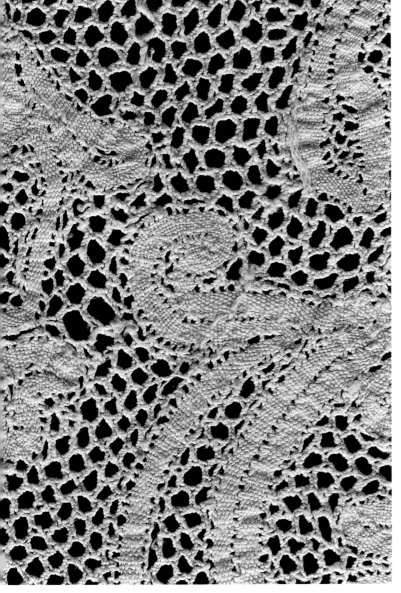

Points to watch

See Flemish bobbin laces (page 134).

History

We have already seen how designs changed gradually from the geometric to the baroque style in the 17th- century Venetian needlepoints and this trend occurred simultaneously in the North Italian bobbin laces. As early as the late 16th century, floral motifs had been introduced into the symmetrical designs of pointed and scalloped edgings and by the early 17th century these had developed into more flowing designs of curving, trailing stems bearing small leaves and flowerheads. These could easily be created by the bobbin technique as the narrow tapes required only a small number of bobbins and the motifs could be worked by the bobbin-tape or the part technique (**Plate** 134).

As technical abilities improved and the more expensive needlepoint laces were elaborated, so were the bobbin laces; the clothwork pattern areas expanded and holes and filling stitches which had played a minor role in earlier laces assumed greater importance. By the 1650s the baroque style was fully fledged and is seen more clearly in the Milanese bobbin laces than in the Venetian needlepoints where the heavy raised work and later rearrangement of motifs frequently conceal the original design.

Plate 133: Detail of the back of the lace in **Plate** 137c showing the Italian round mesh ground. The ground threads are linked by sewings into the edge of the previously made pattern and occasionally carried loosely over the back.

125

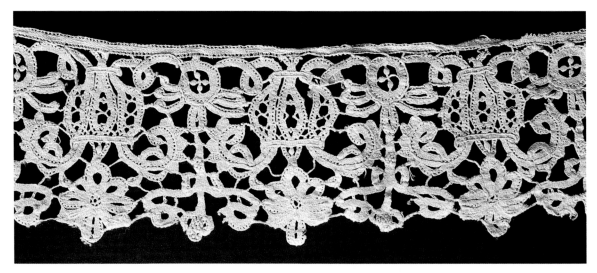

Plate 134: Milanese edging: about 1640-50. Depth 8cm (3.2in); pattern repeat 8.5cm (3.4in).
This piece shows the transition from the simpler, symmetrical plant designs of the early 17th century to the later baroque designs. The slightly wavy headside has replaced the scalloped edge of earlier laces.
Note the slight variation in the width of the clothwork forming the leaves and the minor use of filling stitches and raised work on the surface.
From the collection of the late Mrs. Valerie Cliffe.

As in the needlepoints, the bolder designs of the 1650s to 1670s required few connecting bars and, in Milanese laces, the clear spaces between the smoothly rounded outlines of the motifs were often complemented by large apertures in the clothwork (**Plate** 137a). In more elaborate forms, the scrolling tapes were patterned by a seemingly endless succession of diverse stitches. These bolder designs were often made by the part technique.

Towards the end of the century, as the scale of the motifs decreased, the variety of filling stitches and the breadth of the clothwork diminished to an almost uni-form width in all but the more exceptional cases: the use of the bobbin-tape technique became much more prevalent. A further change was an increase in the number of connecting bars and the introduction of net grounds; these appear to have developed slightly later than, but were used alongside, the bar grounds. At first the meshes were irregular both in shape and direction but by the 1670s a more organized round or diamond mesh ground had developed. Alternative nets, such as the kat stitch ground (page 201), were also used occasionally.

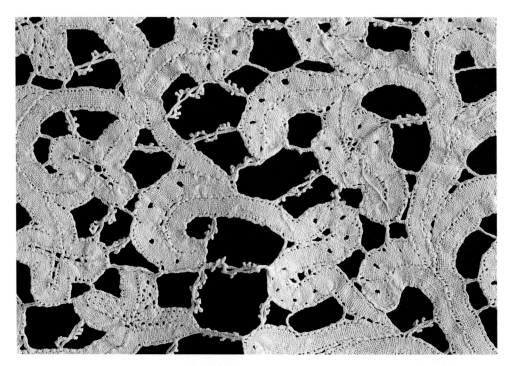

Plate 135: Detail showing a double-bar ground including bars formed simply by twisted pairs of threads, four-thread plaits with and without picots, and interwoven plaits. The threads are sometimes carried over the back of the lace but less frequently, and over shorter distances, than in Flemish work and are often neatly plaited rather than left loose.

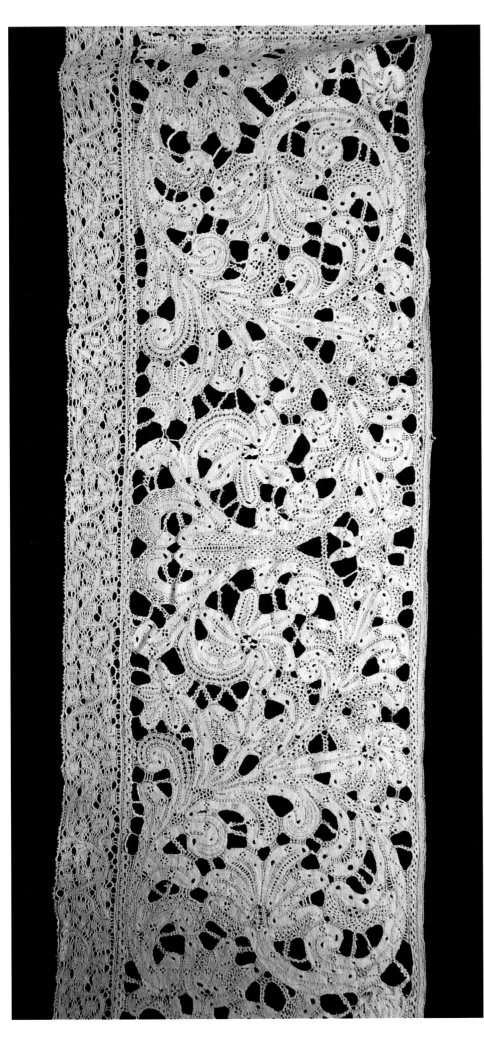

Plate 136: Milanese flounce with a later
Flemish bobbin lace edging: flounce
about 1650-80; edging probably about
1680-1700 (see comment on **Plate** 196).
Depth of flounce 22cm (8.5in); pattern
repeat 74cm (29in); length shown 36cm
(14in); depth of edging 4.5cm (1.6in).
The flounce is made up from separate
panels each comprising a single pattern
repeat with a central axis of symmetry: a
secondary axis is created at the join.
Despite its apparent complexity, the
design is formed essentially by a single
scrolling tape joined by sewings along
touching edges. The contrasting effects
are given by variations in the width of
the tape itself and in the arrays of holes
and filling stitches within it. As is
typical of Italian work, the leaves and
flowers are formed by the tape branching from a stem and doubling back to
form the stem again.

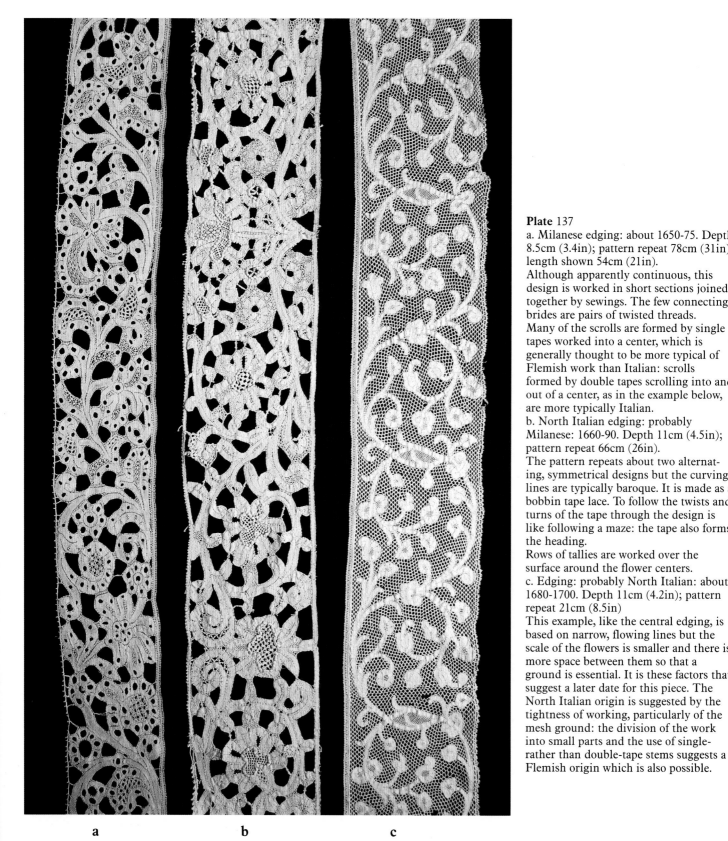

a   b   c

Plate 137

a. Milanese edging: about 1650-75. Depth 8.5cm (3.4in); pattern repeat 78cm (31in); length shown 54cm (21in).

Although apparently continuous, this design is worked in short sections joined together by sewings. The few connecting brides are pairs of twisted threads. Many of the scrolls are formed by single tapes worked into a center, which is generally thought to be more typical of Flemish work than Italian: scrolls formed by double tapes scrolling into and out of a center, as in the example below, are more typically Italian.

b. North Italian edging: probably Milanese: 1660-90. Depth 11cm (4.5in); pattern repeat 66cm (26in).

The pattern repeats about two alternating, symmetrical designs but the curving lines are typically baroque. It is made as a bobbin tape lace. To follow the twists and turns of the tape through the design is like following a maze: the tape also forms the heading.

Rows of tallies are worked over the surface around the flower centers.

c. Edging: probably North Italian: about 1680-1700. Depth 11cm (4.2in); pattern repeat 21cm (8.5in)

This example, like the central edging, is based on narrow, flowing lines but the scale of the flowers is smaller and there is more space between them so that a ground is essential. It is these factors that suggest a later date for this piece. The North Italian origin is suggested by the tightness of working, particularly of the mesh ground: the division of the work into small parts and the use of single- rather than double-tape stems suggests a Flemish origin which is also possible.

By 1700 the Italian baroque style was out of favor in fashionable dress but lace continued to be made in the lighter designs of the late 17th century (**Plate** 137c) through much of the 18th century. At the same time, designs influenced by the new French classical style were seen (**Plate** 141). In these, narrow tapes meander almost continuously through the lace, defining areas of indeterminate shape filled with fancy stitches, and organized in repeated symmetrical arrangements about vertical axes.

Much of this 18th-century bobbin lace was made in wide flounces for church use whereas narrower, coarser edgings were made and used in the peasant communities. This manufacture spread out from Milan, where the finest of the 17th-century lace was made, north to the Alps and into the southern parts of Austria. Derivatives were also made in Germany and Eastern Europe as will be seen in a later chapter.

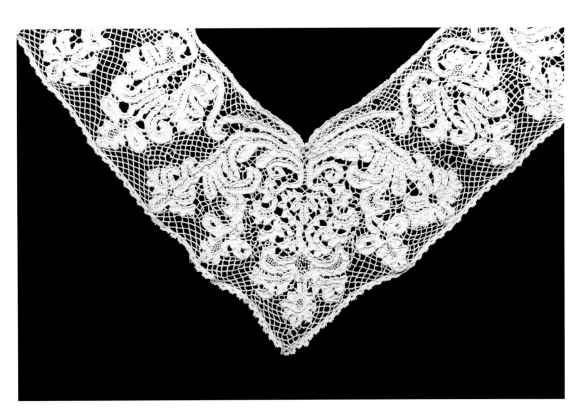

Plate 138: corner flounce of Milanese bobbin tape lace with a coarse, plaited, diamond-mesh ground: late 17th century. Depth of corner 17cm (6.7in). The obvious symmetry in the motifs of this design displays a northern influence but the tape incorporates a cord on its upper surface (see detail in **Plate** 139) in imitation of the raised work of the prestigious Venetian needlepoints of the period.

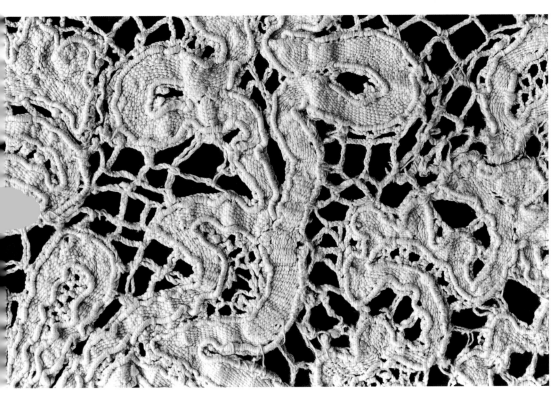

Plate 139: Detail of **Plate** 138 showing the surface cords. The bobbin-made tape appears puckered but this is because of the tightness of working, not because it is pre-made like machine-tape laces.

129

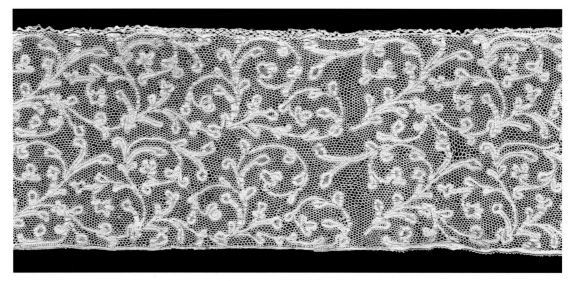

Plate 140: Flounce made by the part technique; North Italian or possibly Flemish; late 17th-early 18th century. Depth 19.5cm (7.6in); pattern repeat 30.5cm (12in).
This flounce was clearly worked in separate panels but, on close inspection, it is found that the tapes within the repeats are not continuous. Unusually there are two pattern repeats within the depth of the flounce.

Plate 141: Flounce: probably North Italian: about 1700-40, but possibly Flemish. Depth 28cm (11in); pattern repeat 23cm (9in); length shown 40cm (16in)
A comparison of this flounce with the Flemish flounce in the 'candelabra' style (**Plate** 149a) will show the influence of French designs. The differences are that here the branching motifs are created, and joined, by a bobbin-made tape which meanders almost continuously through the design and many of the budlike flowers are created by loops in the tape.
The scalloped headside is a typical feature of point de France; Italian baroque laces normally have a straight edge. The motifs in the scallops are worked separately, as are the major panels. These are joined by the ground and the fillings along secondary axes of symmetry in the design.

In the 19th century the peasant traditions continued in Italy to a limited extent, with a revival at the end of the century. Among the revival laces was a derivative of Venetian needle and bobbin laces of about 1700, in which trails of narrow clothwork fork and scroll in opposing, inward spirals to terminate in tiny trefoils or flower buds worked in a combination of cloth stitch and half stitch.

The 19th-20th century version of this lace is particularly associated, in Italy, with Cantu, near Lake Como, but similar laces were also made in Belgium along with copies of laces in the late 17th century Milanese high baroque style. Examples of these are shown and discussed at the end of the chapter on Brussels and Belgian bobbin laces.

Plate L: Unknown Gentleman; English provincial; about 1770.
By about the 1730s, men had ceased to wear cravats with elaborate lace ends except on formal occasions. The lace seen in this portrait consists solely of the shirt ruffles, i.e. gathered frills around the cuffs which fall over the wrists and matching frills down the front opening of the shirt. At least the top buttons of the coat and waistcoat were normally left undone so that the lace would be seen. By the early 19th century even this use of lace had ceased except for formal wear.

Flemish laces in the Italian baroque and French styles

Characteristics

1. Usually a part lace but occasionally made by the bobbin-tape technique.
2. Uniform threads (no gimp).
3. Mainly flat but with some Brussels-type raised work after about 1700.
4. Clothwork pattern areas with some half stitch after about 1700.
5. Right and wrong sides differ: the wrong side has groups of threads passing loosely across the motifs from one area of working to another.
6. Grounds:

    a. Bobbin-made bars, often decorated with picots (**Plate** 143).

    b. Round mesh ground (**Plate** 144): hexagonal mesh with four threads plaited or crossed on all six sides, enclosing an almost round hole with pinholes usually visible at each corner. A very open variation, similar to kat stitch (see page 201) is often found, particularly in 18th-century examples.

NOTE: The division between the laces described here and those described on pages 173-175 is somewhat arbitrary because of the mixture of techniques and styles current in 17th century Flemish laces. Those I have termed 'Flemish-style' are, for the most part, straight laces or their direct predecessors and lead conveniently on to the straight laces considered in the later chapters.

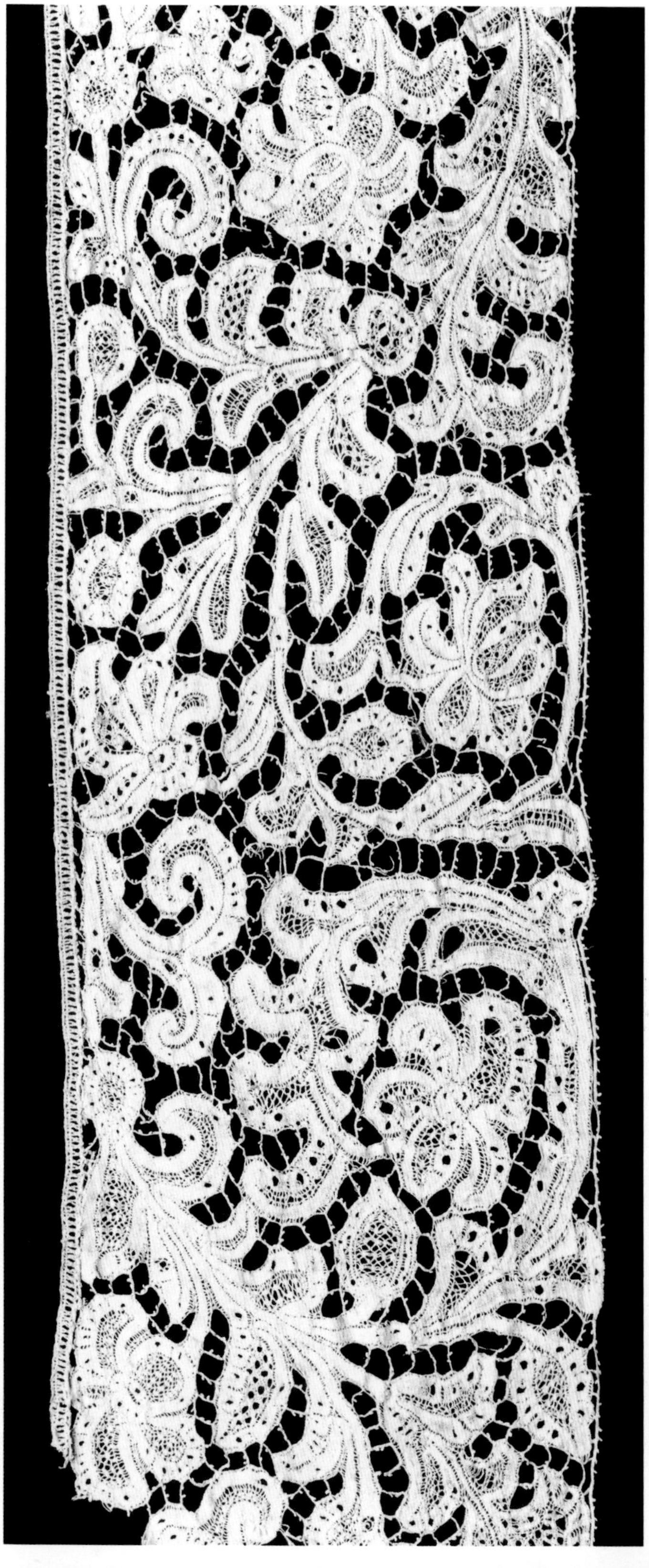

Plate 142: Flounce of Flemish bobbin lace: about 1650-80. Depth 19cm (7.5in); pattern repeat 57cm (22.5in).
The design of this flounce exemplifies the Italian baroque with its sweeping curves, large, exotic flowerheads and abundance of filling stitches but a Flemish origin is suggested particularly by the ground: this comprises fine picoted bars which snake back and forth across the open areas (see **Plate** 143).

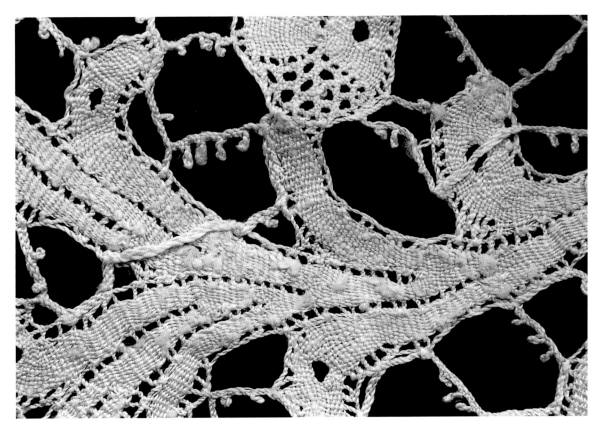

Plate 143: Detail of the reverse of the lace in **Plate** 148b showing the typical Flemish bar ground: the bars are worked in continuous lengths after the pattern has been completed and are joined by sewings into the edges of the motifs. They are decorated with picots where they cross the spaces between motifs and are worked along the edges or carried across the backs of the motifs from one point where they are needed to the next.

Note the cut ends of thread in the clothwork areas where threads have been removed during working as the clothwork is narrowed.

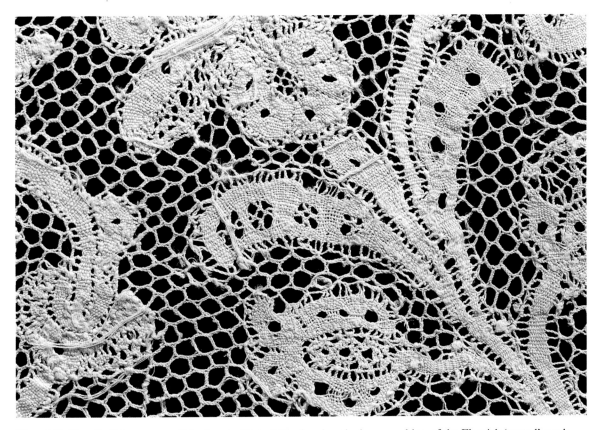

Plate 144: Detail of the reverse of the lace in **Plate** 148a showing the loose working of the Flemish 'round' mesh ground. Like the bar ground, the threads of the mesh ground are joined by sewings to the threads outlining the design and are occasionally carried loosely over the backs of the motifs from one area of working to the next.

Points to watch

Flemish bobbin laces in Italianate baroque designs are confusingly similar to their Italian counterparts and, indeed, not always distinguishable but the following indications can help:

(a) Italian laces tend to be more tightly worked than Flemish ones; this may be noticeable in densely packed clothwork, strong bars and tightly plaited meshes in which the pinholes at two corners disappear.

(b) Italian bars are often complex and/or worked in pairs: Flemish bars tend to be slighter and made in continuous lengths, crossing open spaces then running alongside a motif before crossing anothergap.

(c) Flemish designs tend to include more intersecting stems: Italian designs have a more continuous flow and backward-curving motifs rarely cross other motifs.

(d) Flemish designs tend to be broken into smaller parts for working.

(e) Flemish scrolls are often formed by a clothwork tape which spirals into a center whereas Italian scrolls more often have a double tape spiralling into and out from the center.

(f) Flemish laces are often in a finer thread and tend to be softer and more supple than Italian laces. It must be remembered that these are tendencies, not hard rules; there are exceptions to all of them.

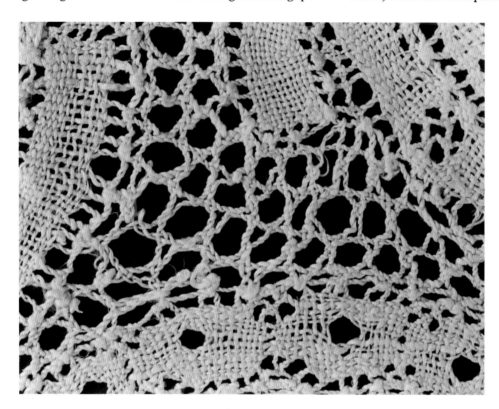

Plate 145: Closer detail of the Flemish round ground.

Plate 146: Flounce of bobbin tape lace with the Flemish round ground; probably Flemish, mid-late 17th century. Depth 12.5cm (5in) – this incudes the integral bobbin tape footing but not the additional later footing; pattern repeat 17cm (6.7in).

Despite the flow of the bobbin-made tape throughout this design, the pattern is one of repeated upright floral motifs defining a scalloped headside, with secondary motifs defining axes of symmetry between them. This shows the continuity of designs fashionable in the mid 17th century in the northern European market. Other examples of this style will be seen in the chapter on Flemish laces in the Flemish style.

Note the oversized, stylized birds on either side of the main motif.

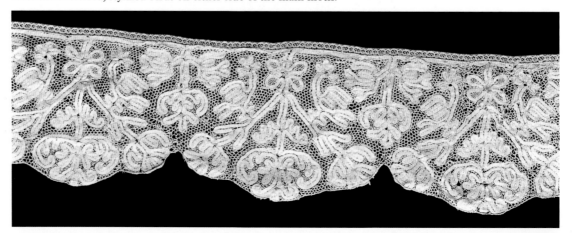

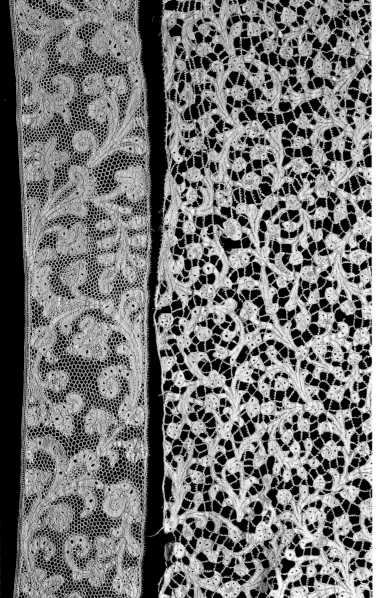

Plate 147: Edging of Flemish part bobbin lace: mid – late 17th century. Depth 8.5cm (3.5in) – excluding the later heading.

Unlike the flounce of **Plate** 146, this edging is made by the part technique but achieves a much greater feel of baroque movement in its bold curves and flamboyant central motif.

Plate 148:

a. Flemish edging: about 1670-90. Depth 9.5cm (3.7in); pattern repeat 73cm (29in); length shown 35.5cm 14in)
Although the design flows continuously, the lace is made in relatively small parts.

b. Part of a Flemish flounce (altered): about 1690-1700. Depth shown 15cm (6in)
This example is very typical of Flemish lace in the Italian style of the late 17th century; the thread is finer, the clothwork broader than in Italian lace; the rounded flower buds divided into lobes, each with a central hole, are characteristic and also found in contemporary Flemish laces in the French style (**Plate** 149a).

History of Flemish laces in the Italian baroque style.

The term Flemish bobbin laces is used very generally to identify all those 16th- and 17th-century laces made in the Low Countries, particularly in Flanders, before the various lace-making towns such as Brussels, Mechlin and Valenciennes developed their own peculiar characteristics. It therefore includes the early geometric laces already described as well as laces in the Italian baroque manner and laces in floral designs peculiar to Northern Europe (see pages 173-175). It also includes late 17th-century laces in the French manner and some 18th century laces.

In the earlier years, while techniques were developing, there was no clear distinction between straight, part and bobbin-tape laces but in the mid-17th century their paths started to diverge. Although the baroque style influenced the straight laces, it is seen in perhaps its most accomplished form in the part laces. Here the division of the work into separate motifs enabled each to be patterned with intricate detail while the essential rhythm and movement of the baroque could be achieved by their subsequent combination into large, flowing designs.

Naturally the Flemish baroque laces followed the same design trends as their Italian counterparts and the origins of many surviving examples, especially those of poorer quality, are unclear. Some indications of differences are given under 'Points to Watch' but qualities such as the tightness of working can be judged only by experience.

Perhaps one innovation of the Flemish industry was the net ground. This had started to develop before 1650 and was formed in various ways before it settled into the most common form, known as the round ground. The Italian ground is very similar; did it develop independently? As yet there is no clear answer.

By 1700 the Italian baroque designs had dwindled into patterns of branching, curving stems carrying tiny bud-like flowers but, in Flanders, a different influence had already been felt: that of France. The new French designs started a fresh fashion to which we shall return later. In the meantime, continuously scrolling tape designs similar to that shown in **Plate** 137c continued to be made into the 18th century and were joined by designs, such as that in **Plate** 151, combining the Italian and the new French styles.

It was not until the late 19th century that interest in the Italian baroque style returned. The major demand at this time was for heavy Venetian needlepoints but bobbin laces in imitation of the Milanese were also made.

By now the Italian industry itself was moribund but distinct efforts were made to revive it. Although

these had some success in the period up to the First World War, many of the later copies were made in Belgium where the part-lace tradition had survived through many changes in style since the 17th century.

As with other antique laces that were copied in this period, some close imitations were made but many 19th-century examples are easily identifiable by their shapes, their mixture of styles from different periods, their thread, or their workmanship. Examples of these late derivatives are seen in the chapter on Brussels and Belgian laces.

The French influence in Flemish part laces

The influence of French designs on Brussels needlepoints in the late 17th century was mentioned in an earlier chapter and their effect on her bobbin laces, and on those of neighbouring Flanders, will come as no surprise. The earliest laces derived from the new French classical style date from the 1680s or 1690s. In these, the sense of continuous movement in the preceding baroque style has gone and only the tiny scale and curving nature of its later motifs remain. The scattered branches, ideally suited to the part technique, are grouped about vertical axes centered on candelabra-like motifs and are joined by a bar or net ground. Even the smooth outlines of the earlier strong, baroque curves are broken by feathery leaves and buds which sprout in all directions.

The subsequent changes which occurred in this style are difficult to follow but in the 1700s the designs appear to have turned briefly from repeated symmetrical designs to asymmetric arrangements such as that illustrated in **Plate** 149b. The symmetry of the classical style may never have been abandoned entirely; certainly it is seen again in the early 18th century as the motifs gradually expanded to fill the space previously taken up by the ground.

Opposite page:
Plate 149:
a. Flemish flounce (possibly Brussels) with the round Flemish mesh ground: 1690-1710. Depth 21cm (8in); pattern repeat 54cm (21.5in); length shown 71cm (28in)
This shows a typical example of what is known as the 'candelabra' design, with its symmetrical groupings of motifs about candelabra-like features. It appears to have been derived from the French Bérainesque designs of point de France but is by no means a direct copy.
b. Flemish flounce with a bar ground: 1700-20. Depth 24cm (9.5in); pattern repeat 47cm (18.5in)
This design lacks the symmetry of the flounce above and the bud and leaf motifs are on a slightly larger scale and more crowded, indicating a slightly later date. The bar ground was largely superseded by net grounds in the early 18th century but was still used occasionally even in the second half of the century.

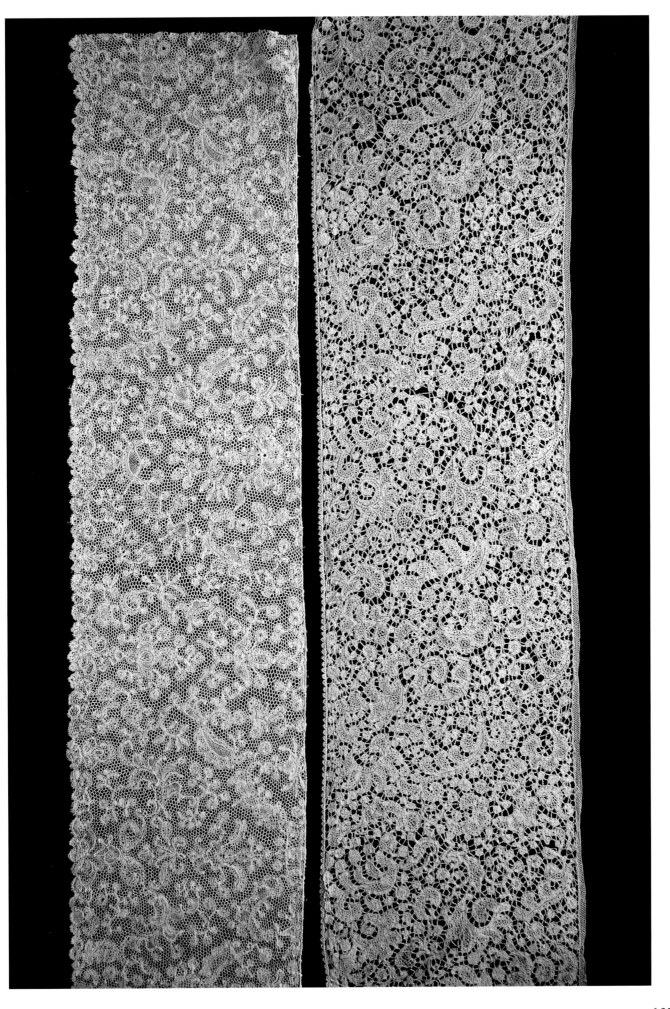

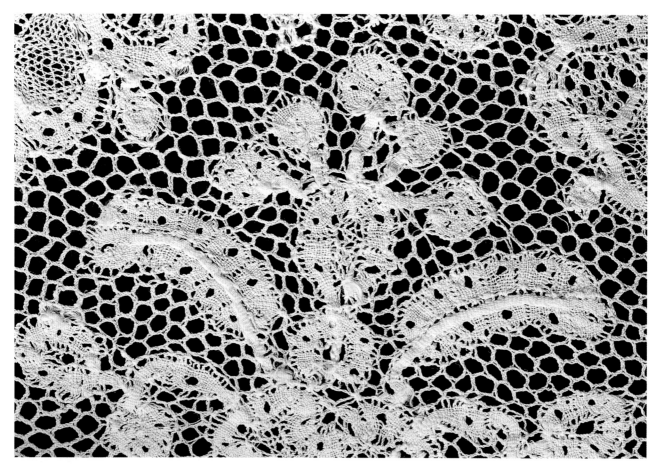

Plate 150: Detail of Plate 149a. Note the loose working of the round Flemish ground and the narrow band of clothwork forming the centers of the leaves: these are raised over the surface and typify later Brussels bobbin laces.

Plate 151: Flounce, probably Flemish: early 18th C. Depth shown 16.5cm (6.5in); pattern repeat 25cm (9.5in); length shown 33cm (13in).

The scrolling pattern is very similar in style to that of the flounce in Plate 141 but the tape is not continuous; the pattern is worked as a part lace. This, and the looseness of working of the round mesh ground, as well as the multitude of loops in the tape suggest that this is probably of Flemish rather than North Italian origin.

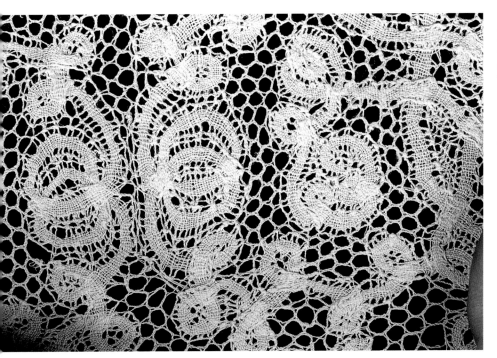

Plate 152: Detail of **Plate** 151.

By this time the fineness of the Brussels laces distinguished them from the overall group of Flemish part laces and changes in design in the 18th century will be considered more fully in relation to this more fashionable lace. In general the poorer-quality laces, which were made in enormous flounces often for furnishing purposes, followed substantially the same trends but often with some time lag because of the persistence of old designs in less organized industries. Many of these flounces, such as that in **Plate** 153, have in the past been attributed to Brabant, a province north and east of Brussels, but may equally well have been made in the smaller Flemish towns or perhaps even in England, by the East Devon industry.

Plate 153: Flounce of a type generally known as 'Brabant' but possibly made in Brabant or in Flanders: about 1740-60. Depth shown 57cm (22.5in); width shown 81cm (32in); full depth 60 cm (24in); pattern repeat 48cm (19in).

The naturalistic floral design of this flounce is completely different from the stylized designs in **Plates** 149 and151 and follows the new trends introduced in the early 18th century and discussed in the needlepoint section and in the bobbin sections which follow. It is made in a far coarser, poorer-quality thread and with much looser workmanship than the related Brussels laces; this enabled such large pieces to be made comparatively quickly and cheaply.

Central and Eastern European bobbin laces

This chapter is concerned mainly with those central and Eastern European laces derived from Italian baroque laces but often influenced by the French style like the Flemish laces we have just seen. These comprise or include convoluted meandering bobbin tape designs, usually made with continuously flowing tapes but sometimes made by the part technique. Examples dating from the 18th century often incorporate a multitude of filling stitches, either within the tapework or in spaces between the tapes. 19th Century tapes are usually very simple but often incorporate colored threads. Designs frequently include naively-drawn animals, birds and flowers.

The illustrations used in this chapter are based purely on what I happen, by chance, to have in my collection. They are too few to be representative of the wide range of laces made across central and Eastern Europe and are certainly too few for any generalization which could enable one to distinguish laces made in different regions. I hope, however, they give some flavor of an Eastern style which is distinct from that of the West.

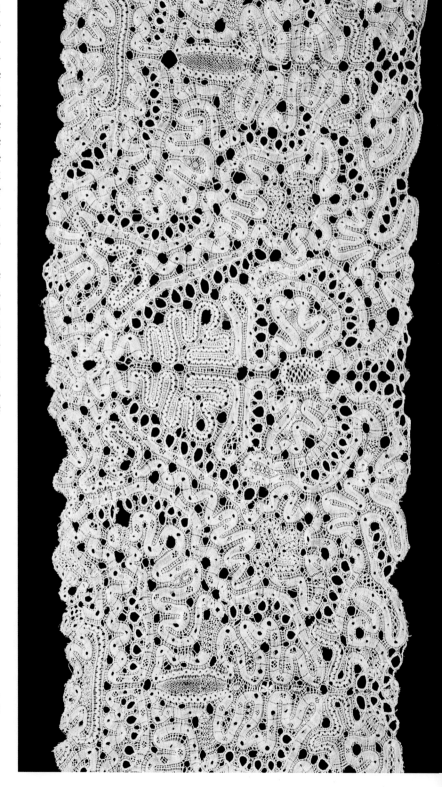

Plate 154: Flounce of Eastern European bobbin-tape lace: 18th century. Depth 30cm (12in); pattern repeat 53cm (21in).
The more convoluted, crowded, and decorated nature of this design distinguishes it from the North Italian laces from which it is derived.

Plate 155: Group of Eastern European laces: all 19th-early 20th century: probably Russian.

a. Torchon in red and white cotton (See **Plate** 7 for detail). Maximum depth 6.5cm (2.5in); pattern repeat 9.5cm (3.7in).

b. Bobbin tape lace in red and white cotton. Maximum depth 5cm (2in); pattern repeat 6.5cm (2.5in).

c. Bobbin-tape lace in red, white and blue cotton. Maximum depth 10cm (4in) pattern repeat 12cm (4.7in). (See **Plate** 11 for detail)

d. In white cotton with black detail. Maximum depth 9cm (3.5in): pattern repeat 6cm (2.4in).

e. Part lace in white cotton with details in red and blue cotton. Maximum depth 17cm (6.7in); pattern repeat 30cm (12in).

History

In the late 17th and 18th centuries the Italian baroque fashions spread northward into the Austro-Hungarian Empire and on into Russia. The French influence was also felt and the flowing tape designs were modified, becoming more convoluted and ornamented with filling stitches, but often arranged to define axes of symmetry. Many laces from this early period are found in wide flounces, suitable for furnishing and church use, and are worked in relatively fine, soft thread.

Gradually fashions in the West changed but meandering tape designs had become firmly rooted in the Eastern cultures. They continued through the 19th and into the 20th century but the tapes were gradually simplified, worked in coarser thread, and color was introduced. Enormous quantities were made to decorate peasant dress, complementing the multi-colored embroideries of the different regions, while much was also required for household linen.

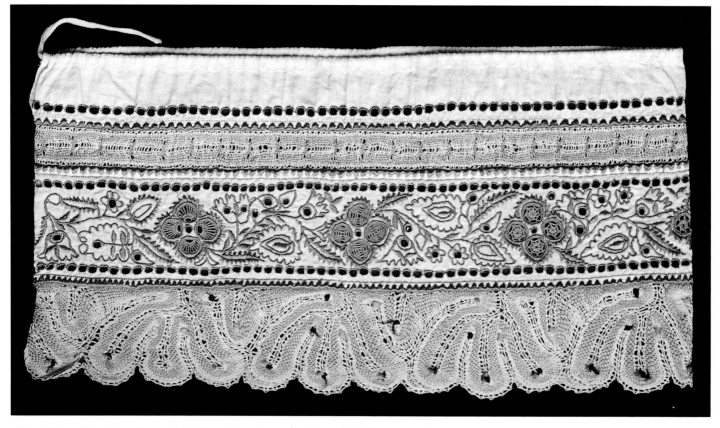

Plate 156: cuff or sleeve decorated with an insertion and edging of bobbin-tape lace in yellow and white thread, with embroidery in orange silk thread including needlepoint lace fillings: late 19th-20th century; probably Czech.

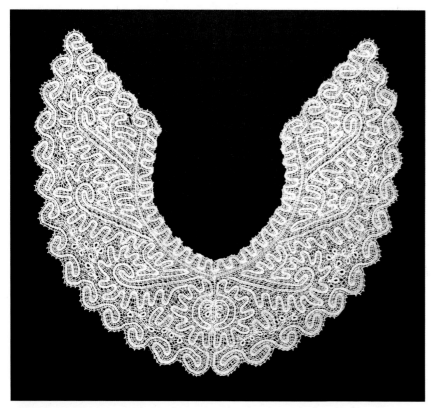

Plate 157: Collar: about 1880-1890. Diameter of neck opening 14cm (5.5in); maximum width 38cm (15in).
This collar is of the type known as 'Russian' lace despite the fact that it was made in Western Europe. Its style followed that of eastern European laces which were still being made in convoluted designs derived from North Italian laces of the 17th to 18th centuries.

By the mid-19th century this style of lace was all but forgotten in the West. Examples brought back by travelers were hailed as novelties and soon copies were being made. These were not direct copies as Western fashion still had little place for colored lace. Instead, all the fashionable accessories of the period were worked in coarse white or black thread, in narrow, open-textured, convoluted tapes joined by a coarse mesh ground. These were sold as 'Russian' laces.

While colored laces continued to be made in the East, the interest of the Western market in the late 19th century stimulated production of more fashionable goods in Russia, still in the meandering tape designs but in monochrome. The industry continued through the 20th century, particularly in the Vologda region of Northern Russia.

Plate M: Fashion Plate; about 1840.
This fashion plate shows various forms of the wide collar which stretches from shoulder to shoulder and is known
as a bertha. It was in fashion in the late 17th century and was revived, as we see here, in the 1830s to continue in use
into the 1860s. The mid 19th century berthas usually have a boat-shaped neckline, as seen in **Plate** 241; a slightly
different form, with the circular shape seen in **Plates** 177 and 254, came into use in the 1890s.

Brussels

including mixed bobbin and needlepoint laces and Belgian part laces

Characteristics

1. Part lace.
2. Pattern areas mainly in clothwork but with some half stitch.
3. Right and wrong sides differ:

    a. Right side often has raised work in the form of narrow bands of clothwork (**Plate** 159) or bundles of threads (**Plate** 174) outlining some edges and features within the design.

    b. Wrong side often has groups of threads passing loosely across the motifs from one area of working to another.
4. Needlework is often incorporated as complete motifs, as decorative fillings and spots, or as the ground.
5. Grounds:

    a. Bobbin-made brides, often decorated with picots, were common in the early to mid-18th century and after about 1850.

    b. Vrai drochel bobbin ground (**Plate** 160-elongate hexagonal mesh with two sides of four plaited threads and four sides of two twisted threads) common from the early 18th century to mid-19th century

    c. Point de gaze (**Plate** 78) and other needle-made grounds after about 1850.

    d. Machine net used from the early 19th century onwards.

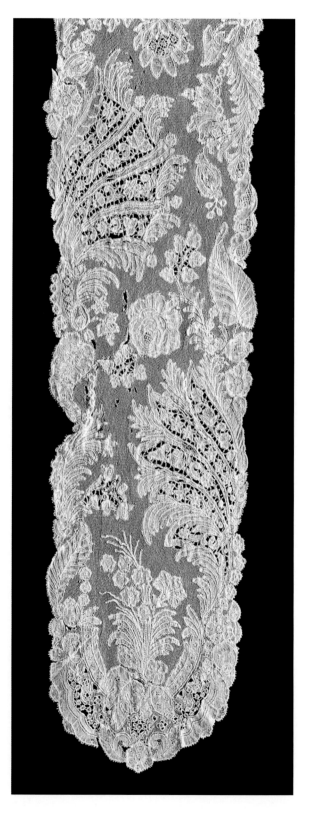

Plate 158: Brussels mixed bobbin and needlepoint lappet: 1745-60. Width 8.5cm (3.3in); length shown 20cm (8in); full length 60cm (24in)

This lappet shows a style between those of the outer lappets in **Plate** 163. Note the contrasting effect of the fine drochel ground in the center and the open bar ground in the feathery leaves which spring from the edge; these form a pattern resembling a typical rococo shell motif.

Although described as a mixed lace, the needlepoint here forms only a small crescent of filling stitches in the end of the lappet (see detail, **Plate** 159).

Lappets formed part of a woman's head-dress. In the late 17th century they were narrow, often with a border of tiny scallops. They then became wider and straight-edged, often narrowing slightly towards the end. By 1730 the straight edge was softening into slight waves but a rounded end and more wavy-edged form had already been introduced. By 1740 the rounded end with a wavy edge was usual but in the later 18th century the straight edges returned.

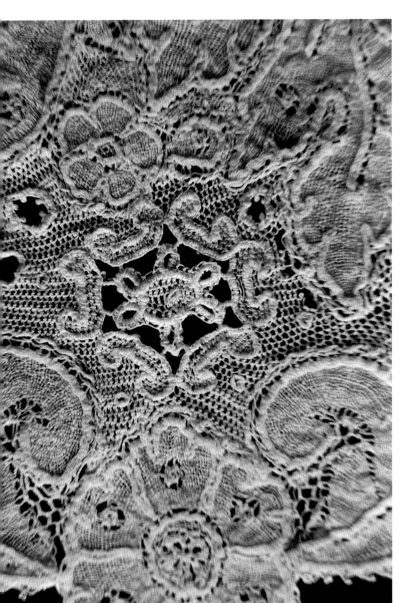

Additional features

A gimp thread is sometimes incorporated in 19th-century designs, particularly in duchesse laces (see **Plates** 173-176 and page 161 for further characteristics).

19th-Century examples often have spots or tiny sprigs scattered over the ground.

Points to watch

The vrai drochel ground is very similar to the Mechlin eis ground (see **Plate** 212 , page 185), but Brussels plaits are longer by one half stitch.

East Devon (Honiton) lace developed along very similar lines to Brussels bobbin lace in the 18th century; it is technically very similar but much less care was taken over design and consistency of workmanship in Devon. It is thus possible to tell many Devon laces from their 18th century Brussels counterparts but I believe we still have much to learn about distinguishing them from the lesser-quality part laces made in Flanders and Brabant.

In the 19th century, Honiton and the finer Brussels laces developed more distinctive characteristics but, again, the Devon products can be confused with cheaper Belgian laces. In particular, the Honiton guipures are most easily confused with the Bruges duchesse laces and the differences between these two types will be discussed more fully in the 'Honiton' chapter. With some examples, however, there can be no definitive answer on provenance since both Devon and Belgium copied features of the other region's products.

Plate 159: Detail of **Plate** 158, showing the different textures of the buttonholed needle-point filling and the surrounding bobbin lace. The raised work around the edges of the bobbin motifs is worked first and then the cloth stitch is worked over them. The motifs are thus worked face down and the lace maker would not have seen the finished result until the lace was lifted from the pricking.

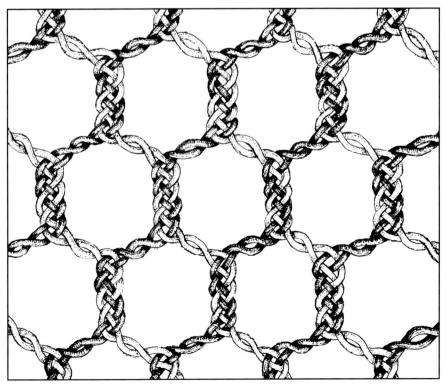

Plate 160: The vrai drochel ground.

The history of Brussels lace in the 17th century is obscured by the confusion that has arisen over the term 'Point d'Angleterre'. This is a name which has long been attributed to the finest Brussels laces. It was certainly used in the early to mid 18th century for lace made specifically in Brussels but was also in use in the late 17th century with no categorical indication of origin.

Arguments currently abound over whether this term was first applied to an English lace later copied in Brussels or to a Brussels lace made largely for the English market, with various amusing variations such as, 'It must have been intended for the French market because of the use of the French language'. The question is not without interest but is of little help to us in distinguishing lace made in Brussels from the technically similar lace of East Devon, generally known as Honiton lace.

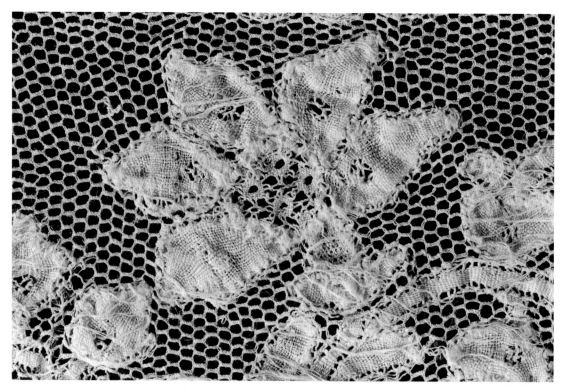

Plate 161: detail of the wrong side of Brussels bobbin lace with the drochel ground showing threads used for the ground carried loosely over the backs of the motifs from one area of working to the next.

Opposite page:
Plate 162: Group of edgings. Length shown 34cm (13.5in);
a. About 1700. Depth 8.0cm (3.2in); no clear pattern repeat
By 1700 the Italian baroque designs had degenerated into confused designs such as this but an interesting feature is the formation of the tape on the surface, around the edges of the half-stitch pattern areas. This probably developed into the raised work of later Brussels laces.
b. About 1700-10. Depth 8.4cm (3.3in); design altered.
Compare this piece with the flounces in **Plate** 149. Its design has the symmetry of flounce (a) but the scale of the motifs in relation to the depth of the lace and their style are more in keeping with flounce (b).
c. About 1745-60. Depth 7.5cm (3.0in); pattern repeat 60cm (23.5in)
The light-hearted feel of this design, with its scattering of birds and butterflies, is typical of the rococo style.
Some fillings are closely similar to needlepoint fillings in appearance; needlepoints were again popular in this period and various features were borrowed by bobbin laces.
d. Edging with shaped ends (not shown): about 1820-30. Depth 6.5cm (2.5in); full length 99cm (39 in); no exact pattern repeat.
Stylistically this lace could almost be of about 1770, but the working is too precise, the fillings too organized for an 18th-century piece. It must be 19th century, but pre-1850 when the drochel ground had almost died out: it dates from the period when designs were just becoming free of the constraints of the classical period.

What is fairly certain is that Brussels was one of the centers for the manufacture of Flemish part laces in the Italian baroque style in the second half of the 17th century. We have followed the gradual degeneration of this style from the bold designs of the 1650s to 1670s (pages 132-139) to the rather fussy style of about 1700 but at this point an interesting development occurred. The crowded designs of this period, with their narrow, curving and branching stems and tiny flower buds, are often found in a form of tape lace seen in **Plate** 162a. Here the tape, which is not pre-made but worked with bobbins on a pillow, is looped over itself and forms a raised edge on the surface around the edges of the tiny areas of cloth stitch or half stitch. This may be the start of the raised outline of Brussels lace which was to become a major characteristic in the 18th and 19th centuries. Raised leaf centers, however, are also seen in the French-style Brussels laces of about the same date (**Plates** 149 and 150).

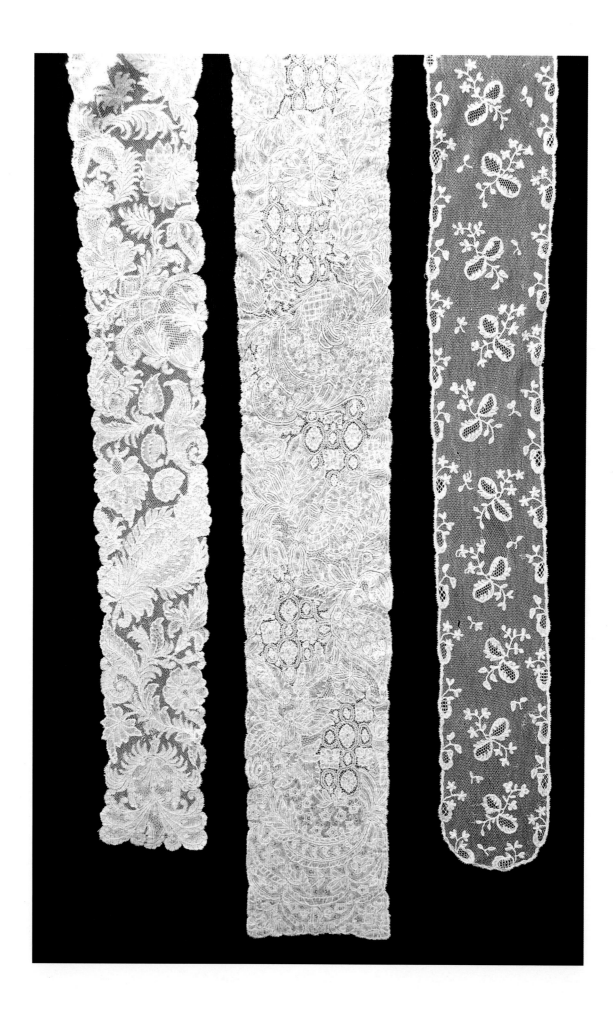

Both of the laces shown in **Plate** 149 are flounces and were probably made for furnishing use since there was little call for lace on this scale for dress in the early years of the 18th century. Much finer laces in this style and technique were also made, however; an example is shown in **Plate** 162b. Laces of this type, with their clear designs and good workmanship and, more particularly, their incredibly fine, firmly-twisted thread, are among the first attributable with any certainty to Brussels. Despite this new style, the Brussels industry went through a difficult period during the first two decades of the 18th century as fashion favored trimmings of plain lawn and gauze. A new impetus was needed and it came in the form of the 'bizarre' designs which had been introduced into French woven silks at the very end of the 17th century.

The belated effect of these designs on French and Brussels needlepoints in the 1720s and 1730s has already been seen but the full impact occurred in the 1710s upon Flemish bobbin laces and particularly those of Valenciennes and Brussels. The new style was in the baroque tradition, with bold designs full of vigor and movement: the large-scale motifs of exotic fruits and flowerheads, feathery leaves and geometric shapes show the influence both of the Far and of the Near East but their treatment is wholly different from that of the 17th-century Italian baroque. Now the motifs are crowded together in abstract patterns, with shapes bounded by odd combinations of angles and re-entrant curves and juxtaposed with leafy sprays. The strongly diagonal movement of the wider, woven silks is translated into a movement to and fro across the narrower lace designs and the vibrant colors of the silks are echoed in the rich patterning of the lace motifs with filling stitches and scatterings of tinier motifs.

The result is seen in the central lappet in **Plate** 163. Here the motifs are so crowded that the lace is almost opaque but this again suited the fashion of the day; the desire for lack of ostentation is catered for by the fact that the pattern is scarcely discernible at distances of more than a few feet while the need to display wealth is satisfied by the extreme intricacy seen at close quarters.

Although little is known of designers in the lace industry itself and few laces are dated, there is a remarkable similarity between these densely patterned laces and the woven silks of the early 18th century, for which dated records are available. This enables the better-quality laces,

made by manufacturers who employed the best designers or who bought in the latest designs, to be dated to within a decade. This cannot be said, however, for the mass of poorer-quality laces, whether made in Brussels or in the minor lace-making regions of Europe where links with France were not so strong.

Gradually, as the bizarre designs were modified, more naturalistic European flowers were introduced and the odd cartouche shapes became less dominant.

The early designs left little room for any ground between the densely-packed motifs but, by 1730, designs were again opening out. The rhythmic movement was still retained but floral or leafy sprigs gained more importance and curved into well-defined spaces bordered by patterned strapwork, cartouches of fancy fillings or by trails of the leaves themselves. Display was again acceptable in dress and the bride ground of the earlier period (**Plate** 162b) was largely replaced by a lighter, net ground which gave a greater contrast with the pattern. This new ground was the 'drochel' or 'vrai drochel' ground which had been known as a filling stitch from the 17th century but was to assume an ever-increasing role in Brussels laces in the 18th century.

As designs grew lighter in the 1740s, they also became more light-hearted with the introduction of rococo scrolls and shell ornamentation, birds and insects (**Plate** 162c). Chinoiserie motifs, such as pagodas, pavilions and figures in Chinese dress, which had occasionally been seen in designs throughout the earlier part of the century became more common.

The rococo style was to last into the 1760s and early 1770s but we have already followed its decline in the French laces of Alençon and Argentan. The only major innovation in the Brussels industry was in the grounding of the motifs. While these were closely spaced, they were arranged on a pattern and the drochel ground was worked between and around them: the threads of the ground are often seen carried across the backs of the motifs as in the drochel-grounded Brussels needlepoints. In the later examples with linear patterns and scattered motifs, the ground was sometimes made separately and the motifs applied to it. In practice, the ground was worked in narrow widths, from about 1 to 2.5cm (1/2 to 1 in) wide, and these were subsequently joined edge to edge to form larger panels. Well before 1800, the joining technique, with a stitch known as point de racroc, was so well developed that the joins were invisible although, with subsequent wear, they now appear as breaks in the lace.

In the late 18th century the Brussels bobbin lace industry suffered the same decline as its needlepoint. The gossamer-fine drochel net suited the fashion and was made in large panels patterned with neo-classical designs for use as aprons, fichus and other accessories but much cheaper fabrics served the same purposes. Only Brussels' name for quality kept the industry alive.

In the early 19th century, Napoleon's patronage was of some assistance: the continuance of the industry is

Opposite page:
Plate 163: Group of lappets
(center). Probably Brussels: about 1720-30. Length shown 48cm (19in); full length 65cm (26in)
This exemplifies the rich patterning of the 'bizarre' designs but is not quite as accomplished as many of the contemporary Valenciennes and Brussels designs. The thread and workmanship are extremely fine but the use of raised work is a little haphazard.
(left). Brussels: about 1730-35. Length shown 43cm (17in); full length 53cm (21in)
(right). Brussels: about 1780-90. Length shown 44cm (17.2in); full length 72cm (28.5in)

Plate 164: Veil: Brussels bobbin motifs applied to drochel ground: 1820-30. Pattern repeat 10cm (4in); pattern depth 21cm (8.5in); full width 141cm (56in); full length 118cm (47in)
The edging of pointed leaves continues around the entire veil which was probably worn draped over the shoulders with the top gathered and tied or pinned into the hair.
Edgings of tiny points were a common alternative to absolutely straight edges from the 1790s through to the 1820s. Small, rounded scallops had also appeared by this time; these broadened into fuller scallops in the 1830s before dwindling to a slightly wavy headside in the 1840s, rather as they had in the early 17th century (see **Plate** 165 for detail).

shown by the number of large veils (**Plate** 164) that survive from the 1820s and 1830s but fashion was not to turn to the fuller designs, most effective in this lace, until the 1840s. By this time it was rarely economic to make the net by hand but the possibilities of machine-made nets had been discovered. The manufacture of the drochel ground ceased by about 1850 for all but the most special orders or exhibition pieces.

The 1840s saw the start of a new boom in the lace trade. With the industrialization of Europe and the wider spread of wealth, more people could afford the lace which fashion now dictated should be worn. Those who could not afford the more prestigious hand-made laces could choose from a growing supply of machine laces or from the cheaper hand-made guipures which were now coming on to the market.

The Brussels industry was well placed to take advantage of the mood. Its manufacturers had close links with Paris where the French court under Louis Napoleon and, more specifically his wife, Eugénie, again led the fashion in Europe. Together with the new needlepoint, point de gaze (pages 74-79), Brussels application laces on machine-made net were among the most sought after in Europe and were to remain so for the rest of the century. They were particularly required in wide flounces for the crinoline dresses of the 1850s and 1860s and as large squares, of up to 2 meters (2 yards), for wedding veils and shawls. Confusingly they were sold under the name 'Application d'Angleterre', possibly because of the prior use of machine-net grounds by the English Honiton lace-makers (see pp 162-172).

The design changes in the application laces were limited but followed the same trends as those already seen in Brussels point de gaze. Indeed, the best of these application laces combined the needle and bobbin techniques. This was not a new departure for the Brussels lace-makers; 18th-century Brussels bobbin laces had often incorporated small amounts of needlepoint while the 18th-century needlepoints were often grounded with the bobbin drochel net. In the late 19th century, their combination was taken to new extremes. In the most expensive fabrics, the mixture of needle and bobbin motifs was even grounded with the hand-made point de gaze net; the name 'point d'Angleterre' was used once more.

150

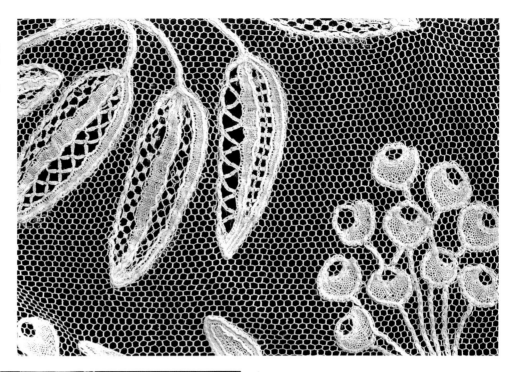

Plate 165: Detail of Plate 164 showing the bobbin-made motifs applied to the bobbin-made drochel ground. The clothwork is more loosely worked than in 18th-century laces. This is a common but not invariable feature of the 19th-century Brussels laces.

The application laces were only one form of Brussels lace. The growing interest in all-over patterns and the reintroduction of guipures in the 1840s also led to the return of Brussels laces grounded with bars, or brides. In some cases the lace was of the same fine quality, made in the same fine thread as the application laces; an example is shown in Plate 167b. More often a much heavier thread was used and the result was a new lace, called 'duchesse' in honor of the Duchess of Brabant, subsequently Queen of the Belgians (see the note below).

Plate 166: Bonnet veil: Brussels bobbin motifs applied to a machine-made net: 1840-50. Width 110cm (44in); length 89cm (35in). There are 5 pattern repeats.
Unlike the veil in Plate 164, this has a draw string along its upper edge for fastening the veil to a bonnet.
Compare the typical, rather tenuous floral edging pattern with that of the contemporary veil in Plate 74 and the sprig design to the earlier examples in Plates 118 and 239.

151

Opposite page:

Plate 167:

a. Edging of bobbin appliqué on drochel ground: about 1815-25. Probably Brussels, but some design irregularities suggest it might be Honiton. Maximum depth 10cm (4in); length shown 56cm (22in).

b. Collar of Brussels guipure with bobbin-made brides: about 1850-60. Depth 6cm (2.3in); full length of inside edge 38cm (15in).

c. Tie of Brussels bobbin appliqué on machine-made net: about 1870-90. Maximum width of ends 9cm (3.5in); full length 96cm (38in).

Shaped accessories like this, with a narrow center broadening into bulbous or splayed ends, are thought to have been worn around the neck and are usually called 'ties' although they could equally well have been used as lappets as occasion demanded.

d. Edging of Brussels bobbin lace with the Alençon needlepoint ground: probably about 1840-60, but possibly later. Maximum depth 7.5cm (3.0in); pattern repeat 26.5cm (10.5in).

This edging is an almost direct copy of an 18th-century rococo design but the thread, the use of the Alençon ground and a less delicate treatment of the design betray its 19th-century origin.

e. Edging of Brussels bobbin appliqué on machine-made net: about 1850-70. Maximum depth 11cm (4.5in); pattern repeat 27cm (11in).

The duchesse laces are generally grouped into two classes; those including needlework fillings or insets of point de gaze, which are known as 'Brussels duchesse', and those without needlework which are known as 'Bruges duchesse'. Usually the former are of finer quality but to what extent they were actually made in the capital is uncertain. By the latter part of the 19th century many of the Belgian lace manufacturers had moved their main premises out of Brussels to smaller towns, such as Bruges and Ghent, which had long lace-making traditions of their own. Records show that much of the cheaper lace was made here while even the fine motifs for the application laces were made at Binche and other centers.

Plate 168: Edging of mixed Brussels needlepoint and bobbin lace with the point de gaze ground: about 1860-80. Depth 4.5cm (1.8in); pattern repeat 4.3cm (1.7in).
The central flower head and its leaves are in bobbin lace; the ring fillings and the rest of the lace are in needlepoint.

Plate 169: Flounce of
mixed Brussels needle-
point and bobbin lace
applied to a machine-
made net: about 1850-75.
Maximum depth 36cm
(14in); pattern repeat
68cm (27in); length
shown 76cm (31in).

The collapse of the French Second Empire in 1870 and the concurrent changes in fashion were not disastrous for the better quality Brussels laces, which were still much in demand for wedding trousseaux, but they did affect the cheaper guipures. Even Belgian manufacturers, with their long traditions of lace-making, struggled to adapt to the changing market.

The revival of the lace industry in the 1880s included the copying of antique laces and, particularly in the Belgian part laces, led to a revival of the late 17th century Italian baroque style. One fine example of this genre is seen in **Plate** 177 but the quality of the reproductions that were made through into the 20th century was extremely varied: some were direct copies, in fine thread; others mixed earlier styles in innovative ways to tempt the now fickle market; and others consisted merely of debased scrolling tape designs with little to commend them. Indeed, the variety and degree of copying of other laces of all types and periods that went on at this time make it impossible to 'categorize' many surviving laces.

Plate 170: Detail of a mixed Brussels lace applied to machine-made net showing the differing textures of the clothwork made by the two techniques. In this example the bobbin raised work consists simply of bundles of threads caught down loosely on the surface although the flower in the bottom right-hand corner is outlined with a thick, or gimp, thread.

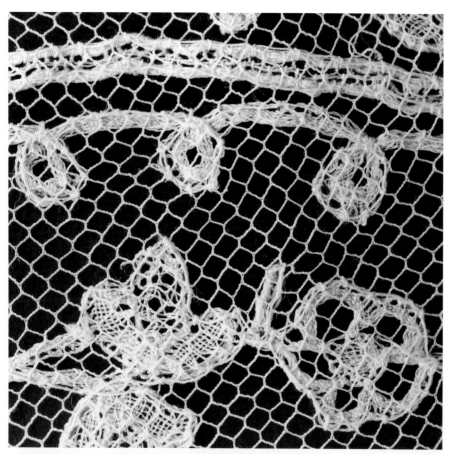

Opposite page:
Plate 173:
a. Edging of Brussels (mixed) duchesse: late 19th-20th century. Depth 8.5cm (3.3in); pattern repeat 16cm (6.5in)
b. Collar of Brussels (mixed) duchesse: 1880-1910. Maximum width 57cm (22.5in)
c. Woman's jabot of Bruges bobbin duchesse attached to machine-made net: about 1900. Maximum width 13cm (5.2in)
Jabots of this type were worn with the high-necked dresses of the late 19th century and into the 20th century.
d. Collar of Brussels (mixed) duchesse: late 19th century. Length of neck edge 22.5cm (9.5in); Center depth 5cm (2in)

Plate 171: detail of the wrong side of Brussels bobbin lace applied to machine-made net: in many examples the net is cut away from the backs of motifs to allow open filling stitches to be seen but that is not the case here.

Plate 172: Fan of mixed Brussels bobbin and needlepoint lace applied to a machine-made net: about 1890-1900. Full width 67cm (26.5in); depth of lace 22cm (8.5in)
The asymmetric floral design interspersed with scrolls and cartouches of fancy fillings is typical of the revived rococo style of the late 19th century: it is fuller and more assured than the 1840 rococo designs and is not a direct copy of an 18th-century design, unlike the design in **Plate** 167d. Large, semi-circular fans are typical of the late 19th - early 20th century.

157

One innovation at the turn of the century, however, was a variety of the Duchesse guipures termed 'rosaline': this has designs reminiscent of late-17th century Flemish laces with highly stylized, bud-like flowers carried on curving, branching stems (see **Plate** 148b). Better examples include needlework, this time in the form of tiny button-holed rings scattered over the surface, giving the form known as 'rosaline perlée'. Variations on this type include the collar shown in **Plate** 178c which, with its symmetrical arrangement of motifs about axes of symmetry, is clearly based on the Flemish 'candelabra' designs (see **Plate** 149a) of about 1700.

A final modification of the duchesse laces was the form sold under the name 'rosaline de fantaisie'. In these, narrow scrolling stems branch into inward

Plate 174: Detail of the collar in **Plate** 173b. Note the needlepoint brides and the raised petals of the needlepoint rose. The bobbin raised work consists of bundles of threads - the more difficult cloth stitch raised work is rarely found in duchesse laces, even in good-quality examples like this.

Below:
Plate 175
(top) Detail of a duchesse lace with a typical floral pattern in which: motifs are worked in whole and half stitch; flowers comprise a ring of lobed petals around an open center; some features are outlined by a thick thread which also separates the petals and is worked within the thickness of the lace (distinguishing Belgian laces from Honiton laces); and some petals have a vein of holes along their centers.
(bottom) Chemical machine-lace copy of duchesse. To the naked eye, this machine copy is extremely similar to a bobbin lace; only the confused, rather fuzzy structure of the bars and net ground give an immediate indication of its machine origin. (See **Plate** 35 for a further example and explanation of chemical lace.)

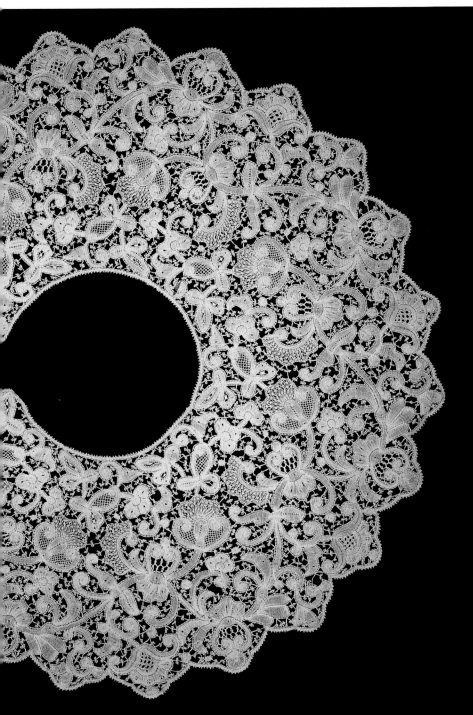

Plate 176: Belgian bobbin lace flounce of the type generally termed 'Bruges duchesse': about 1850-75. Depth 31cm (12.2in); pattern repeat 32cm (12.5in).
Although 'Bruges' duchesse is often inferior to 'Brussels' duchesse, this example is well worked, in fine thread and in a stylish design of swags and flowerheads clearly visible despite the crowding necessitated by the use of a bride rather than a net ground.

Left:
Plate 177: Bertha collar: probably Belgian: about 1890-1900. Maximum outer diameter 60cm (24in); inner diameter 17cm (7in).
The interest in antique laces at the end of the 19th century led to many derivative designs as well as to direct copies of earlier styles. Here, late 17th century Italian baroque motifs are arranged in a circular bertha collar typical of the late 19th century but within the scalloped edge found in early 17th-century laces or in French designs of about 1700.

spirals terminating in tiny flowerheads comprising trefoils or cinquefoils with alternate petals worked in whole and half stitch. The designs are taken from Venetian laces of about 1700 and very similar laces were also made at Cantu, in Northern Italy, where they were called flat Venetian bobbin laces.

The First World War effectively brought an end to the Belgian hand-lace industry. Although lace makers can still occasionally be seen in the streets of Bruges and the thriving lace school attracts new pupils every year, most lace-making is now carried out by amateurs for their own pleasure and the mass of lace on sale in the Belgian towns is machine-made or imported from the Far East.

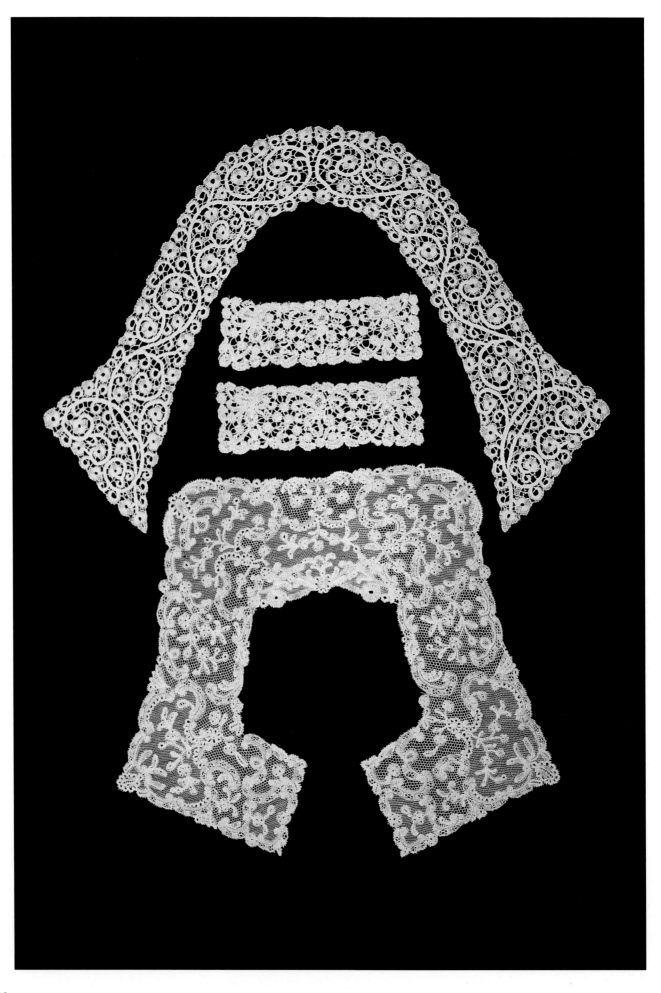

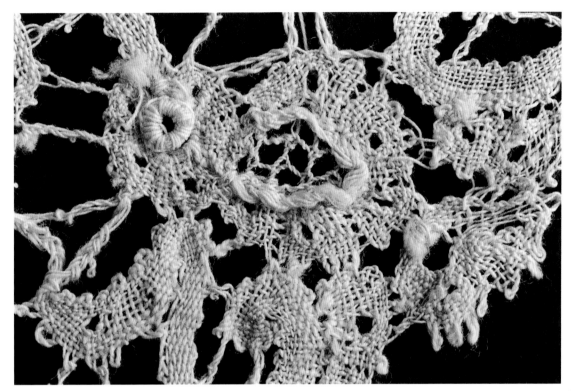

Plate 179: Detail of a cuff of 'rosaline perlée'. Small-scale flowers and leaves with clothwork decorated with holes and bobbin-made raised work typify 'rosaline' laces: this example also has an applied needlepoint ring, or couronne, which gives it the further denomination 'perlée'.

A note on Duchesse Laces

The duchesse laces comprise a group of coarser Belgian part laces, mostly guipures, with the general characteristics of Brussels laces given on page 144. The bobbin work frequently includes: half and whole stitch pattern areas; flowers formed by a ring of lobed petals round an open center; a thick outlining thread which is also used to separate the petals and is incorporated within the thickness of the lace; veins within leaves or petals defined by rows of holes; raised work, usually in the form of bundles of threads on the surface.

Some application laces in which the motifs have the above characteristics, are also classed as duchesse laces.

Points to watch

Duchesse laces with purely bobbin-made motifs are most easily confused with late 19th century Honiton laces discussed in the next chapter.

Opposite page:
Plate 178:
(top) Collar of bobbin lace in a style known as 'rosaline de fantaisie': 1900-15. Maximum width 58cm (23in). Belgian or Cantu, Italy.
The design of this rosaline lace is very closely modelled on Italian designs of about 1700 but the collar shape is the obvious clue to its late date.
(center) Cuffs of Belgian rosaline lace: 1900-15. Depth 6cm (2.3 in); length 18cm (7.2 in). See **Plate** 179 for a detail of a rosaline lace.
(bottom) Collar of Belgian bobbin lace with needle-made ground: 1900-15. Width 43cm (17in).
The designs of both the cuffs and the bottom collar are more reminiscent of late 17th century Flemish laces in the candelabra style (see **Plate** 149a) than of the Italian baroque. The collar is grounded with a needle-made net worked in two different thicknesses of thread and in two mesh sizes.

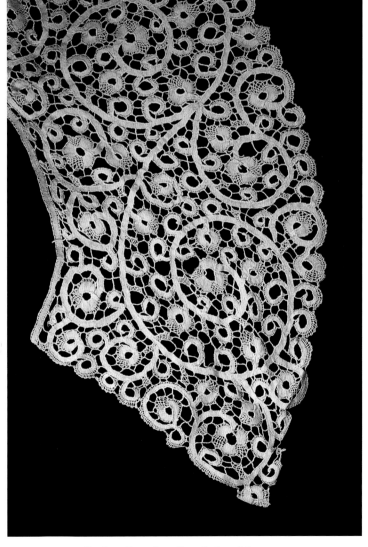

Plate 180: Detail of a collar of rosaline de fantaisie.

East Devon (Honiton)

Plate 181: Devon flounce: about 1750-70. Depth 29cm (11.5in); pattern repeat 69cm (27in); length shown 60cm (23.5in)

The thread and workmanship in this piece are much better than in the flounce in **Plate** 153 but the areas of cloth stitch and half stitch are more loosely worked and there is less raised work than in the lappets and edgings of **Plates** 184 and 185.

Characteristics

1. Part lace.
2. Pattern areas mainly in clothwork but with some half stitch.
3. Right and wrong sides differ.

    a. Right side has raised work in the form of narrow bands of clothwork or bundles of threads outlining some edges and features within the design.

    b. Wrong side often has groups of threads passing loosely across the motifs from one area of working to another.

4. A gimp thread is often incorporated in 19th-century examples.
5. Designs are less skilfully drawn than continental designs, even in most better-quality examples; in poorer pieces, leaves, flowers and other motifs are massed and scattered indiscriminately.
6. Grounds:

    a. Bobbin-made brides, often decorated with picots (common in the early to mid 18th century and again after about 1850).

    b. Vrai drochel bobbin net (**Plate** 183 - elongate hexagonal mesh with two sides of four plaited threads and four sides of two twisted threads) - common from the early 18th century to the early 19th century.

    c. Needle-made net or brides after about 1850 (**Plates** 193 and 194).

    d. Machine-made net from the early 19th century.

Points to watch

East Devon lace is technically very similar to Brussels bobbin lace and better quality examples of English work may be impossible to distinguish from Brussels and other Belgian part laces. The following pointers are guides but not definitive answers.

Design - Honiton designs are often less organized, less sophisticated and less well drawn than Brussels designs and, in the 18th century, the use of old, worn prickings meant that even better motifs degenerated into simple whorls or indeterminate shapes. Similar faults are, however, also seen in poorer-quality continental laces. Poorer 19th century Honiton laces also include indeterminate shapes called 'slugs and snails,' often among better-drawn motifs.

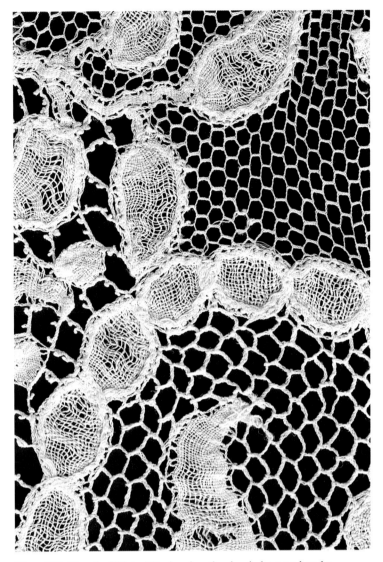

Plate 182: Detail of **Plate** 181 showing the drochel ground and a looped filling stitch which at first glance looks like a needlepoint filling but is, in fact, bobbin-made.

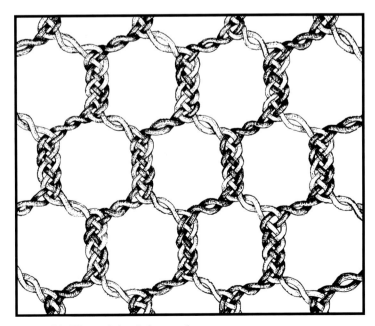

Plate 183: The vrai drochel ground.

163

Plate 184: Group of lappets.
a. (center). About 1725-35. Full length 57cm (22.5in).
This lappet has the same density of design as the central lappet in **Plate** 163 but its more floral character exemplifies a later stage in the development of the 'bizarre' designs. The scalloped edge and rounded end of the lappet are also later features.
b. (left). About 1750-60. Length shown 58.5cm (23in); full length 53cm (21in)
c. (right). About 1760-70. Length shown 58.5cm (23in); full length 77cm (30in).

164

Plate 185: Group of 18th-century edgings and a sleeve ruffle: length shown 53cm (21in); depth a-d 7cm (2.7in), d 3.7cm (1.5in); maximum depth of ruffle 17cm (6.7in).

a. About 1710-40: of good quality and in the 'bizarre' manner but not sufficiently stylish to date accurately.

b. About 1740-60: in very fine thread but showing the haphazard nature of much English design.

c. Mid 18th century: even more confused than edging b and showing an intermediate stage in the degeneration of design and workmanship between that of b and e.

d. About 1760-80: an unsophisticated version of French designs of the period in which asymmetric floral sprays spring from a patterned edge.

e. Mid-late 18th century showing the final deterioration of early 18th century 'bizarre' designs.

f. Sleeve ruffle – about 1760-75.

Plate 186
These two edgings were clearly made to the same pattern but show some of the results of different interpretations of the design and/or of the use of an old pricking in which the pinholes have become enlarged so that the motifs are distorted. One obvious area of difference is the two whorls to the right of the picture which spiral in opposite directions. The upper one also includes a gimp thread crossing over the clothwork: this is a device commonly used in Devon laces to separate flower petals, as seen in the flowerhead at the top of the main motif, and indicates that this feature may, originally, have been intended to be a flower. Leaves which spiral into a center are, however, also featured in Devon laces and in the related Flemish laces; they originated in the baroque laces of the 17th century and recur, usually in rather crude forms, in both English and continental laces through the 18th century.

Consistency of working - Honiton lace often includes: areas worked to different standards by different workers; fillings and raised work placed indiscriminately; and, in 18th century examples, the drochel ground worked in different directions. Brussels work is more consistent in standard.

Thread - the 18th century English thread was whiter and softer than Brussels thread giving the lace a slightly fuzzy appearance and softer feel but this difference has, in many cases, been lost due to wear and washing over the centuries. Imported Flemish thread was occasionally used in England although it was extremely expensive and hard to obtain.

Plate 187: Two edgings: length shown 33cm (13in).
 a. About 1775-1800, with drochel ground. Pattern repeat 32cm (12.5in); depth 7.2cm (2.9in)
b. Early 19th century; probably 1830-50. Pattern repeat 6.5cm (2.6in); depth 12.5cm (5.0in)
The repeated flowerhead forming a scalloped edge was a recurrent theme in 1830s designs but I have seen this carnation in a number of Honiton laces, often of clearly later date. The motifs are applied to machine-made net.

166

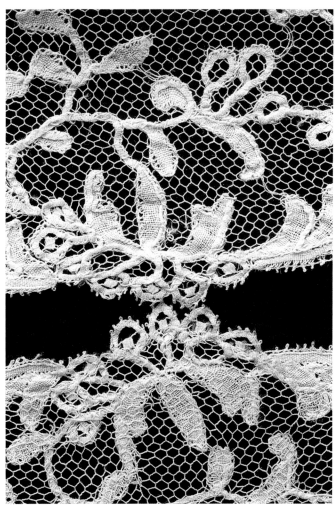

Plate 189: Detail of the stole in **Plate** 188 showing the right side above and the wrong side below.

The cloth-stitch pattern is tightly worked and has good raised edges; this is typical of Honiton laces from the early 19th century before the lace boom of the 1850s caused a rapid deterioration in standards.

A gimp outlining thread is incorporated in the design and a Honiton leadwork filling (square spot) is seen in the edge motif.

Plate 188: Stole of Honiton lace applied to a machine-made net: about 1840-50. Width 35cm (14in); full length of stole 220cm (88in); length of patterned end 47cm (18.5in).

The arrangement of an asymmetric floral design within a triangular shape is typical of the 1840s, as is the weak, straggly nature of the flower sprigs. The similarity of the border design to that of the contemporary Brussels border in **Plate** 166 will be apparent but the Brussels design is better drawn and more orderly.

Honiton v. Duchesse

Honiton laces frequently include cabbage roses formed by a strip of clothwork or alternating half and whole stitch which spirals or snakes around an open center with a leadwork filling (see **Plate** 191). Petals are separated by a thick thread which is worked back and forth loosely over the surface. Duchesse laces do not include the cabbage rose and, in flowers with rings of petals, these are separated by a thick thread worked back and forth but caught firmly between the finer working threads.

Duchesse laces, on the other hand, include leaves or petals with veins defined by rows of holes not frequently seen in Honiton laces.

In the 19th century even the poorest-quality Honiton laces were made in relatively fine thread. In Belgium, on the other hand, the finer threads were reserved for the better quality laces while the poorer duchesse guipures, most easily confused with Honiton laces, were made in coarser threads.

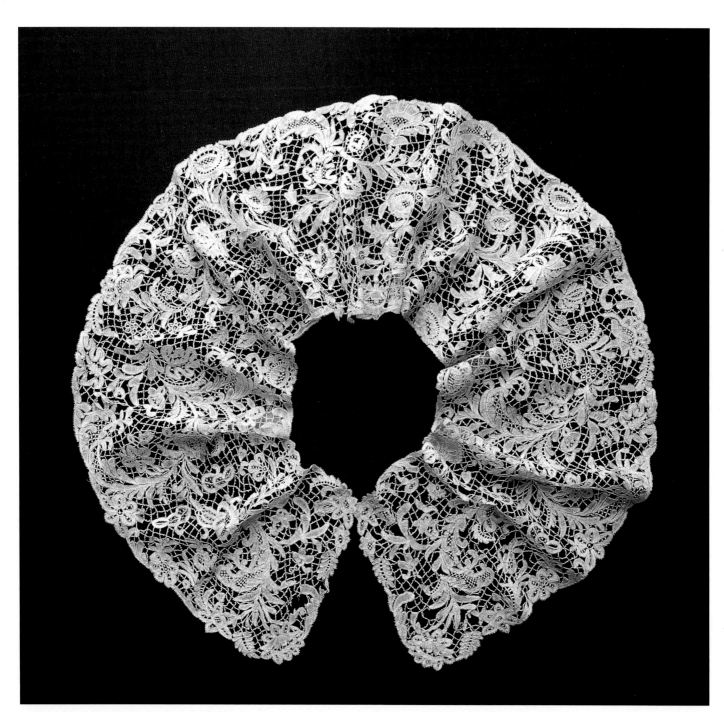

Plate 190: Bertha collar of Honiton guipure with bobbin-made brides: about 1850-60. Depth of lace 20cm (8in); length of inner edge 104cm (41in)
This bertha would have been worn around the shoulders of an evening dress, as seen in **Plate M**. It would have needed very little gathering so that its rich design would have been clearly displayed. When opened flat it is almost the same shape as the bertha in **Plate 241**. Technically the lace is very similar to the lappet in **Plate 191**.

168

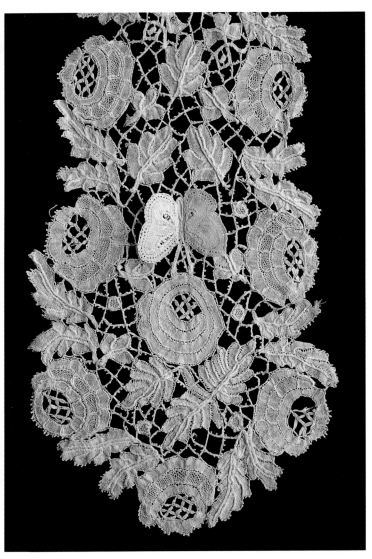

Plate 191: Lappet end of Honiton guipure with bobbin-made brides: about 1850-75. Maximum width 10cm (2.5in); length shown 18cm (7in); full length 96cm (38in)

The pair of lappets is made in 19th-century fashion in one continuous length.

The picoted connecting brides are known as 'purl bars' in Honiton lace.

The cabbage roses of this design are almost ubiquitous in Honiton laces; the petals may be made in a continuous spiral, as in the central example, or in a ring with additional layers worked back and forth, as in the outer flowers. The petals are often divided by a gimp thread carried loosely over the surface and alternate petals or layers of petals are commonly worked in half and whole stitches. The flower centers are normally open but for a leadwork filling as in these examples.

Note the raised wings of the butterfly which are attached to the lace only along their inner edges.

History

Various records show that, by the early 17th century, lace-making was established in the East Devon villages around Honiton but what is not so clear is the type and quality of the lace that was made. Early 17th century English portraiture shows many examples of bobbin laces similar to those of Flanders but with compartmentalized rather than flowing designs, but few actual examples survive. Celia Fiennes, a visitor to the area in the late 17th century, remarked merely that lace made there was as fine as Flanders lace but did not wash so well, and records in the early 18th century are no more specific.

By the 18th century the Devon lace-makers were certainly making part bobbin laces similar to those of Brussels and from comments such as Celia Fiennes', it is perhaps fair to assume that this was so in the earlier period. The problem with washing may well have been due to the poorer-quality English thread and is one factor in the attribution of the edging in **Plate** 185a to Devon.

What is surprising in Celia Fiennes' remarks is her comment on the quality of the English lace. This suggests that Devon work was better than has recently been supposed and we are only now starting to distinguish some of our finer examples.

The difficulty for the English industry was that it operated in an entirely different manner from that of Brussels. In Brussels, the manufacturers were based in a major city with strong links to Paris and the French court, their major market. They controlled large workforces to whom they supplied thread and patterns and whose work they could oversee. They hired their own designers or bought designs from trained designers. In Devon there was no such organization. Many of the cottagers may have bought their own thread and worked their own patterns repeatedly. Others were supplied with thread and patterns by local dealers but it appears that no one manufacturer controlled a large body of workers who worked for him alone so that there was little safeguard against the pirating of new, and expensive, designs. Devon was also remote from London, its major market, and even here the English aristocracy, who spent much of the year on their country estates, were not so fashion-conscious as their French counterparts whose lives were spent at court. In Devon there was thus little incentive to control the quality of workmanship, to train specialist designers, or even to buy in new designs.

The major problem then with much of the Devon lace was in its design, or rather lack of it, and in the rather haphazard attitude to workmanship mentioned above. New designs were, of course, introduced, as shown by the examples in the accompanying **Plates** 183 and 185, and the general design trends seen in the Brussels laces were followed, but even the better examples are distinguished by a certain poverty in the drawing and a general lack of sophistication. Another problem was the reworking of old patterns which may not have been fully understood in the first place; the results of this are shown in **Plate** 186.

In previous chapters we have seen how the changes in fashion at the end of the 18th century led to the abandonment of densely-patterned laces suited to the part-lace technique. The drop in demand for Devon lace was felt particularly keenly because of the recent loss of Devon's other major market, after London: this was the USA which, with independence, was freed from the restriction of being obliged to trade with Britain.

By 1800, of the thousands of lace makers in Devon a decade or so earlier, all but a few hundred had turned to other means of earning a living. The early decades of the 19th century saw little improvement in the situation, despite the move of Heathcoat's machine-net factory from Nottingham to Tiverton in 1816. This provided a cheap foundation for the new Honiton application laces and considerably quickened the making of large items, such as veils and stoles, but even Queen Adelaide's order of Honiton lace could do little to promote the industry while fashion was against it.

By the beginning of Victoria's reign it was only with difficulty that enough workers could be found in and around the little East Devon fishing village of Beer to complete an order for a flounce and matching trimmings of a quality suitable for the Sovereign. These pieces, supplemented with a veil, were subsequently worn by Queen Victoria at her wedding and later at the christenings and weddings of many of her children.

The continuance of royal patronage in subsequent years, together with the reawakened desire for opulent designs suited to the Honiton technique, brought about the revival of the industry. The contemporary interest in guipure laces also saw the return of the bar-grounded lace. This was the start of a new boom and, for a short while, the fame of Honiton lace spread even to the continent. Copies of the new guipure were made at Mirecourt in Lorraine and to some extent in Belgium. Here cross-fertilization with the local 'duchesse' laces resulted in many hybrid versions whose origin is now almost impossible to determine.

The success of the industry in the 1850s and 1860s without any strong organization to sustain it was the main cause of its downfall. In order to satisfy the enormous demand for Honiton lace, the majority of workers lowered their standards and quickened their production. The difficult cloth-stitch raised work was replaced by bundles of threads loosely bound to the surface or was omitted altogether. Such rudimentary designs as there had been were soon abandoned in favor of agglomerations of unrelated motifs or, at worst, an indeterminate mass of squiggles and curls often called 'slugs and snails'. Even the poorest of the laces shown in **Plate** 192 is not as bad as much of the production of this period.

To put all the blame on the workers would be unfair. They were working long hours to scrape a living in the teeth of machine competition and were exploited by the many unscrupulous dealers who acted as agents for the sale of the lace in London and other cities. Only a very few establishments such as that of Mrs. Treadwin in Exeter and John Tucker in Branscombe were concerned to maintain standards of quality and workmanship.

When the slump came in the 1870s, Devon's lace-makers were again forced into other forms of employment. Many of the Branscombe workers turned to a form of tape lace which we have already seen (pages 62-3) while Mrs. Treadwin's workers were taught to repair and re-order antique laces which were becoming ever more popular. Even the 17th-century Venetian needlepoints were included in their repertoire.

When the final lace revival came in the late 1880s a few lace-makers returned to the industry but the lace schools which had provided new blood had been closed under the Education Act of 1870. With few children available for training, the impetus which led to some better-quality work at the turn of the century soon died. Although lace continued to be made until the First World War, little has been made professionally since then. Honiton's renewed popularity is as an amateur craft hobby.

Opposite:
Plate 192: Group of Honiton laces with different grounds.
a. Collar with a needlepoint ground (see **Plate** 193): late 19th century. Depth of lace at center 8cm (3.2 in); length of inner edge 99cm (39in).
The collar has organized, repetitive designs around its outer and inner edges but, between them, is a scattering of unconnected motifs, including birds and butterflies. This lack of order is far more typical of Honiton laces than the organized design of the bertha in **Plate** 190.
It has been pointed out to me that the outer leaves, seen more clearly in the detail in **Plate** 193, are hop leaves rather than the more usual vine leaves.
b. Cuff of Honiton lace with a knotted needlepoint ground (see **Plate** 193): about 1855-70. Depth of lace 7.5cm (3in)
This cuff would probably have been worn under a flared outer sleeve of a dress of the late 1850s or 1860s.
c. Modesty piece of Honiton lace with a needlepoint ground inset in machine-made net: about 1910-30. Triangle side 17cm (6.5in)
Modesty pieces were used to fill in low-cut necklines; they were particularly common in the 1910s-20s when necklines fell after the very high style of the 1890s-1900s.
The tape-like design around the central flower sprig is commonly known as 'slugs and snails'.
d. Pair of mittens of Honiton appliqué on machine-made net with cream silk-satin ribbon trim: late 19th-20th century. Length 15cm (6 in)
The mittens are designed to cover only the palm and base of the thumb and were probably made for a wedding.

a

b

c

d

Plate 193:
Above - detail of the cuff in **Plate** 192
Below - detail of the collar in **Plate** 192.

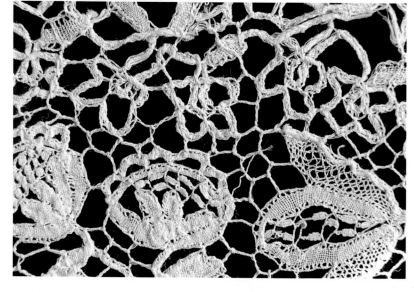

Plate 194: Detail of a Honiton lace
with a coarse needle-made ground.

Flemish bobbin laces including potten kants

Plate 195:
a. Scallop from a flounce: about 1630-40. Maximum depth 11.5cm (4.5in)
Width 9.5cm (3.7in).
The broad areas of clothwork, with little relief in the way of filling stitches, are typical of North European laces of the 1630s. The poor delineation of the stylized floral design may be due in part to the technical difficulties found in working more complex designs at this date. There is also a possibility that this lace is English rather than Flemish. It is worked by the part technique.
From the collection of the late Mrs. Valerie Cliffe.
b. Flemish edging: about 1640-50. Maximum depth 3cm (1.2in); pattern repeat 5cm (2in).
This is worked by the straight technique. The footing and picoted heading are integral. From the collection of the late Mrs. Kathleen Tipping.
c. Flemish edging: about 1640-50. Maximum depth 4.5cm (1.7in); pattern repeat 5.5cm (2.5in).
This is worked by the part technique. The footing and the picoted heading are later additions. The picots are replacements for the original ones which have worn away.
In addition to the design and workmanship, the extremely fine thread used in this example and in examples (b) and (d) indicate their Flemish origin: no other country in Europe grew the high-quality flax needed to produce it, nor had the workforce skilled enough to spin it.
d. Flemish edging: about 1660-80. Depth 6cm (2.5in); pattern repeat 17.5cm (7in).
This is worked by the straight lace technique with a kat stitch ground (page 201).
The repeated cloud-shaped motifs set off against a mesh ground and alternating with symmetrical floral motifs are typical of one branch of Flemish design reputedly made near Antwerp for sale in the Low Countries. This and edging (a) in **Plate 196** have often been called 'Dutch' laces for this reason. An example in the Exeter Museums' collection (Catalogue No. P327-Palliser Collection) has a design of a double-headed eagle picked out by holes in the clothwork instead of the stylized floral motif seen here. The double-headed eagle was the badge of the Hapsburgs who ruled part of the Netherlands at the time.

a

b

c

d

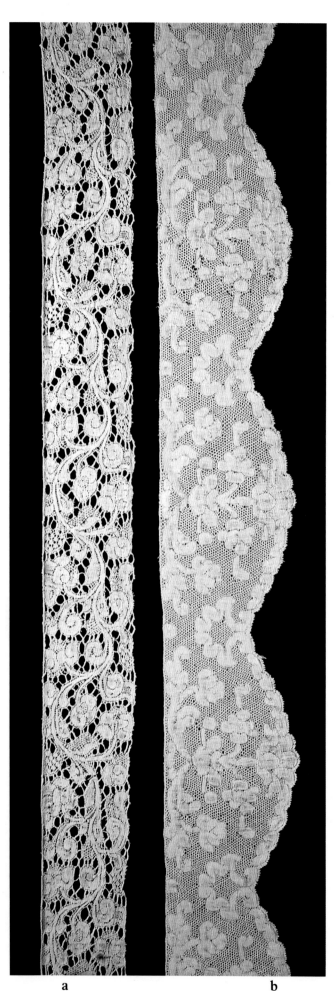

a   b

Plate 196:
a. Flemish edging: about 1670-90. Depth 7cm (2.7in); pattern repeat 15cm (5.7in).
The design is a peculiarly Flemish version of the Italian baroque style. It is worked as a straight lace with plaited connecting brides (many are repaired).
This type of design was introduced in the mid-17th century but the scale of the motifs in this example and a loss of boldness in the design suggest the later date. An even later version is seen in the edging added to the Milanese flounce in **Plate** 136.
b. Flemish edging: about 1660-90. Maximum depth 11cm (4in); pattern repeat 20.5cm (8in).
This is worked as a straight lace with a round Flemish ground, but the ground is worked tightly in the manner of the 18th-century straight Valenciennes laces rather than loosely in the manner of the 17th- and 18th-century part laces. Although the scalloped edge of this piece might suggest a date in the 1640s, the open nature of the design indicates the rather later date.

Note and Characteristics

This chapter deals with those Flemish laces not considered on pages 120-123 and 132-139 and, in particular, with laces which developed from the very early bobbin laces considered on pages 120-123 which have repetitive designs defining axes of symmetry within scalloped edgings. By the 1620s stylized floral designs were included and it is these that became established in the Flemish repertoire under the name 'potten kant', meaning 'pot' or 'vase' lace because of their stylized design of a pot of flowers.

The early 17th century examples of this genre are flat guipures, made with uniform threads but in any bobbin technique. Later examples are mesh-grounded straight laces, often with a gimp thread outlining their design. The mesh grounds vary, the round Flemish ground (**Plate** 199) or kat stitch (**Plate** 222) being common in the 17th and 18th centuries and kat stitch or Lille ground (**Plate** 227) in the 19th.

History

The early development of bobbin laces in the geometric style has already been discussed (pages 120-123) and we have also seen the introduction of floral motifs into needlepoints and into Milanese bobbin laces by the early 17th century. Naturally, such changes also occurred in Flemish bobbin laces but here the Flemish manufacturers developed styles which appealed directly to the northern market and were followed in other parts of northern Europe.

The new trend appears to have started with the scalloped edgings of about 1620. The earlier and contemporary geometric laces tended to be very fine and spidery and, at first, the floral designs were also depicted by narrow bands of clothwork but these were much flatter, softer and more supple than the Milanese bobbin tapes (**Plate** 134). Some of the areas of clothwork soon broadened out and by the 1630s the deep scallops were filled with an intricate pattern of stylized flowerheads and leaves, sometimes still linked by, or interspersed with, narrow trails of clothwork. The overall arrangement was, of course, one of symmetry about the axis of the scallop as in all other laces of the period. By the 1640s, the scallops were shallower and the pattern had again broken into spidery lines, but now these were closely spaced and separated only by open linear areas crossed by a multitude of threads. The basic floral motif is often scarcely discernible in the resulting dense patterning.

The paucity of remaining examples of mid-17th century Flemish lace makes it difficult to follow subsequent changes but the dense patterning appears to have continued into the 1650s and 1660s as the edge of the lace gradually became straighter. The baroque influence is also seen in the introduction of curving stems but the underlying preference for symmetry is retained as the flounces are divided into panels filled with repeated symmetrical motifs.

One feature of the later Flemish laces which may, in part, be attributable to these dense designs is the mesh ground. Examples (b) and (c) in **Plate** 195, show that these designs were created in both part and straight laces and it is in the latter, in particular, that the primitive mesh is seen. Here, in order to form and, at the same time, to bridge the open areas between the pattern motifs, the threads are plaited and twisted together around irregular voids. The creation of this complex patterning must have taxed the ingenuity of workers in the 1640s to their utmost.

A further example of these early meshes is seen in the baroque lace of **Plate** 196a. This is again a straight lace despite its flowing design which would be easier to execute by the part technique. It is interesting to compare this lace with the almost contemporary Flemish part lace in **Plate** 148a: they both have the

same curving stems and spiralling leaves and, although the use of filling stitches is slightly different, a few of the stitches themselves are identical.

By the 1650s or 1660s more regular mesh grounds had developed as seen in **Plate** 195d and **Plate** 196b. Both of these laces display a continuation of the symmetrical, floral designs which filled the scallops of the 1630s and the 'potten kant' laces of the 18th and 19th centuries (**Plate** 197); this is one of the few laces named for its design rather than its place of origin.

The 'potten kants' were marketed particularly in the Netherlands and they show the remarkable strength which tradition can have in a community. Although the design developed in the mid-17th century, and its treatment changed gradually over the centuries, it survived, still recognizable, through the 19th century.

a

b

Plate 197:
a. Flemish potten kant: late 18th-early 19th century. Depth 9.5cm (3.7in); pattern repeat 16cm (6.3in).
This is worked as a straight lace with the Mechlin ground and typical soft Mechlin gimp thread (**Plate** 211). The fineness of the thread used, the openness of the design and the scattering of subsidiary motifs are typical of laces of the 1760s to 1780s, but the traditional nature of the potten kant design means that it could be of substantially later date.
Many potten kant laces of the 19th century were worked with the Lille ground (**Plate** 227).
b. Upper insertion - Flemish potten kant: early 18th century. Depth 11cm (4.5in); pattern repeat 17cm (6.7in).
This is worked as a straight lace with the round Flemish ground. The clumsiness of the pattern shows that this was a peasant lace: the care and density of the working and use of the round Flemish ground proclaim it to be of earlier date than 19th-century.

Central insertion - Lille bobbin lace: mid-19th century; about 1830-50. Depth 10.5cm (4in); pattern repeat 12.5cm (5in).
This insertion is of the type known in continental Europe as 'Lille' (pages 194-198) but is in a design particularly associated with the Belgian town of Beveren which made lace for the Dutch market. Here it is combined with the earlier potten kant and a narrower edging, probably of similar provenance and date, to form a cap (incomplete).
Lower edging: depth 3.5cm (1.4in); pattern repeat 2cm (0.8in).

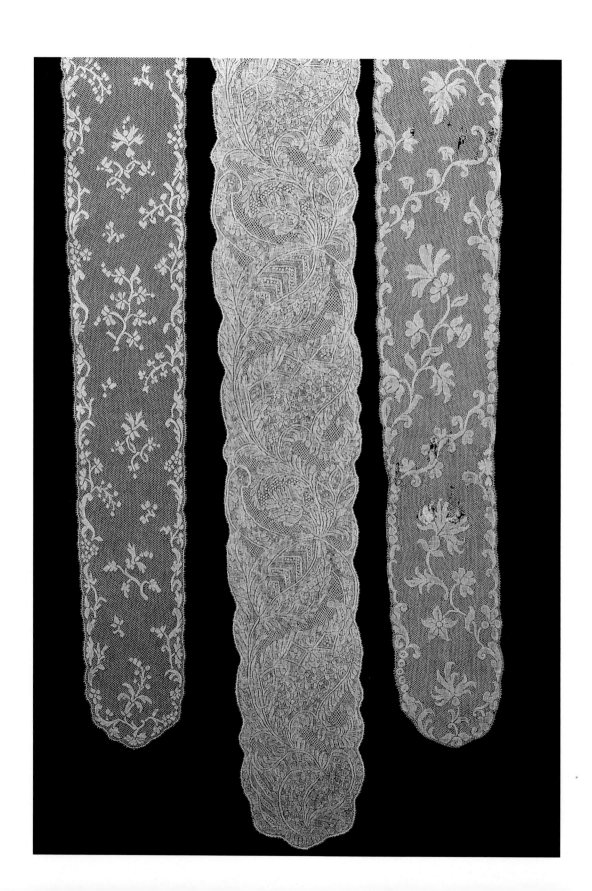

Plate 198: Group of lappets.

(center). About 1725-35. Length shown 39cm (15in); full length 63cm (25in).

A later form of the 'bizarre' patterns is shown here; the design is less crowded than those of the late 1710s-early 20s but the motifs are still richly patterned with filling stitches and geometric shapes and there is strong movement from side to side. The ground is a 'five-hole' ground (see **Plate** 203).

(right). About 1765-80. (See **Plate** 202 for detail.) Length shown 33cm (13in); full length 67cm (26.5in).

Here is the classic form of Valenciennes lace: the design is in dense clothwork with internal features picked out by rows of holes; the ground is the round Flemish ground and no filling stitches are used.

(left). About 1780-90. Length shown 33cm (13in); full length 55cm (22in)

Note the lightness of the mesh ground compared with that of the right-hand lappet in this Plate. This results from the use of the diamond ground instead of the round ground. The density of the clothwork is enhanced by the introduction of a few extra threads which do not continue into the ground but are cut off at the upper edges of the motifs: this shows that the lappet was started at the rounded end.

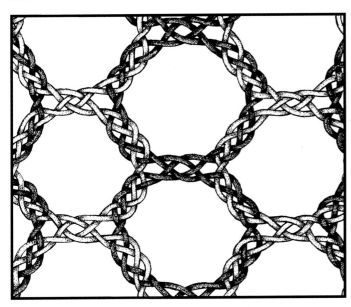

Plate 199: The Valenciennes round ground.

Plate 200: The Valenciennes diamond ground.

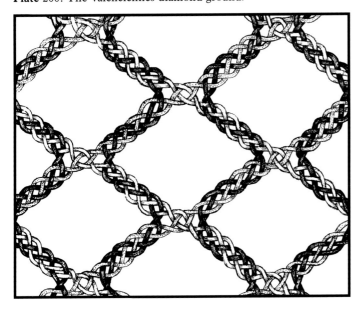

Valenciennes characteristics

1. Straight bobbin lace.
2. Fine, uniform threads - no raised or gimp outline.
3. Pattern of closely woven clothwork.
4. Rows of generally rectangular holes outline the pattern and define features within it.
5. Little use of fancy fillings or grounds after the early 18th century.
6. Cut ends of thread at one or each end of pattern motifs in some late 18th century and in most later examples. This is due to additional threads introduced to increase the density of the clothwork.
7. Grounds:

   a. Round Flemish ground (**Plate** 199). A hexagonal mesh with four threads plaited or twisted on all six sides enclosing an almost round hole - most common in the mid- to late-18th century.

   b. Diamond ground (**Plate** 200). Diamond-shaped mesh with four plaited sides - most common in the 19th century.

   c. Snowy (point de neige) ground of complex arrays of interconnected spots common in the early 18th century.

   d. Other complex grounds also used in the 18th century.

Points to watch

The only constant factors in Valenciennes lace are the very fine thread used and the total lack of thick outlining which makes it completely flat.

The 'snowy' ground which was common in the early 18th century was long thought to have originated in Binche, a Flemish town about 50 km (30 miles) from Valenciennes, but there are no clear records of this town's products in the early 18th century. By the mid-18th century Binche was certainly making straight laces similar to those of Valenciennes but so were many other lace-making towns and Binche was also making motifs for Brussels part laces.

What may have originated in Binche is a flat lace, similar to Valenciennes, but with a more open, confused structure including the snowy or other complex grounds, and a frequent use of half-stitch pattern areas and tallies in the design. These laces were fashionable in the very late 17th-early 18th centuries. As designs changed through the 18th century, it is thought that the Binche workers continued using the snowy ground after it had been given up in Valenciennes; the Binche products may be distinguished by their slightly poorer quality, with less firm clothwork and much less regular use of Valenciennes' outlining rows of holes to differentiate the pattern motifs from the ground.

Very close copies of Valenciennes laces were made by machine in the 19th century.

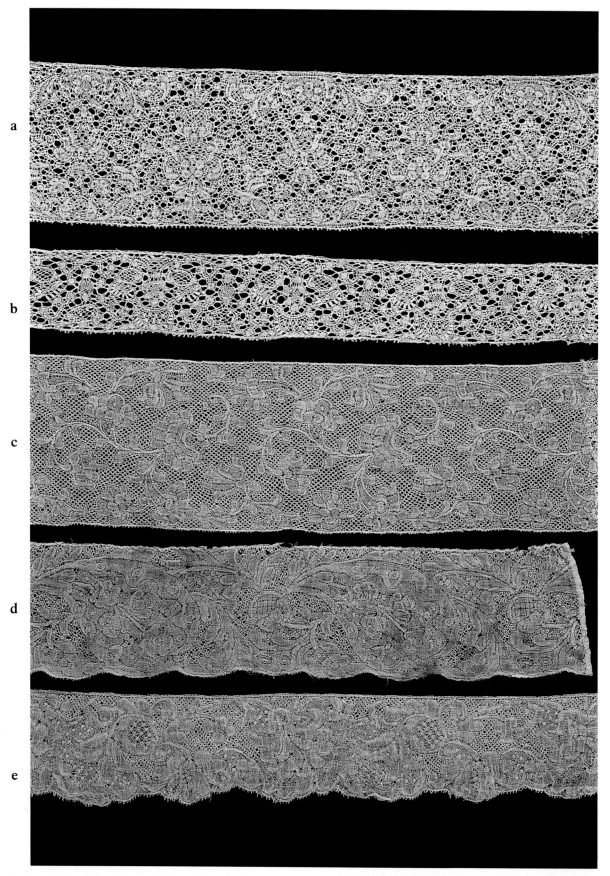

Plate 201: A group of edgings: length shown 21.5cm (8.5in).
a. About 1700. Depth 6.5cm (2.6in); pattern repeat 9.5 cm (3.8in).
The design, although confused, is essentially a 'candelabra' pattern
(see **Plate** 149a). The ground is a very open, irregular form of the
snowy ground used in example (d) below. This, and edging (b),
below, are of a type commonly ascribed to Binche.
b. About 1700. Depth 3.5cm (1.4in); pattern repeat 6cm (2.4in).
Note the use of half stitch and tallies.

c. About 1700-20. Depth 7cm (2.8in); pattern repeat 9 cm (3.6in).
This light design of separate, curving, asymmetric sprigs is quite
common in Valenciennes laces and appears to date from the early
18th century. This has the five-hole ground better seen in **Plate** 203.
d. About 1715-25. Depth 5.5cm (2.2in); pattern repeat 11cm (4.4in).
This is in the bizarre style with a snowy ground.
e. About 1725-40. Depth 4.5cm (1.8in); pattern repeat 11.5cm (4.6in).
This has the five-hole ground with snowy ground used as a filling.

178

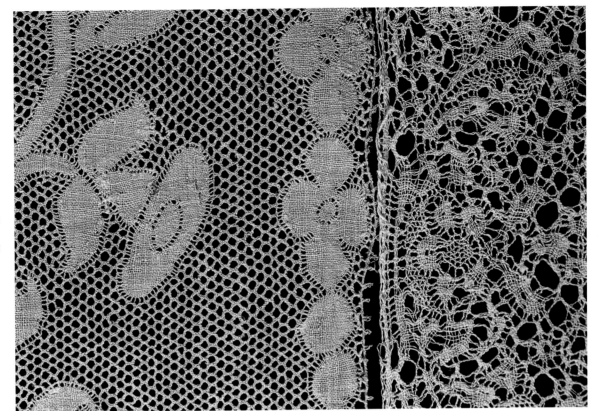

Plate 202:
a. (left). Detail of the right-hand lappet in **Plate** 198
b. (right). Detail of edging a in **Plate** 201 showing the extremely complex bobbin work formed by the straight technique including areas of half stitch and whole stitch.

Below:
Plate 203: Detail of an edging similar to **Plate** 201c with the 5-hole ground.

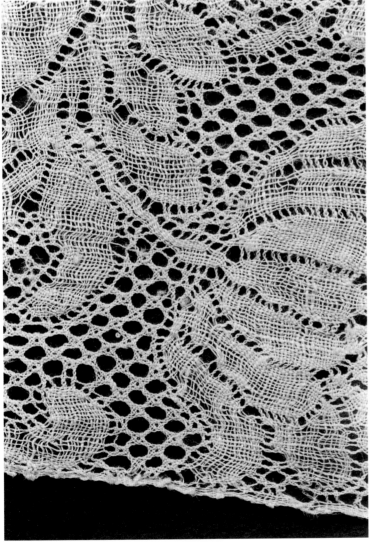

History

It is rare that history relates the names of those involved in the lace trade but records indicate that the first important manufacturer in Valenciennes was one Françoise Badar. She herself was a lace-maker, having learnt the craft in Antwerp, and she taught the Valenciennes people to make both bobbin and needle laces. In the late 1640s and 1650s, the industry grew under her direction and she was soon joined by other manufacturers.

This early prosperity was not to last. In the wars between France and Spain for dominion over the Low Countries, Valenciennes became a battlefield and the settlement of 1678, which ceded Valenciennes to France, brought little relief. The heavy taxes imposed on Valenciennes' products made them uncompetitive and it was not until the 1720s that fashion and the economic climate again turned in Valenciennes' favor.

In the intervening years, changes had occurred within the Flemish industry and the products of various of the lace-making towns had diverged. Whereas Brussels had become known for her fine quality part laces, Valenciennes' workers had specialized in a straight lace. This in turn was differentiated from straight laces of the Antwerp area by the introduction of new French designs. These at first followed the Bérainesque style but it was the introduction and development of the 'bizarre' designs which coincided with, and perhaps brought about, the revival of the industry.

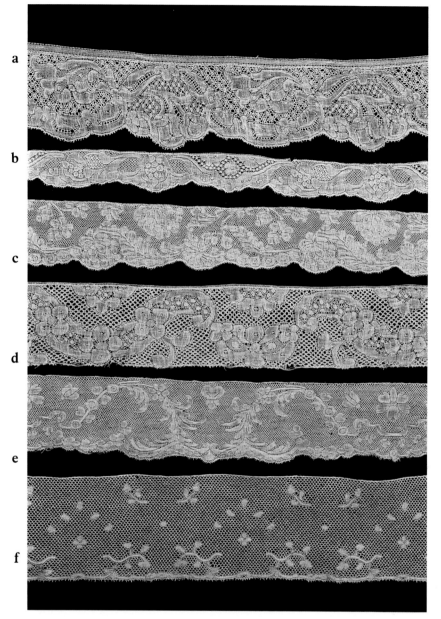

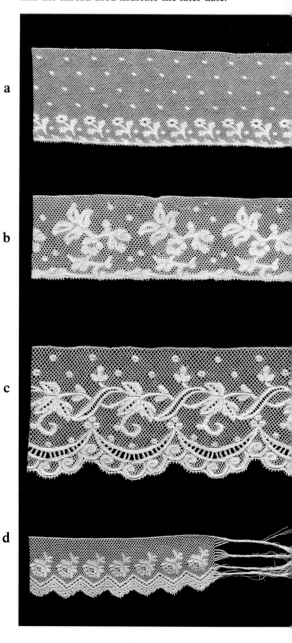

Plate 205: Group of 19th-20th century edgings. Length shown 20cm (8in).
a. About 1800-10. Depth 7.5cm (2.9in); pattern repeat 2cm (0.7in)
b. Mid-late 19th century. Depth 6.5cm (2.6in); pattern repeat 7 cm (2.8in)
Although the pattern of this piece probably dates from about the 1840s, it is worked in a fairly heavy thread, for the lower end of the market, and could be of a much later date. The ground is a rather open version of the round Flemish ground which is associated with 19th-century Valenciennes laces made in Dieppe (see **Plate** 207).
c. Late 19th century; probably about 1855-75. Depth 10cm (4in); pattern repeat 6.5cm (2.6in)
d. Late 19th-early 20th century. Maximum depth 4.5cm (1.8in); pattern repeat 2cm (1.9in)
This is yet another example of a late 19th-20th century lace copying an early style. Here the dentate edge common in early 19th-century edgings is mixed with a repeated sprig motif also used at that time, but the larger scale of the design and the thread used indicate the later date.

Plate 204: Group of edgings with various grounds.
a. About 1730-50. Depth 5.5cm (2.2in); pattern repeat 11.5cm (4.5in).
b. About 1730-50. Depth 2.5cm (1in); pattern repeat 13.5cm (5.3in).
c. About 1740-60. Depth 3.5cm (1.4in); pattern repeat 13cm (5.2in).
d. About 1745-70. Depth 4.5cm (1.8in); pattern repeat 19cm (7.5in).
e. About 1765-80. Depth 5cm (2in); pattern repeat 12cm (4.8in).
f. About 1780-1800 or 19th century. Depth 6cm (2.4in); pattern repeat 10cm (4in).
Edgings b, c, and e in this group are well executed in the very fine thread associated with Valenciennes laces. Edgings a, c and f, on the other hand, are less competent, being worked on a slightly larger scale and in a coarser thread although this is obvious only when they are seen alongside the better-quality laces. Being aimed at the lower end of the market, these may date from slightly later in the 18th century than suggested by their designs. Edging a, with its snowy ground, may be a Binche product.

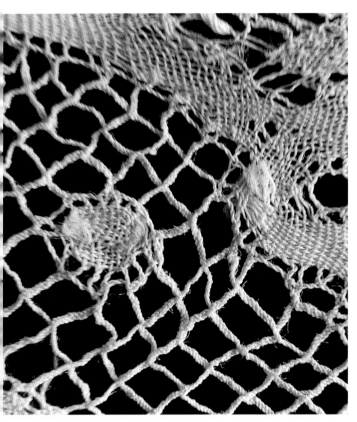

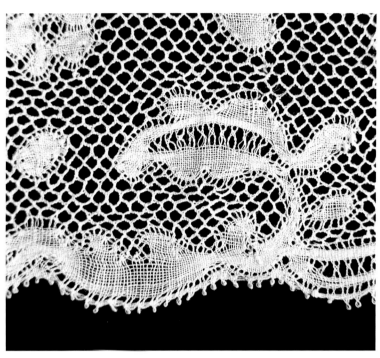

Plate 206: Detail of a 19th-century Valenciennes edging showing the diamond-mesh ground and cut ends of thread at each end of the clothwork where extra threads, added to increase its density, have been cut away.

Plate 207: Detail of a Valenciennes lace with the 19th century round ground.

A further major contribution to the advances of the lace industry in this period was the refinement of the thread manufacture. Flanders had long been renowned for the quality of her linen but now her workforce was able to produce thread only a few fibers thick and with a count which has been estimated at about 1200 (the finest linen thread now available is far coarser, with a count of about 320). It was this thread which was used in many of the exquisite edgings and lappets of the early 18th century which required up to 800 bobbins to create a width of only 4in (10cm).

Throughout the middle decades of the 18th century, Valenciennes was in great demand with the aristocracy who prized it not only for the delicacy and beauty of its designs but also for the strength and firmness of its structure which made it very durable even through repeated washings. The success of the Valenciennes industry naturally led to copying in other lace-making centers but it was always said that the refinement of true Valenciennes lace distinguished it from imitations, or 'fausses Valenciennes'. Certainly, at the time, the industry within the city was highly organized and it is said that great care was taken over the quality of thread used, the consistency of workmanship and over design but we cannot now be certain of the origin of surviving examples.

In the later 18th century, as fashion turned to lighter fabrics, Valenciennes' popularity waned but efforts were made to compete. Additional threads were introduced into the clothwork to increase the contrast between the pattern and the ground which could thus be made more open and, in some cases, the lighter diamond-shaped mesh was used. These changes could not, however, halt the decline and the French revolution effectively brought lace making in the town itself to an end.

In the 19th century, the Valenciennes tradition was continued in other centers, but particularly in Belgium. The diamond-shaped mesh became more firmly established and its scale increased to heighten the contrast with the pattern and to quicken production. The extra threads which had at first been added into the clothwork at the beginning of each new pattern area and taken out at the end, leaving cut ends at one edge, were now carried loosely over the back of the ground from one motif to the next. When the lace was finished they were then cut at both ends of the motif.

Despite these changes, Valenciennes was still a slow and difficult lace to make and much of its production in the nineteenth century was in the form of narrow trimmings and insertions. Compared with other laces it was always expensive but its smoothness and strength made it particularly suitable for underwear and babies' wear and there was always a ready market.

In the lace boom of the 1850s and 1860s some manufacturers were able to increase their range of Valenciennes laces, even to the extent of producing wide flounces. Shading was introduced by the contrasting use of whole and half stitch, as it was in other laces of this period, and the better manufacturers even took to dividing more elaborate designs into sections for working by the part technique. This type of lace came to be known as 'Valenciennes de Gand', after Gand (or Ghent) the home of the more influential manufacturers who made these products.

As with other hand-lace industries, the manufacture of Valenciennes lace could not survive long after 1900 but the interest in antique laces at the turn of the century brought a curious revival. This was the return of the complex laces ascribed to Binche, with the snowy ground and sprinklings of points d'esprit. These are still made commercially to a limited extent and sell under the name of 'point de fée'.

Plate 208: Valenciennes flounce: about 1850-75. Maximum depth 26cm (10in); pattern repeat 25cm (9.7in).

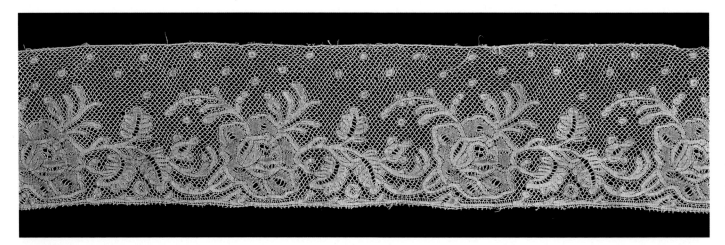

Plate 209:
Edging: about 1870-1900. Depth 6.5cm (2.6in); pattern repeat 8 cm (3.2in)
In the later 19th century, half stitch was introduced into the pattern to give a more naturalistic effect as it was in many other laces of the period.

December 1852. THE WORLD OF FASHION. Plate 2.

Plate N: Fashion Plate from '*The World of Fashion*'; 1852.
In the late 1840s to 1850s many day dresses fitted close around the neck and were worn with a neat, round collar of lace or muslin. This might have a 'van Dycked' edge, i.e. an edge shaped with a row of points similar to those seen in so many of van Dyck's portraits of the early 17th century.

To be properly dressed a married lady would always have worn some sort of head covering, whether a simple cap in the morning or a more elaborate confection with lace and flowers in the evening. Fall caps, such as those seen in **Plates** 77, 241 and 251, belong to this period.

183

Mechlin (Malines/ Mechelin)

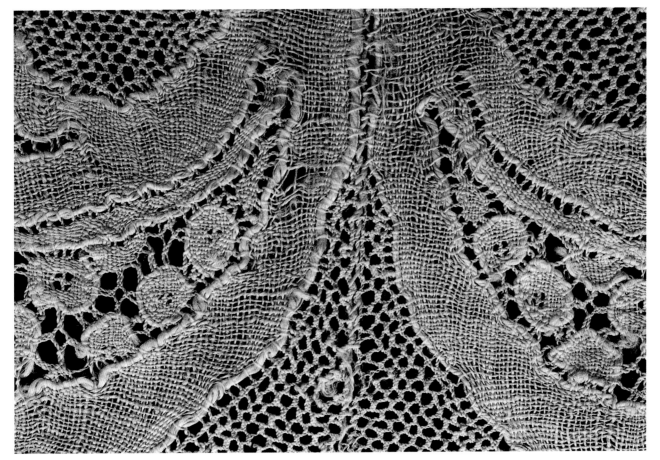

Opposite page:
Plate 210: Cap back: 1735-45. Width 8cm (3.1in); Depth 9cm (3.5in)
This is clearly made in two panels; the technique of joining panels invisibly by the point de racroc had not yet been invented. The cartouches of fancy filling stitches are particularly characteristic of mid-18th-century Mechlin laces.
The cap back formed the center of a woman's formal headdress: a gathered edging sewn around the curved edge would have formed a frill framing the face while a pair of lappets would have hung from the sides or from the straight edge at the back.

Plate 211: Detail of **Plate** 210 showing the Mechlin ground and untwisted gimp outline to the pattern.

Characteristics

1. Straight bobbin lace in fine, soft, white thread.
2. Clothwork pattern.
3. Gimp thread outline to the pattern. The gimp is usually slight, soft and silky but a heavy, twisted thread was sometimes used in the mid-18th century.
4. Frequent use of cartouches and other areas filled with fancy stitches.
5. Ground (see **Plate** 212): hexagonal mesh with two sides of four plaited threads and four sides of two threads - these threads are usually crossed in 18th century examples but the sides were lengthened by the introduction of a twist in the 19th century.

Points to watch

The Mechlin ground is very similar to the Brussels vrai drochel (**Plate** 160) but the Mechlin plaits are shorter by one half stitch giving the mesh the appearance of a regular hexagon.

History

Mechlin (Malines in French) is a small Flemish town to the north of Brussels and not far from Antwerp. As early as the 16th century it was a center of the lace-making industry and by the late 17th century its name was probably in use as a generic term for Flemish straight

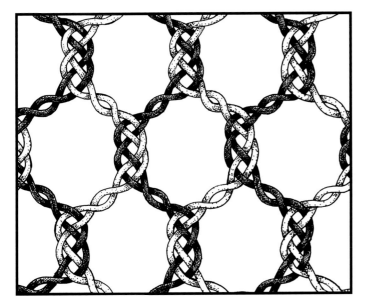

Plate 212: The Mechlin 'eis' ground. The ground is shown with twisted threads on four sides, but these threads are often simply crossed, particularly in 18th century laces.

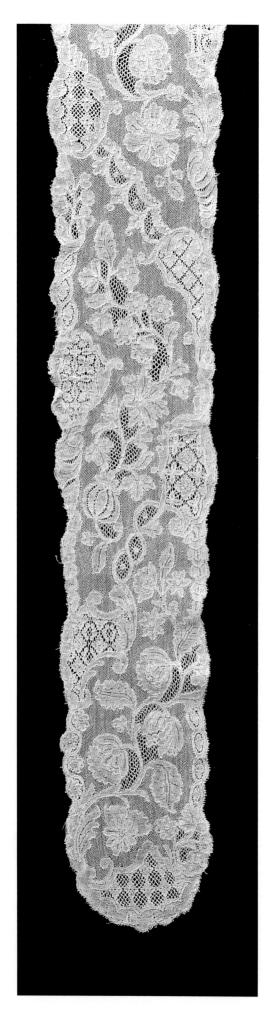

laces. In the early 18th century, as laces from the various towns acquired the distinct characteristics now associated with them, Mechlin became known for its straight lace made in a fine, soft, white thread. It was this, as much as the gimp introduced in this period, that distinguished Mechlin lace from that of Brussels and Valenciennes which were worked in a more tightly twisted, creamy thread.

In other respects there was little difference between the early products of Mechlin and Valenciennes: they were both worked in the intricate designs of the period and with a variety of complex meshes. Not until the 1740s did the fine hexagonal mesh we associate with Mechlin laces become firmly established but this was retained for the rest of its history save always, of course, for the occasional exception.

From its early period, Mechlin retained one other feature: the use of complex fillings often arranged in the odd cartouche shapes of the bizarre period. These are seen in their most accomplished form in the cap back and lappet of **Plates** 210 and 213 and continued well into the second half of the century.

Throughout this early period Mechlin was widely regarded as the 'Queen of Laces' and was particularly popular in England. Its soft texture had suited the styles even of the 1700s but, by the 1760s and 1770s, the crisper texture of needlepoint was again in fashion. It is probable that the thicker, corded gimp was introduced into some Mechlin laces at this period in imitation of the stiff cordonnet of the French needlepoints: an example is seen in **Plate** 216.

Plate 213: Lappet: 1735-45. Length shown 51cm (20in); full length 58cm (23in)

Plate 214: Group of Mechlin edgings: length shown 27.5cm (11in).
a. About 1720-40. Depth 4.5cm (1.8in); pattern repeat 16.5cm (6.5in)
The footing is 18th century and may even be the original one.
b. About 1730-50. Depth 4cm (1.6in); pattern repeat 18cm (7in)
The footing is of much later date. A complex ground is used here but the gimp thread and use of fillings in the design are typical of Mechlin laces.
c. About 1745-60. Depth 4.5cm (1.8in); pattern repeat 21cm (8.3in)
Many mid-18th-century edgings were worked in designs which could be sewn edge-to-edge, as shown here, to form a double frill with the pattern continuing across the join.
d. About 1755-70. Depth 3.5cm (1.4in); pattern repeat 16cm (6.3in)
A complex 'armure' ground is used and the footing is of later date.

Below:
Plate 215: Late 18th century edgings: length shown 27cm (10.5in).
a. About 1755-75. Depth 4.5cm (1.8in); pattern repeat 18 cm (7in)
The extremely thick corded gimp thread used here stands proud on the right side of the lace, in imitation of the raised work of French needlepoints which were particularly fashionable at the time. A detail of a similar lace is shown in **Plate** 216.
b. About 1765-80. Depth 5cm (2in); pattern repeat 18.5cm (7.3in)
c. About 1770-85. Depth 5cm (2in); Pattern repeat 17cm (6.7in)

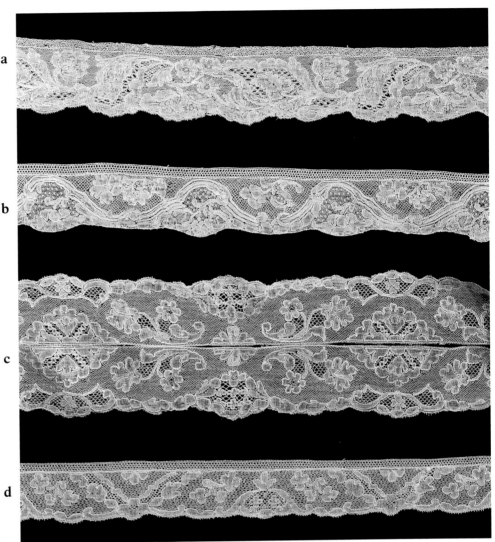

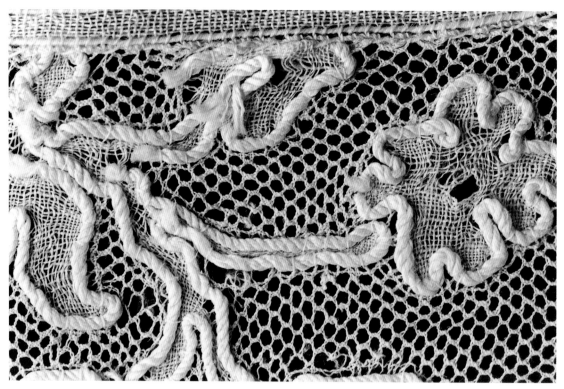

Plate 216: Detail of a Mechlin lace with a corded outline.

It was also in this period that Mechlin came to be regarded as a 'summer' lace by the French court; it suited the softer, lighter fabrics worn in the summer months whereas French needlepoints were *de rigueur* in the winter. No doubt this usage, together with its popularity in Britain, enabled its production to continue, if on a reduced scale, through the slump at the end of the century.

Naturally by this time its designs had changed. The rich patterns of earlier decades were replaced by simple, repeated classical motifs and flowerheads. In these there was little room for Mechlin's accustomed virtuosity of filling stitches.

The early 19th century brought continued change in design as it did in other laces but the Mechlin technique could not cope successfully with the larger fashion accessories required in the second half of the century. Being a straight lace, it could not, like the Brussels laces, make use of machine nets to quicken production. Nor was it strong enough for the accustomed uses of Valenciennes lace.

It remained a slow and laborious lace to make, and commensurately expensive, despite a slight change in the structure of its net ground (see characteristics). Although its production continued in the later nineteenth century and occasionally wide flounces were made, it never regained its former importance and little was made in the 20th century.

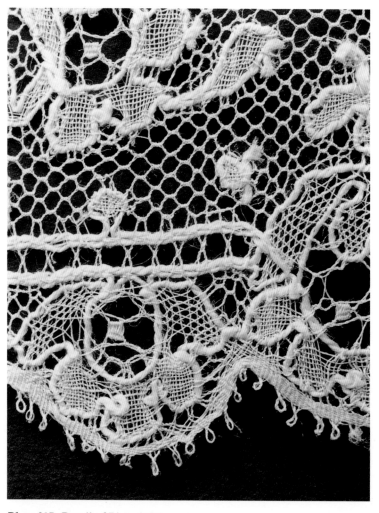

Plate 217: Detail of **Plate** 219d.

188

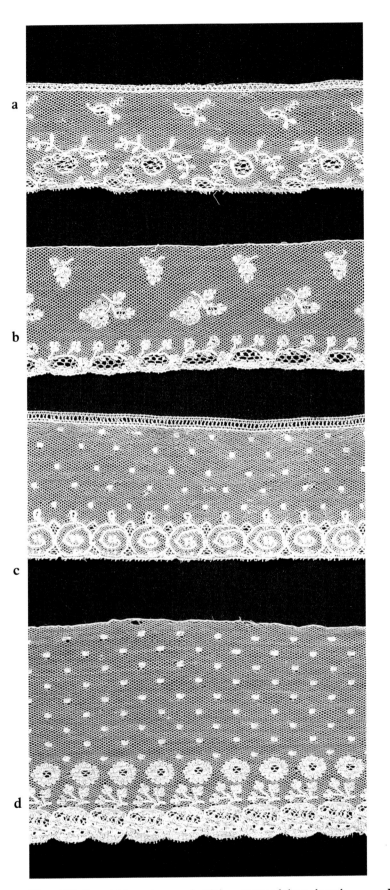

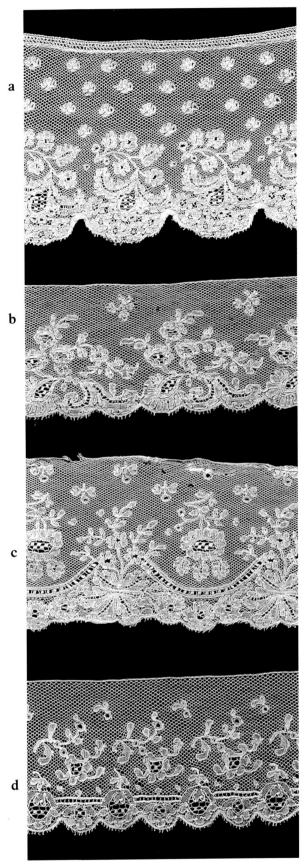

Plate 218: Late 18th century-early 19th century edgings: length shown 14cm (5.5in).
a. About 1775-1800. Depth 4cm (1.6in); pattern repeat 4cm (1.6in).
b. About 1775-1800. Depth 5cm(2in); pattern repeat 3.5cm (1.9in).
c. About 1800-1810. Depth 6cm (2.5in); pattern repeat 1.5cm (0.6in).
d. About 1810-1820. Depth 9cm (8.5in); pattern repeat 2cm (0.8in).

Plate 219:19th century edgings: length shown 15cm (6in).
a. About 1820-30. Depth 8.5cm (3.9in); pattern repeat 4cm (1.6in).
b. About 1830-45. Depth 5.5cm (2.2in); pattern repeat 5cm (2in).
c. About 1850-75. Depth 6.5cm (2.6in); pattern repeat 7cm (2.8in).
d. Late 19th-early 20th century. Depth 6cm (2.4in); pattern repeat 3cm (1.2in).

Point de Paris

Plate 220: Group of straight bobbin laces with the point de Paris ground.
(left) Insertion: second half 18th century; probably 1760-80. Width 6.7cm (2.6in);pattern repeat 4cm (1.7in).
Strips of this type were joined edge to edge to form larger costume accessories or other articles.
(center) Lappet end: about 1780-1800. Width 8.5cm (3.5in); full length (two lappets now joined) 134cm (52in).
(right) Edging: probably early 20th century. Depth 7cm (2.8in); pattern repeat 2.5cm (1in).
Although this example has a repeated sprig design which could date it to the early 19th century, the relatively large scale of the design suggests this is a later copy.

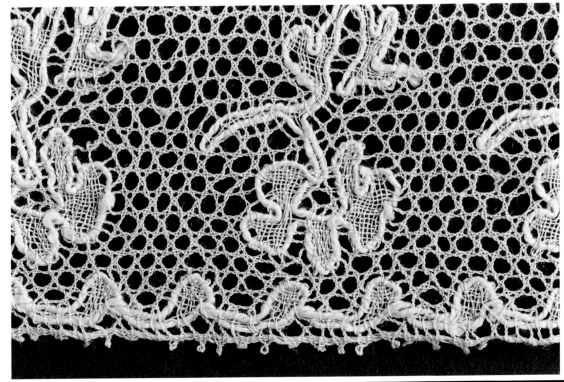

Plate 221: Detail of the edging in Plate 220.

Characteristics

1. Straight bobbin lace in linen or cotton thread.
2. Gimp thread outline to the pattern.
3. Clothwork pattern areas.
4. Paris ground (also known as kat stitch etc. See **Plate 222**). The meshes give the appearance of a six-pointed star, with pairs of twisted threads defining a central hexagonal hole surrounded by six smaller triangular holes

Points to watch

The characteristic ground of this lace is also known as 'fond chant', or 'Chantilly ground', because of its association with Chantilly lace (see pages 212-217), and as 'kat stitch' in Great Britain. It occurs in a wide range of laces made by both the part and the straight techniques, both as a ground and as a filling stitch. It is only when it is combined with all the other features listed above that the resulting lace is generally called 'point de Paris'. For example, similar laces made in silk rather than linen or cotton are termed 'blondes'.

History

The name 'point de Paris' is ascribed to laces with the above characteristics made in the Île de France, including Paris itself, which was a lace-making region certainly as far back as the 17th century. Its ground, however, probably developed in Flanders along with other mesh grounds and is seen in early Flemish part and straight laces.

In the early 18th century, the lace-makers around Paris generally made relatively cheap products with simple patterns set off against light, open grounds. These

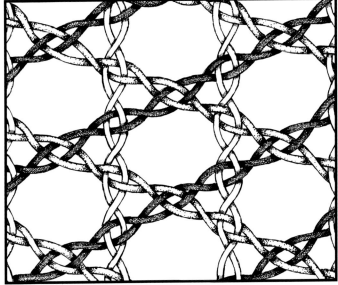

Plate 222: The point de Paris or kat stitch ground.

were made in silk and linen threads, of a coarser standard than used for the high-fashion laces of their times, but found a market both at home and abroad.

By the early second half of the century, these lighter laces were themselves becoming fashionable, particularly for the inner parts of flowing sleeve ruffles that were then in vogue and for larger dress accessories, such as capes and fichus. Gradually it seems, as the taste for open designs and light nets developed, more refined versions of the 'Paris' laces were made in finer linen, suitable even for smaller accessories such as caps and lappets.

The taste for this style of lace continued into the 19th century and, of course, copies were made elsewhere so that, as with so many other laces, it is no longer possible to be certain of the actual place of manufacture of surviving examples.

Opposite page:
Plate O: Fashion Plate from '*The Englishwoman's Domestic Magazine;*' about 1860.

The late 1850s-early 1860s saw skirts, supported on the frame crinoline, at their fullest and lace designs at their most opulent. Deep flounces, mantles and square shawls, six feet (2m) wide. were all made in hand-made lace or machine fabrics.

Plate 223: Group of flounces each with the point de Paris ground in the major part adjacent the footside and the Lille ground (see next chapter) near the headside.
a. Probably late 19th-20th century. Depth 8cm (3in).
b. About 1810-20. Depth 16cm (6in); pattern repeat 11cm (5in).
c. Mid 19th century. Depth 12cm (4.5in); pattern repeat 10cm (4in)

Below:
Plate 224: Circular mat with a point de Paris edging: probably Belgian; early 20th century. Outer diameter 17cm (6.8in). Figural motifs of this type were very popular in the early 20th century and are found particularly on small mats, like this, for the table or dressing table or on handkerchiefs, all of which made useful presents for the tourist. Another example is shown in **Plate 231**.

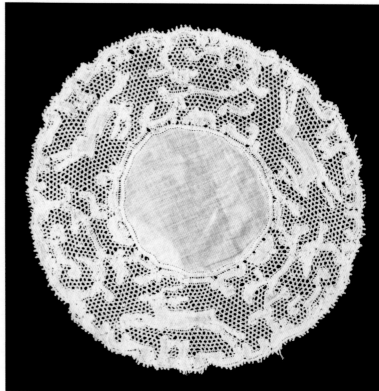

THE FASHIONS

Expressly designed and prepared for the

Englishwoman's Domestic Magazine.

AUGUST 18

193

Plate 225: Veil or apron: probably Lille: about 1800. Depth shown 38cm (15in); full depth (center) 73cm (29in); ends 98cm (34in); pattern repeat 21.5cm (8.5in); full width 135cm (53in).

18th-century aprons are typically deeper at the ends than in the center which suggests that this piece may be an apron but the difference may be due simply to uneven stretching from wear and washing. The pattern is sliced through at the ends rather than being arranged with side borders: the top edge is turned over to take a draw string.

In the late 18th and early 19th centuries most lace was made in the form of narrow edgings patterned with repeated flowerheads or tenuous, classical motifs along the headside but the occasional larger articles often had classical designs such as this. The spiky nature of the sprigs suggests a Lille origin although similar work was carried out in England.

Characteristics

1. Straight bobbin lace.
2. Clothwork pattern frequently including narrow and/or branching lines in early examples.
3. Gimp thread outline to the pattern.
4. Few filling stitches used but often of large scale leaving relatively large openings.
5. Ground (**Plate** 227): fond simple (also known as fond clair or Lille ground or, in the UK, as East Midlands or Buckinghamshire point ground) - hexagonal mesh with four sides of two twisted threads and two sides of two threads crossed.

Note and Points to watch

The fond simple ground may well have originated in Lille but was in use throughout Europe in the 19th century. Apart from Lille, noted centers were the English East Midlands counties of Buckinghamshire, Bedfordshire and Northamptonshire, where the lace came to be known as Buckinghamshire (or Bucks) point, Tønder in Denmark, Neuchâtel in Switzerland and the Erzgebirge in Germany, but these are to name but a few.

The products of all these regions can supposedly be differentiated from each other by minor technical differences in their working ; in practice this is rarely true. A study of laces in my collection has shown that, in many antique laces, which are now well over one hundred years old, characterizing features can no longer be discerned; in other examples, features purportedly restricted to specific regions are mixed together in the same lace.

Design features, including usage of filling stitches, are also supposed to be characteristic of certain regions and this is, to some extent true; for example, Beveren, in Belgium, is particularly associated with lace having flo-

Plate 226: Detail of **Plate** 225.

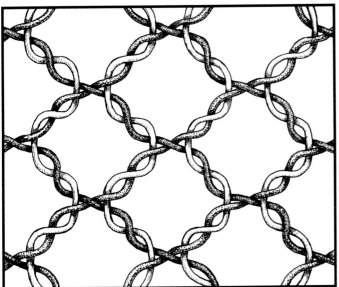

Plate 227: Fond simple or Lille ground.

ral sprig designs like that shown in **Plate** 230e, which was made for a very conservative Dutch market. In the majority of cases, however, designs were common throughout Europe; narrow edgings in very simple, repetitive designs were a staple of all industries and continued in use for many decades whereas better quality articles were aimed at a Europe-wide, fashion-conscious market for which styles had to change if they were to meet the demand.

It is not possible, in this book, to show examples from all the regions that made Lille-type laces and to elucidate their similarities and differences. I have therefore chosen a few laces to illustrate the basic characteristics, including some which can be ascribed with some certainty to specific regions. In addition I include a chapter on the 'Bucks point' laces which, naturally, predominate in my collection and which show something of the evolution of fashionable styles through the 19th century.

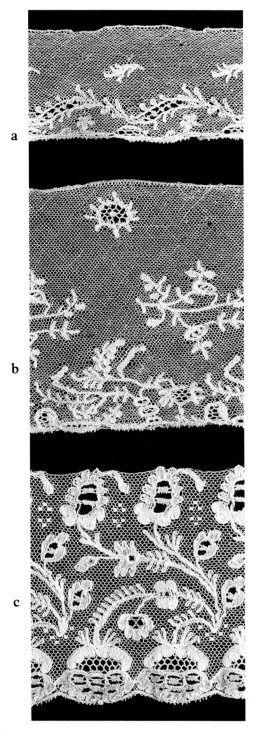

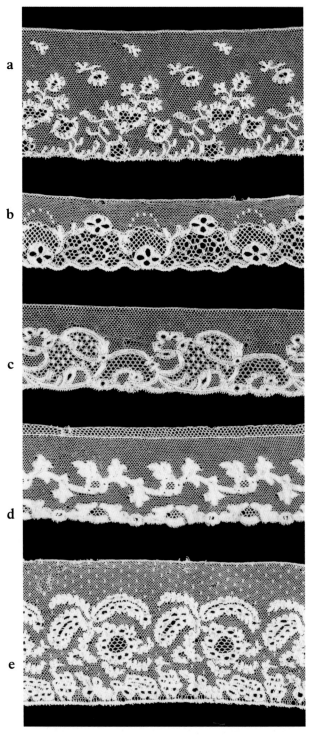

Plate 228:
a. Edging: about 1775-1790. Depth 4.5cm (1.7in); pattern repeat 4cm (1.5in). This edging could have been made in Lille or in the English East Midlands.
b. Lille edging: about 1780-1800. Depth 10cm (4in); pattern repeat 7cm (2.8in).
Branching designs formed by extremely narrow areas of clothwork bounded by gimp thread, with minor areas of very open filling stitches, are thought to be particularly characteristic of late 18th century Lille work.
c. Lille edging: mid-19th century. Depth 9cm (3.5in); pattern repeat 6cm (2.4in).
The thread used in this 19th-century example is much coarser than that of the 18th-century examples and the net ground has larger meshes. It was thus quicker to work, cheaper and more suited to compete with machine products. It is worked without a footing and was probably intended to be joined along the footside to an insertion strip to make a wider flounce. Interestingly, some of the clothwork is worked in the ground thread and some in the gimp to give different densities.

Plate 229: Group of edgings with the Lille ground.
a. Depth 8.5cm (3.2in); pattern repeat 6cm (2.5in).
b. Depth 5cm (2in); pattern repeat 7cm (2.7in).
c. Depth 6cm (2.25in); pattern repeat 9cm (3.5in).
d. Depth 6.5cm (4.3in); pattern repeat 9.5cm (3.8in).
e. Depth 10cm (4in); pattern repeat 7cm (2.7in).
a – d: probably 2nd quarter of the 19th century but possibly later. The thread and character of design of all these examples are not typically English; they might have been made in any of various regions of continental Europe. Example d is of a type in which the gimp thread is used in the center of the motifs rather than as an outline; a detail of another example is seen in **Plate** 232.
e. Mid-late 19th century. This was probably made at Beveren in Belgium for the Dutch market (see **Plate** 197 for a further example).

History

Lille, like Valenciennes, was a Flemish lace-making town ceded to France in the late 17th century. Its workers continued to make lace in the Flemish tradition and in the early 18th century made inferior copies of the Mechlin and Valenciennes laces.

Their other major product was a poorer-quality linen lace for the peasant markets which was worked in simple, often geometric patterns against a variety of light, open grounds similar to those of the Île de France considered in the previous chapter. In the 1760s and 1770s these laces became fashionable and, as dress continued to simplify with the introduction of neo-classical styles, the market for lightly-patterned trimmings grew.

It was during this period that a stitch, previously used only as a filling, came to be used as a ground. This was the fond simple, a simple twist net which, along with the straggly, branching designs of the period, we have come to associate with Lille lace.

Over the next 40 years the Lille industry did not suffer as greatly as other parts of the French lace industry but it did see a succession of declines and resurgences as it competed against revolution, war and the growing market in machine-made nets. By the 1830s it was again flourishing and the neo-classical designs had given way to patterns of floral sprigs. The subsequent changes to richer, more elaborate patterns were not so successful. This essentially lightweight lace could no longer compete with the luxurious needlepoints and heavier bobbin laces of Brussels. The development of the machine industry was a final blow. This had copied the Lille ground from an early date and the attachment of the Jacquard device to the lace machines in the 1840s enabled the net to be patterned at will.

Although lace continued to be made in northern France and Belgium by the Lille technique in the later 19th century, much of the production was again for the lower end of the market. Designs became stereotyped, workmanship deteriorated and the quantity produced gradually fell away. Despite some improvements in the early 20th century, little was made commercially after the First World War.

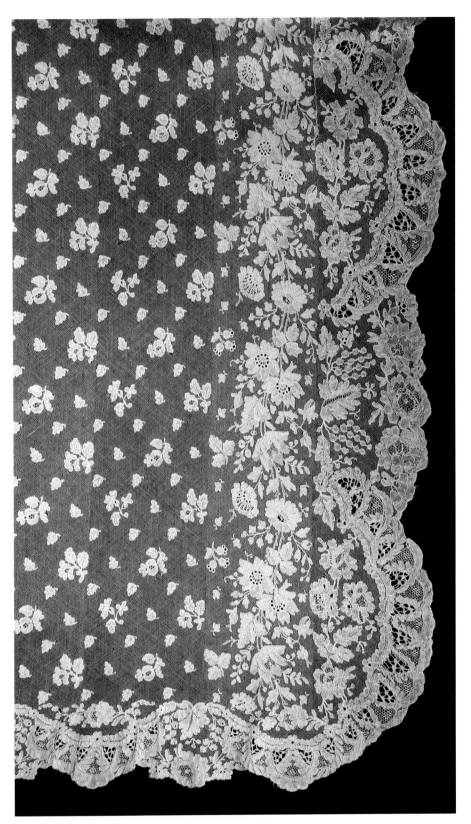

Plate 230: Bonnet veil: about 1850-60. Depth shown 40.5cm (16in); full depth of veil 48cm (19in); length shown 58cm (23in); full length of veil 114cm (45in).
The top edge is finished with a footing. The strips from which this veil is made are clearly visible; the floral band above the scalloped edge is of much higher quality than the sprigged ground above it while the edge itself is of intermediate quality. The organization of the design within the scalloped border, the beautiful drawing of the flowers, and their naturalistic rendering with the use of half stitch together with the cloth stitch to give the effect of shading all combine to suggest a French origin: indeed, a similar treatment of the flowers can be seen in some designs from Caen, but it has been suggested by a highly reputable expert that this piece might be English.

Plate 231
(top) Handkerchief with a Lille-ground edging: early 20th century; probably Belgian. Maximum depth of edging 4.2cm (1.6in).
(bottom) Lille ground edging probably from Tønder in Denmark because of the openwork trail which is frequently found in Tønder designs. The gimp thread sometimes outlines the design and sometimes runs through it, as seen in the detail in **Plate** 232. Depth 6cm (2.25in); pattern repeat 8cm (3in).

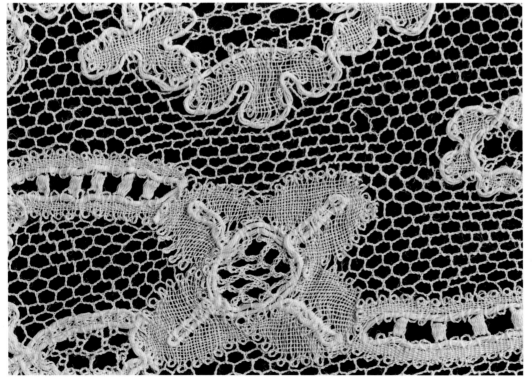

Plate 232: Detail of the Tønder edging in **Plate** 231.

Opposite page:
Plate P: Fashion Plate; about 1870
The 1870s saw a reaction against the use of lace in dress and in favour of ruched and gathered fabric trimmings but lace is still seen in the fashion plates, in particular, as ruffles and frills round the neck and cuffs, as long, narrow collars that extend down the front of the lengthening bodices, or as square collars round the low necklines of evening wear.

Fig. 1. No. 6. EVENING TOILETTE AND CARRIAGE TOILETTE. Fig. 2.

Fig. 1. PINK SILK, TRIMMED WITH LACE AND CRÊPE.—The skirt is trimmed *on tablier* with lace and crêpe bouillonnés, and at the back it is plain and trained. The sash, which is point d'Angleterre like the flounces, is fastened at the side under a trail of pinks and jessamine. Low bodice, with square basques back and front, and ornamented with bouillonnés and lace to correspond with the skirt. Pattern of skirt, 3s. 7d. ; of bodice, 2s. 7d.

Fig. 2. SCABIOUS VELVET, TRIMMED NATURAL OSTRICH FEATHERS.—The train skirt is bordered with a gathered flounce, which is headed in front with three rows of feather trimming. Tablier draped at the side, and likewise ornamented with feathers. A square Medici tunic at the back, with a jetted châtelaine bag on the left side. The bodice is made with a waist-coat front. Pattern of bodice and tunic, 3s. 1d. ; of skirt, 3s. 7d.

East Midlands (Buckinghamshire) point

Characteristics

1. Straight bobbin lace.
2. Clothwork pattern is most common except in black laces where half stitch is more usual.
3. Gimp thread outline to the pattern.
4. Areas of fancy filling stitches common, particularly honeycomb and honeycomb with mayflowers (small blocks of whole stitch).
5. Grounds:

a. Point ground (fond simple, see **Plate** 235). Hexagonal mesh with four sides of two twisted threads and two sides of two threads crossed.

b. Kat stitch (also known as wire ground, point de Paris, Chantilly ground, fond chant - see **Plate** 236). The meshes give the appearance of a six-pointed star, with pairs of twisted threads defining a central hexagonal hole surrounded by six smaller triangular holes.

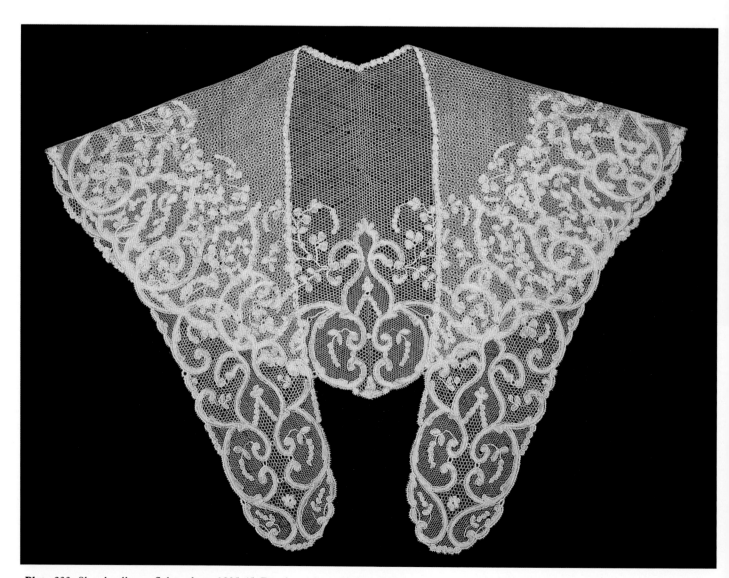

Plate 233: Shawl collar or fichu: about 1835-45. Depth at center 28.5cm (11in).
The design shows the mixture of influences that were current in the late 1830s-40s. The major area of the ground is worked in kat stitch while point ground is used in the stylised edge motifs. (See **Plate 234** for detail).

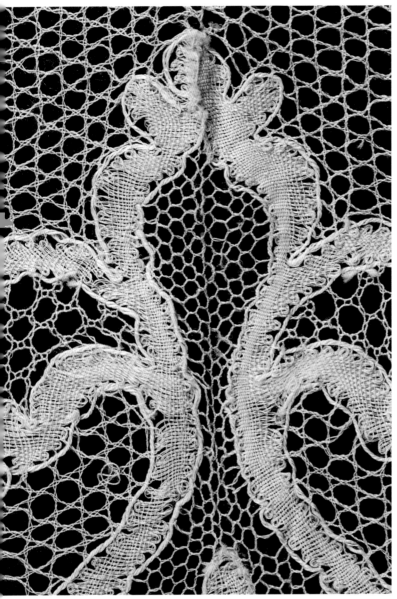

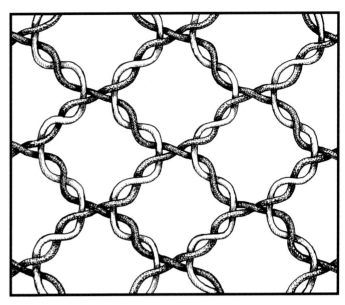

Plate 235: East Midlands point ground (fond simple etc.)

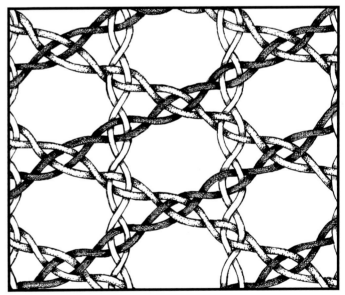

Plate 236: Kat stitch ground

Plate 234: Detail of the shawl collar in **Plate** 233 showing: the central join between the two halves of the collar; an area of point ground in the center; the kat stitch ground at the top; and areas of honeycomb filling (right and left center).

Points to watch

See Lille lace pages 194-199. Similar laces with the kat stitch ground were also made throughout Europe.

Good machine copies of point ground were made in the early 19th century, shortly followed by the kat stitch ground.

Simple needle-run, or darned, machine nets (see pages 111-112) can easily be mistaken for East Midlands bobbin laces.

The tradition of lace-making in the English East Midlands counties of Bedfordshire, Buckinghamshire and Northamptonshire goes back to the late 16th century but the products of the early years are no longer specifically identifiable and the same is true for much of the 18th-century production. By this time lace in the style of the poorer-quality continental products, with light, open grounds and simple patterns, was being made although the Mechlin laces, so beloved of the English aristocracy, were copied as well.

If one studies the portraiture of the 1750s and 1760s one sees a greater use of these lighter laces. Large accessories, such as capes and flounces, were made up from strips joined edge to edge while flowing sleeve ruffles often consisted of a lighter, cheaper product with perhaps an edging of more expensive lace.

In the 1770s the American War of Independence was as much a blow to the Midlands industry as it was to Devon. Lace making, which had spread to surrounding counties in the previous years of prosperity, drew back into the major centers. This was to be a recurring process over the next hundred years or more as the trade struggled against the vagaries of fashion and the growth of the machine industry.

In the 1790s and early 1800s, revolution and war were for once in the East Midlands' favor. With the diminishing flow of lace from the continent and the continuing interest in lighter laces, particularly in wide expanses of net, the East Midlands industry was stimulated to greater production.

During the previous decades the lighter Lille ground, known in England as point ground, had been introduced and this was now used to create veils, stoles, shawls or even overdresses. These, in the style of their time, were sprinkled with spots or tiny motifs and edged with a light pattern of repeated flowerheads or delicately drawn motifs. Usually these were arranged along a straight edge but a pointed edge was also common.

Surviving pieces of Midlands lace enable one to follow the development of design through the early 19th century. The pointed edges of the 1800s to 1810s became gradually more rounded as the simple flowerheads or upright sprigs developed a curving form, then grew in size to fill the broader, scalloped edges of the 1830s. At the same time, flowing linear patterns or repeated examples of the curving sprig motif developed inside, but spaced from the decorative edge. Usually the major proportion of the lace was still composed of sprigged net but, occasionally, floral designs snaked vertically or at an oblique angle up the ground. In the 1830s these gradually widened at the bottom until the broad triangular form of the 1840s was reached.

Throughout this period the design was expanding gradually up into the net and becoming ever more elaborate. By the 1840s a desire for all-over patterning had returned but the expertise required to draw the necessary designs had long since vanished. Earlier laces, particularly those of the mid-18th century, were looked to for inspiration. The result was a mixture of naturalistic floral designs, often intermingled with light rococo scrolls or ribbonwork, of more stylized designs with cartouches of fancy fillings and occasionally of stylized classical designs.

Unfortunately for the Midlands industry, the competition from machine laces had now reached a climax. The point ground, which was the simplest of the hand-made nets, had been copied by machine at an early stage. In its infancy, both fashion and the novelty of machine-made net had made it desirable and the hand-lace industry had declined but, in the late 1820s and 1830s, the tables were turned as machines could not yet produce the patterned fabrics fashion demanded. For a while the Midlands laces, but more especially the French blondes, could compete in price and popularity with the hand-embroidered nets and muslins and it was the machine-lace industry that suffered.

Plate 237: Baby's bonnet: about 1770-1800. Diameter of lace cap back 3cm (1.3in); depth of edging 1cm (0.5in).
Narrow, lightly patterned edgings and insertions constituted a major proportion of the East Midlands output in both the 18th and 19th centuries. Many were used as in this example to decorate babies' wear and were known as 'baby laces'.

Enormous efforts were now devoted to the patterning of machine-made net and in the 1840s, the Jacquard machine, which had been developed to quicken the production of woven brocades, was applied to lace manufacture. Although many developments had yet to come, from this point on, machine-made lace could, effectively, be patterned at will.

By the late 1840s the Midlands point lace could no longer compete in price with machine-made copies. Its light ground and straight technique were not, in any case, suited to produce the heavier, more richly patterned laces that were coming into fashion. Many of its workers turned to making the guipure laces discussed in a later chapter; many others left the industry altogether.

Although the production of point-ground laces continued through the second half of the 19th century, the making of larger accessories disappeared. Only the narrow edgings, in simple versions of the earlier designs, remained.

The 1890s and early 1900s brought something of a revival, both in the East Midlands region proper and in isolated, former lace-making areas, such as Downton near Salisbury in Wiltshire. Many of the patterns of the earlier years were revived and, although they were usually worked in a slightly coarser thread and on a slightly larger scale, they can make dating of surviving examples difficult.

Plate 238: Group of 19th-century point ground edgings: length shown 30cm (12in).
a. About 1805-15. Depth 7.5cm (3in); pattern repeat 6.5cm (2.6in)
Note the straight edge, finely drawn classical motifs including a laurel wreath, and the crowns picked out by tallies in the ground.
b. About 1820-40. Depth 5.5cm (2.1in); pattern repeat 9.5cm (3.7in).
The gimp thread is used within the motifs rather than as an outlining thread. This form is sometimes called 'Regency point' but its design indicates that it is of later date than the Regency period.
c. About 1840-50. Depth 6.5cm (2.6in); pattern repeat 13cm (5.1in).
Designs of odd-shaped cartouches outlined with stylized flowers and filled with fancy stitches in the mid-18th-century manner are particularly common in East Midlands laces after about 1840.
d. Post-1850. Depth 4cm (1.6in).
This is an example of the much simplified designs current in the later part of the 19th century.

Plate 239

a. Baby's bonnet of East Midlands point lace with a circular back of darned machine net: mid-19th century. Diameter of cap back 6cm (2.2in).

The bonnet is made up from a series of narrow insertions of point lace and a circular cap back of embroidered net. Simple designs such as these continued in use for decades and are impossible to date with any accuracy.

b. Lower part of an East Midlands point flounce of about 1820-30. Width shown 38cm (15 in); depth shown 29cm (11.5in); full depth 106 cm (42 in).

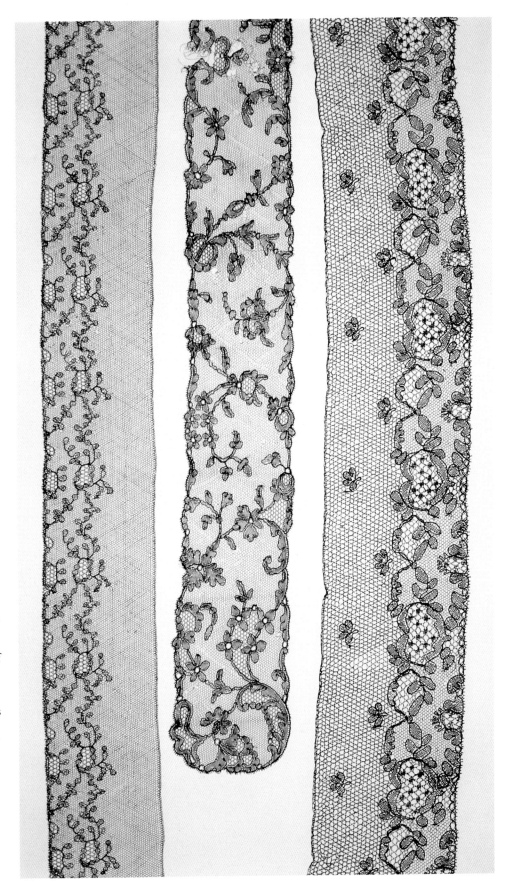

Plate 240: Group of East Midlands black point laces.

(left) Edging with the point ground and honeycomb fillings: about 1830-40. Depth 9cm (3.5in); pattern repeat 7.5cm (3in).

(center) One of a pair of lappets made in a single length: about 1840-50. Width 9cm (3.5in); length shown 53cm (21in); full length 112cm (44in).

(right) Edging with the kat stitch ground near the footside and the point ground near the headside and with honeycomb and honeycomb-with-mayflower fillings. Depth 12cm (4.5in); pattern repeat 11.5cm (4.5in).

These are technically similar to Chantilly laces with their use of half stitch instead of cloth stitch for the pattern. The two edgings are, however, worked in a shiny thread and their designs are typical of English manufacture. The central lappet is in the dull grenadine thread of Chantilly but is still likely to be of English manufacture.

205

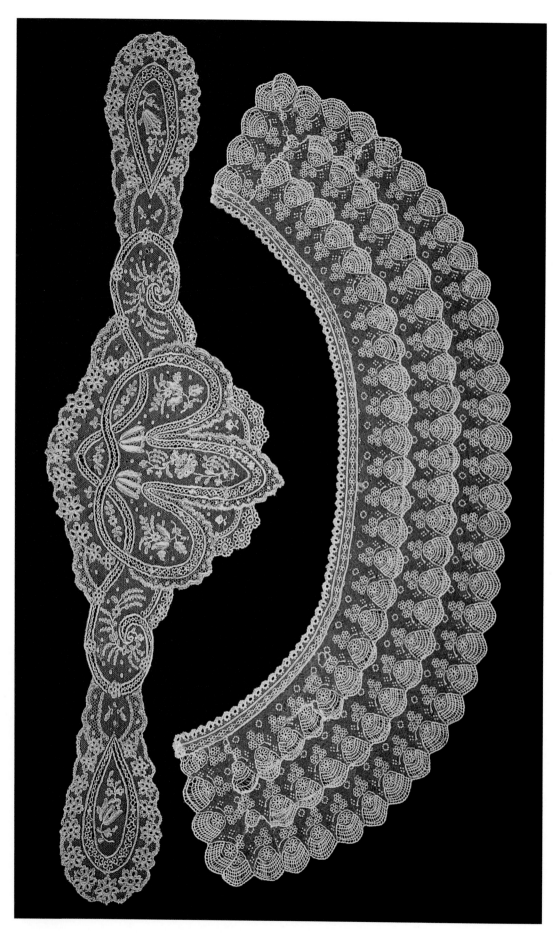

Plate 241:
a. Fall cap: about 1850-60.
Length 100cm (40in); depth at
center 29cm (12in).
b. Bertha collar: 1840-60. Length
of inner edge 79cm (31.5in);
depth 22.5cm (9in).
Tiered berthas made up from
several overlapping lace edgings
like this were very popular in the
mid-19th century in addition to
berthas made from a complete
panel of lace like that in **Plate**
190.
The design of the lace edging was
in use over several decades.

Opposite page:
Plate Q: Portrait Photograph by
Alexander Bassano, London
(sitter unknown); about 1900-05
Lace was much in evidence in
early 20th century dress though
much of it was machine-made.
This lady is wearing a collar of a
type much worn in the 1890s and
1900s which stands high around
the neck and is probably
supported by internal stiffenings.
Her jacket is also trimmed with
lace and has a wide part-circular
collar, also typical of the period.

Blonde

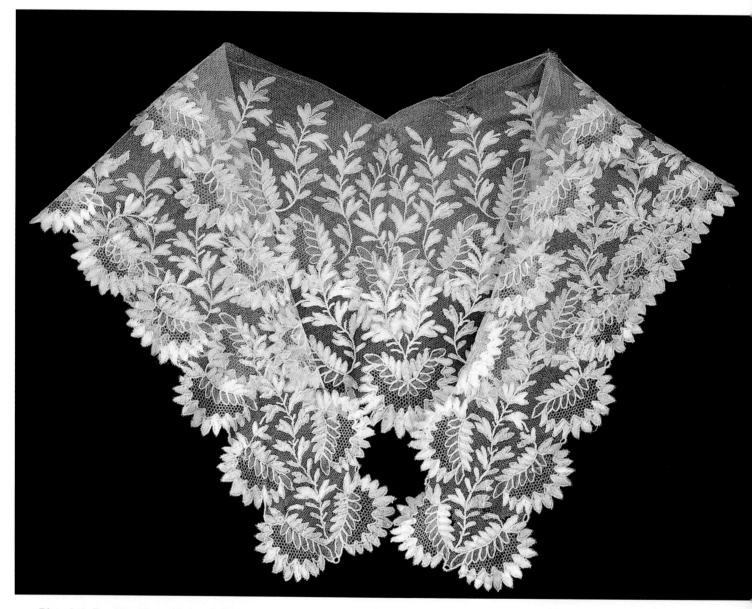

Plate 242: Double collar or fichu of silk blonde lace, probably from Caen or Bayeux: about 1835-40. Maximum width as shown 64cm (25in).

Large double collars of this type were extremely popular from the 1820s to the 1840s; the shape varied gradually to suit the shoulder outline created by the dress underneath. This example has the typical scalloped edge of the late 1820s to early 1830s, with each scallop filled with a single flowerhead, but the spread of the leafy sprigs into the net ground suggests a date in the late 1830s. When unfolded it does not lie flat; it is definitely shaped to be worn folded and to fit the curve of the shoulders.

Plate 243: Detail of a blonde lace showing the contrast between the extremely fine thread used for the ground and the half stitch pattern areas, the floss silk used for the cloth stitch and, in this case, the even thicker gimp thread. The ground, though much worn, is of the simple Lille type.

Plate 244: End portion of a blonde shawl or scarf: 1830-50. Width 40cm (15.5in); full length (not shown) 196cm (75in).
This is a good example of the curving sprig designs that were growing larger in the 1830s-40s. The scarf might have been worn round the shoulders or draped from the hair.

Characteristics

1. Straight bobbin lace in silk thread - cream, black or ivory.
2. Dense, shiny pattern areas in thick floss silk set off against a very light ground in a very much finer, twisted thread.
3. Floss silk or corded silk used to outline the pattern or to form linear patterns.
4. Some half-stitch pattern areas in the fine ground thread.
5. Grounds:
   a. Fond simple (East Midlands point ground, **Plate** 235, page 201). Hexagonal mesh with four sides of two twisted threads and two sides of two threads crossed.
   b. Paris ground (also known as kat stitch etc, **Plate** 236, page 201). The meshes give the appearance of a six-pointed star, with pairs of twisted threads defining a central hexagonal hole surrounded by six smaller triangular holes.

Points to watch

Close copies of blonde laces were made by darning silk machine nets with a floss silk thread (see **Plate** 119): in darned work, the floss silk is seen passing in and out of the meshes of the net but, in true blonde, the floss silk is trapped between the finer threads of the ground.

Large blonde articles were made from strips of blonde joined invisibly, edge to edge, by the point de racroc or were made with a machine-net center to which a blonde edging was joined almost invisibly. The machine net might be left plain or decorated with darned patterns or, in some cases blonde motifs, worked separately, are applied to a machine net.

History

Silk laces were made throughout the 17th and 18th centuries but the perishable nature of the thread has meant that little has survived and we must look to written records and to portraiture for their history. The type known as 'blonde', from its natural, creamy color, became popular in the 1750s when it was admired for its delicacy and sheen. Like the linen-thread laces of Lille, it was made with open grounds and light, geometric patterns, often in a chenille thread.

The center for the industry at this time was the region around Paris but other centers and, indeed, other countries made their own blondes. As lace designs generally grew lighter, blonde became ever more favored and was even found suitable for trimming the neo-classical dress of the early 1800s.

By the 1810s and 1820s, its popularity had grown to such an extent that it was used for flounces, pelerines, stoles and veils and even for whole dresses. Here was the reaction against the earlier simplicity of dress; when everyone wore muslin, mistress and maid were indistinguishable but an overdress of silk lace was only for the wealthy.

In the early 1800s, Chantilly, a small town to the north of Paris, and Caen in Normandy produced the finest blondes but in the late 1820s their manufacture was taken up in Bayeux. Here Lefébure, a leading manufacturer of his day, developed the trade with Spain and the Spanish colonies by producing a more heavily-patterned blonde, suited to their taste. This became known as 'blonde matte' or 'Spanish blonde' and was made in the usual cream or white silk, but also in black.

In the late 1830s and 1840s black lace was also becoming popular in northern Europe but the taste for blonde was waning or being satisfied by machine-made copies. The French workers were adaptable; they turned their skills to the 'Chantilly' laces and their prosperity continued as we shall see in the next chapter. Laces combining the two techniques were also made as seen in the fall cap in **Plate** 251.

In the later 19th century, blonde regained some favor, particularly in its black form, but, in a highly competitive market, manufacturers needed new ideas to survive. One innovation was the use of colored silk; this was developed in the Normandy town of Courseulles but it needed a highly skilled lace maker to achieve a successful result.

As regards black lace, Spain was still a major consumer. It had its own blonde industry in Catalonia and made shawls, mantillas and other articles, both for home use and for its colonies. Often these can be distinguished from the French products by their less regular workmanship, coarse thread and uneven coloring, often tending to brown rather than black with age.

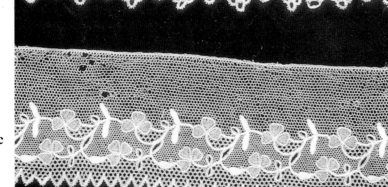

Plate 245: Group of blonde edgings.
a. About 1820-40. Depth 17cm (7.2in); pattern repeat 6cm (2.2in).
b. Probably early 20th century. Depth 10.5cm (4in); pattern repeat 5.5cm (2in).
In this example some of the pattern areas are in half stitch in the 'Chantilly' style and some in cloth stitch, worked with floss silk.
c. About 1860-75. Depth 10cm (4in); pattern repeat 4cm (1.5in).
Here the pattern is created almost entirely by the gimp thread.

Plate 246:
a. Black blonde shawl; probably Spanish: 2nd half of the 19th century. Depth shown 36cm (14.5in); width shown 55cm (21.5in); actual width 97cm (38in); actual length 220cm (86in).
This stylized floral design is seen as early as the 1840s, but it appears to have continued in use throughout the second half of the 19th century when it appealed particularly to the Spanish market. The end strip is clearly worked in a different direction from the strips which make up the main body of the shawl.
b. Black blonde shawl; probably Spanish: about 1880-1900. Depth shown 39cm (15.5in); width shown 57cm (22.5in); actual depth 70cm (28in); actual length 200cm (78in).
The pretty but rather vapid floral motif is a common feature in late 19th-century designs.

Chantilly

Characteristics

1. Straight bobbin lace, usually in dull black silk (grenadine) thread but sometimes in ivory.
2. Half stitch pattern areas.
3. Thick gimp outline to the pattern usually formed by a bundle of threads.
4. Splits often found in large pieces - these form along joins between pattern pieces. (The 'point de racroc' joining stitch is usually invisible to the naked eye.)
5. Grounds:

   a. Chantilly ground (kat stitch, point de Paris, **Plate** 249). The meshes give the appearance of a six-pointed star, with pairs of twisted threads defining a central hexagonal hole surrounded by six smaller triangular holes.

   b. Fond simple (East Midlands point ground, Lille ground, **Plate** 250). Hexagonal mesh with four sides of two twisted threads and two sides of two threads crossed. This is more common in the second half of the 19th century.

Plate 247: Chantilly bonnet veil: 1850-70. Width 95cm (37.5in); depth 49cm(19.3in). Semi-circular bonnet veils were popular with the smaller bonnets of the 1850s-60s.

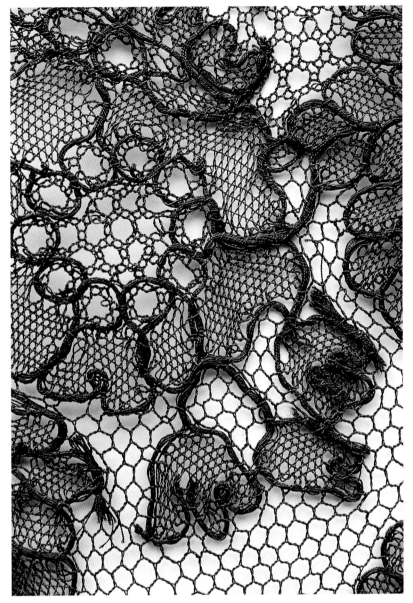

Some black East Midlands point laces are technically similar but sometimes distinguishable by their patterns or their thread.

Extremely close imitations of Chantilly lace were made on various machines (see **Plate** 289). The gimp thread is usually the clearest distinguishing feature: in some machine laces it is darned in by hand; in others it is incorporated by the machine but is caught on to the surface of the lace rather than within the thickness; in yet others it is incorporated by the machine but has cut ends at two places where it surrounds a motif; a hand-made lace normally has cut ends at only one place.

Plate 248: Detail of a Chantilly lace showing the half stitch pattern, the gimp outline, the fond simple ground, and a 'honeycomb' filling.

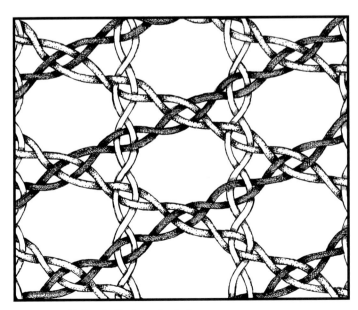

Plate 249: Point de Paris or fond chant

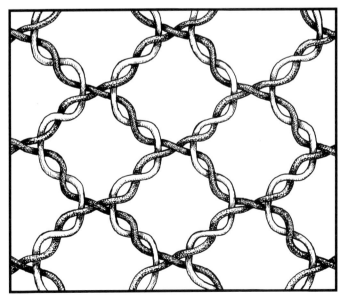

Plate 250: Lille or point ground

213

We have already seen that Chantilly was a center of the blonde lace industry in the early 19th century and references to 'Chantilly' lace up till that time most probably relate to these shiny silk laces rather than to the lace we have come to associate with the name. It was not until the 1840s that tastes in northern Europe turned away from the cream laces and towards the black and the Chantilly manufacturers developed the use of the dull black silk thread known as grenadine. Had the new, fuller designs been worked with the dense clothwork of blonde laces, the name of Chantilly might never have been fêted across Europe. As it was, the working of naturalistic floral designs in the light texture of half stitch created a delicate fabric which displayed to dazzling effect over the pale or the richly colored dresses of the period.

Plate 251: Fall cap: 1860-70. Depth of central cap portion 24cm (9.5in).
This style of fall cap was particularly suited to the hairstyles of the 1860s in which the hair was swept back into a chignon. The lace is worked in a mixture of the blonde and Chantilly techniques: the latter is discussed in the next chapter. Lefébure, a manufacturer based at Bayeux, is said to have introduced this combination and was certainly a noted exponent of it.

Plate 252: Bonnet veil: about 1850-60. Depth 47cm (18.5in); width 103cm (41in).

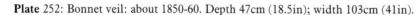

Plate 253:
(right) End of a pair of lappets or scarf: about 1870-90. Width 16cm (6.3in); length shown 33cm (13in); full length
of single lappet 80cm (31in).
This is one end of a pair of lappets made in one piece in the 19th-century manner. The design is stiffer and more
formal than those of the veils in **Plates** 247 and 252 and suggests a later date.
(upper left) Edging: about 1880-1900. Depth 9cm (3.5in); pattern repeat 9cm (3.5in).
The late date of this lace is suggested by the weakness of the design, particularly of the opposing C-shaped scrolls.
(lower left) Edging: about 1855-75. Depth 12cm (4.7in)
I have included this piece with the Chantilly laces because its thread, particularly the gimp outline, and its use of
the fond simple ground in the central band are what one associates with Chantilly lace. Clearly its geometric design
is utterly different from the floral designs one expects of Chantilly laces but during the lace boom of the 1850s and
1860s many styles of design coexisted and were transferred from one technique to another. As we shall see in the
next few chapters, geometric-styled guipures were particularly popular during this period and copies in lighter laces
were by no means uncommon.

215

Plate 254: Bertha collar in white cotton: 1890-1900. Diameter of neck opening 33cm (9in); depth of lace 16cm (6.5in).

Although this example is not worked in the black grenadine silk thread typical of Chantilly laces, its pattern is worked in the Chantilly manner, in half stitch on a Lille ground. The design, with its many cartouches of fancy fillings, is typical of the late 19th century revived rococo style.

Collars of this size and circular shape were worn over the large sleeves of the 1890s.

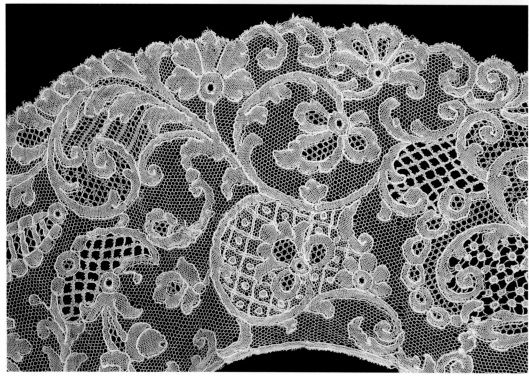

Plate 255: Detail of **Plate** 254.

Plate 256: Fan with tortoiseshell sticks and a leaf of Brussels bobbin motifs with needlepoint fillings applied to black machine-made net with a border of hand-made Chantilly lace: about 1860-80. Overall depth of lace 14.5cm (6in); length of sticks 28cm (11.2in).
In the late 19th century 'Chantilly' laces were made in various centers in Europe and it is most likely that this fan leaf was made by a Belgian manufacturer

By the 1850s the manufacture of Chantilly lace had spread to Caen and Bayeux and even to Belgium but Chantilly still kept the reputation for the highest quality. By now every manner of dress accessory was made in this fabric, even to the huge flounces and shawls needed to cover the full skirts worn over the ever-expanding crinoline frame. Such large pieces could not, of course, be made in one piece by the straight bobbin technique and designs were split into smaller, manageable parts for working.

In the late 1850s and 1860s Chantilly was one of the favorite laces at the French court but the collapse of the Second Empire in 1870 and the accompanying changes in fashion brought about a drastic reduction in its market. Much lace from this period went into store, not to be sold until its return to fashion in the 1890s.

The production of this later period was often in slightly stiffer versions of the earlier designs, much of it in a coarser thread, but it never reached the volume of the earlier periods and little was produced in the 20th century.

Maltese

Opposite page:
Plate 257
(top) Maltese plastron: about 1900-1915. Depth at center front 28cm (11in).
(bottom) Maltese collar: about 1900-1915. Maximum width 44cm (17.5in); width of neck opening 15cm (6in).
Both of these articles are worked in fine cream silk thread but the looser working of the massed wheatears in the plastron gives a lustrous, three-dimensional appearance compared with the flatness of the collar. The collar is worked in three sections: a central ring and two outer bands which are sewn together. In the plastron, the center and scalloped edge are worked separately.
The plastron would probably have been worn with a matching standing collar.

1. Straight bobbin lace, usually in floss silk thread - cream, black or ivory - but also in cotton.
2. Uniform threads - no gimp or raised work.
3. Clothwork pattern areas, usually including the Maltese cross.
4. Frequent use of fat wheatears with pointed ends, often grouped in star formations.
5. Splits often found where pattern pieces are coming apart due to breaks in the overcasting thread used to sew adjacent edges together.
6. Grounds: varied arrangements of twisted and plaited brides combined with wheatears.

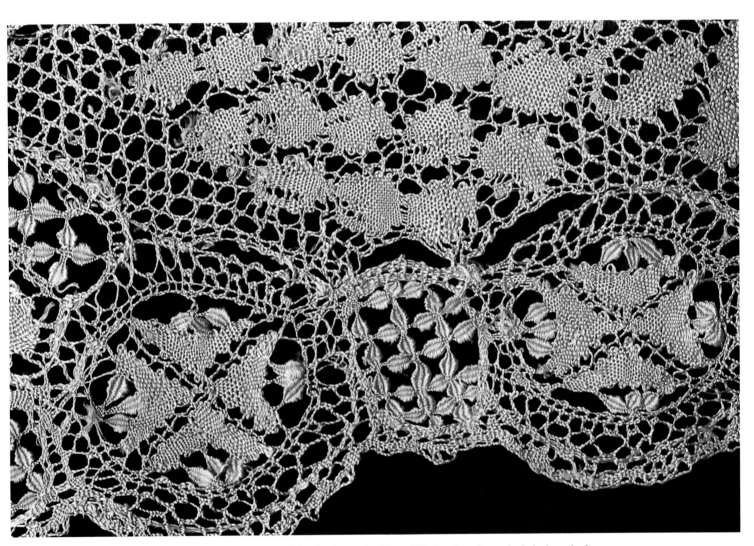

Plate 258: Detail of the edge of one of the lappets of the fascinator in **Plate** 260 showing the typical clothworked Maltese cross, pointed wheatears and loosely-worked, open ground around the crosses. The area of kat stitch on the left is much less common.
The gaps between the scalloped edge and the central part of the lappet are due to the breaking of the thread used to sew the two parts together.

Points to watch

Maltese lace can be very difficult to date because its designs remained substantially unchanged throughout its history. Two factors can help: the style of the costume item which it forms and the quality of the thread and workmanship.

The Maltese cross is usually, but not invariably, found in the design. It was probably introduced in the 1850s to distinguish true Maltese lace from the copies which proliferated throughout Europe as a result of its extraordinary rise in popularity. When the cross is absent, the presence of fat, pointed wheatears may indicate a Maltese origin.

History

It may be thought that the stylized floral and geometric designs of Maltese lace, and particularly the use of wheatears, are reminiscent of early 17th century Italian bobbin laces. This is probably not just coincidence. In the 1830s Malta was suffering from famine and it is said that lace-makers from Genoa, where the old traditions survived, were introduced to pass on their skills.

The timing was apt. Fashionable taste was tending towards fuller designs and the display of Maltese lace at the Great Exhibition at Crystal Palace in London in 1851 excited the whole of Europe. The industry flourished; flounces, fichus, parasol covers and the huge triangular or square shawls worn over the wide crinolines of the 1860s were all made in this boldly patterned fabric.

Plate 259

a. Maltese bonnet veil: about 1850-70. Maximum depth 40cm (16in); maximum width 78cm (31in).

b. Ends of a Maltese bobbin lace scarf worked in a dull black silk thread: late 19th century. Overall length (not shown) 150cm (59in).

Both the scarf and the veil contain the Maltese cross in their designs but the open centers of the crosses in the veil give a much lighter appearance.

Semi-circular bonnet veils which draped closely round the face were popular with the smaller bonnets of the 1850s and 1860s.

220

Plate 260: Maltese fascinator: second half of the 19th C; probably 1850-75. Overall length (when flat) 145cm (57in); depth of central piece 59cm (23in).
The 'fascinator' is simply one name for this shaped head covering with a wide central piece which drapes over the head and lappets which are long enough to be tied beneath the chin. Its large size distinguishes it from the fall caps seen in **Plates** 77 and 241.
Fascinators can sometimes be confused with double fichu collars (**Plate** 242), which have a similar shape when opened out, but the fascinator will usually lie flat when spread whereas the double collar is often shaped to curve around the shoulders and will not lie flat. Naturally, a fascinator might have been worn around the shoulders or a double collar over the head if it suited the fashion of the moment.
This fascinator is carefully worked in a very fine, cream floss silk which suggests a date in the early second half of the 19th century. It is worked in seven parts: the central cross; three concentric areas around the cross; the scalloped border; and the two centers of the lappets.

In the 1870s, when many of the lace industries of Europe were suffering from competition with machine-made products, the Maltese industry was able to continue because of the popularity and comparative cheapness of its laces. These were, in any case, relatively quick to make but the standards of workmanship dropped and coarser threads were introduced.

The revival of interest in handicrafts in the 1890s and 1900s led to some better work being done. Laces from this period can often be distinguished by their thick, very lustrous thread which gives the proliferation of wheatears an almost three-dimensional appearance; laces of this type always remind me of modern bubble-pack wrapping.

Another innovation in the 1890s or 1900s was the introduction of a bleached white silk thread. Nearly all the earlier silk laces had been in cream or black and these colors continued to be used although black was considerably less popular in the 20th century.

The disappearance of lace from dress in the First World War marked the death of many of the lace industries of Europe. The Maltese industry survived, if on a much reduced scale, by supplying souvenirs to the British troops stationed on the island and to the tourist trade which followed. It was in the period between the two World Wars that much of the household lace, dressing table sets, place mats, etc, in white or ecru cotton, was made and imported into Britain with thousands of silk handkerchiefs with skimpy edgings barely recognizable as Maltese lace.

Le Puy

Characteristics

1. Straight bobbin lace, usually in black silk but also in blonde or white silk or in cotton.
2. Uniform threads except for Chantilly-style insertions in finer thread.
3. Designs of small clothwork areas and trailing lines defining areas filled with other stitches, particularly fond simple and rows of long, narrow wheatears, usually with pointed ends.
4. Grounds: various well-ordered arrangements of plaited and twisted brides forming large-scale, often complex meshes.

Plate 261: Cape or fichu: about 1860-80. Depth of lace at center 40cm (16in); width of neck opening 14cm (9.5in).
This piece has all the characteristics of a true Le Puy lace: complex ground, Chantilly-like panels, and an organised design with strapwork around the edge.

Plate 262: Detail of a Le Puy lace showing a cloth stitch pattern motif surrounded by a complex bar ground and separated from a Chantilly lace insertion by a line of strapwork. The Chantilly motif has tallies raised over its surface.

Points to watch

Le Puy lace is closely related to Maltese lace (see pages 218-221) and similar guipures, such as the English East Midlands (Bedfordshire) guipure (see pages 226-229), were made all over Europe in the late 19th-20th centuries. The simpler guipures from these areas are often indistinguishable from each other; it is the better quality examples, with stylish designs and Chantilly insertions that are termed 'Le Puy' lace although even some of these were made elsewhere.

Apart from the laces to which Le Puy has given its name, the Auvergne lace-making region produced numerous other types of lace.

History

Le Puy and the surrounding region of the Auvergne have a long lace-making tradition, stretching back at least to the 17th century. Then, and in the 18th century, the Auvergne produced many of the simpler, cheaper types of lace, including the blonde laces, which became popular in the second half of the 18th century. The region suffered greatly from the decline at the end of the 18th century and it was not until the 1820s and 1830s that various manufacturers took the organization of the industry in hand and the tide turned. Workers were trained in more skilled techniques, new designs were supplied and new ideas tried and tested.

One of the innovations of this period was a black silk guipure lace, closely followed by a white guipure in imitation of the Maltese lace when this became popular on its showing at the 1851 Exhibition, London (see page 220). The Le Puy manufacturers put their own interpretations on the designs and the result was the new lace, described above, for which Le Puy was to become famous: not that this was the only lace then made in the area, nor that these guipures were made only around Le Puy. Many lace-making areas of Europe took to copying the Maltese laces more or less closely since their bold designs were fashionable at the time and they were quicker and cheaper to make than the previous net-grounded laces.

A major advantage of the Le Puy region was that its more influential manufacturers had Parisian bases with access to the latest fashions and the best designers. While the designs of Malta and other minor lace-making areas fossilized, the Le Puy workers had a constant supply of the most up-to-date patterns. These included formal designs of cartouches and fan shapes defined by patterned strapwork closely resembling that of the best Chantilly and Brussels laces. What was omitted in these guipure laces was the floral aspect of the more opulent designs, and even this was to some extent remedied by the introduction of panels of Chantilly-type lace.

In the 1860s a simpler version of the geometric Maltese lace was introduced; this was known as 'Cluny' lace (see pages 120-123) and was made alongside the better quality laces. With the fall of the French Second Empire in 1870 and the consequent depression in the French industry, the renowned adaptability of the Le Puy workers enabled them to maintain a certain degree of prosperity by turning to other types of lace, including torchon and simple guipures in cotton, wool and metal threads, much of it for export. This was sufficient to keep the industry alive until the First World War but there was little recovery afterwards and now the Le Puy shops are filled largely with machine-made lace.

Plate 263: These two pieces date from the second half of the 19th century, probably about 1860-80.

a. Edging in black silk. Depth 8cm (3.7in); pattern repeat 6cm (2.4in).

I include this edging with the Le Puy laces since it has several characteristics typical of the so-called Le Puy type, i.e. a ground of large-scale meshes formed by picoted brides; long wheatears with pointed ends; and inserted panels of Chantilly-type lace. Narrow edgings of this type with comparatively simple designs were made in various areas of Europe; this may be an English piece.

b. Flounce. Depth 15.5cm (6in); pattern repeat 10cm (4in).

The stylish design including a motif resembling a fleur de lys suggests a French origin for this piece. The complex ground in the upper part is typical of the Le Puy lace but there are no wheatears or areas of Chantilly lace; the simple Lille net ground is used as a filling in the elongate teardrop shapes, but is worked in the same thread as the rest of the lace.

Plate 264: Cape or fichu: about 1860-80. Depth of lace at center 40cm (16in); width of neck opening 14cm (9.5in).

The design and work involved in this piece are poorer and less skilled than in the fichu in **Plate** 261 but the use of patterned strapwork and the contrast given by different densities of stitching are typical of Le Puy work.

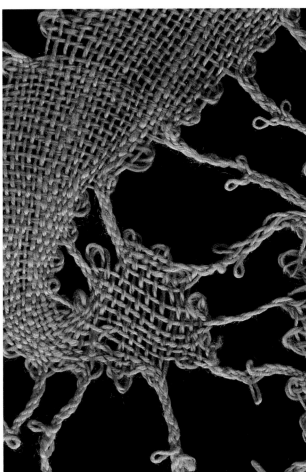

Plate 265: Flounce with shaped headside and footside in white and pale blue cotton. Pattern repeat 31cm (12in). This flounce may well have been made in the Auvergne as its design and quality are typical of the stylish Le Puy guipures and the Le Puy manufacturers were noted for their innovativeness, here shown in the use of colored threads. I have no positive provenance for the piece, however, and it could have been made elsewhere.
The flounce is made in two shaped strips sewn edge to edge.

Plate 266: Detail of **Plate** 265. The use of two colors enables one to see clearly that this is made as a straight lace as the threads continue from the clothwork pattern into the plaited brides and on into the adjacent pattern area.

East Midlands (Bedfordshire) guipure

Characteristics

1. Straight bobbin lace.
2. Clothwork pattern areas sometimes incorporating gimp threads within or outlining the design.
3. Frequent use of tallies (wheatears), most commonly with square ends, and areas of point ground (see **Plate** 235, page 155) as a filling.
4. Designs of trailing lines and simple leaf and flower shapes.
5. Ground: irregular arrangements of plaited and twisted brides.

Points to watch

See Le Puy laces (pages 222-225) and early bobbin laces (pages 120-123). Some techniques more common to part laces, such as the use of sewings, were used in more complex designs.

History

The name of Bedfordshire is now associated with the guipure lace just described but this was a comparatively recent introduction. In the 18th and early 19th centuries the English East Midlands counties had been involved in the making of straight laces with open net grounds and it was not until the 1840s that guipures started to return to fashion.

As we have seen in an earlier chapter (pages 200-206), by this time the making of point lace was in decline because of competition from machine laces and because of the renewed interest in more richly designed continental laces. Many of the English lace-makers turned to alternative forms of employment while others turned their talents to the guipure laces which were quicker and easier to make than point lace.

Impetus for this change was given particularly by the success of the Maltese laces at the Great International Exhibition in 1851. This resulted in copies of the Maltese style which have come to be known as 'Bedfordshire Maltese' although some were, in fact, also made in the neighboring counties of Buckinghamshire and Northamptonshire.

Opposite page:
Plate 267:
a. Corn motif: late 19th century. Depth 31cm (12.3in)
b. Collar: about 1870-90. Length of inside edge 87cm (34.5in); maximum width 63cm (25in).
Both of these pieces are of good quality; the collar is exceptional. Designs of this complexity could not be worked purely by the straight technique and include sewings to join touching edgings. (See **Plate** 268 for detail.)

Above:
Plate 268: Detail of the collar in **Plate** 267, showing the dense clothwork and picoted bar ground which are typical of East Midlands guipures. The use of a gimp thread is quite common but the very neat, raised tallies worked over the surface are particularly fine.

The general trend in the 1850s and 1860s was to increase the rate of production as the demand for lace increased but competition from machine products forced prices down. As in the Devon industry, the quality of design and workmanship declined: the earlier, more intricate patterns of stylized flowers and trailing clothwork set against complex grounds were largely replaced by the simpler 'Cluny' laces.

Only a few manufacturers held out. The firm of Thomas Lester in Bedford was noted for its efforts to provide good designs and to ensure a high standard of workmanship from its employees. Many of these designs, with their naturalistically drawn flowers, are similar to those of the Honiton guipures of the period. Their complexity necessitated the splitting of the design into small areas for working or the borrowing of techniques, such as the use of sewings to join touching edges, from the part laces.

A few manufacturers followed Thomas Lester's lead but the quantity of these higher-quality products was small compared with the mass of poorly-made lace. Like Devon, the Midlands suffered from the poor organization of the industry. Many of the middlemen who distributed lace patterns to the cottagers for working saw their workers once in a few weeks. They had no control over standards of workmanship nor over where the lace made on their patterns was sold. With pay so low that many could scarcely earn a living wage by working 14 hours a day, no loyalty could be expected, nor was there any incentive to provide new, better and more expensive patterns.

With conditions as they were, it is surprising that the industry survived the recession of the 1870s but, as in other regions, there was a resurgence at the end of the century. Lace continued to be made commercially into the 20th century though on a very reduced scale.

Plate 269: Group of black East Midlands edgings from the second half of the 19th century. Length shown 18cm (7in). These are typical products of the East Midlands industry but could equally well have been made in Belgium, France or other lace-making areas of Europe. Examples c and d are of the type referred to as 'Bedfordshire Maltese' and probably date from the 1850s to 1870s. Examples a and b are probably later.
a. Depth 5.5cm (2.2in); pattern repeat 3cm (1.2in).
b. Depth 8cm (3.2in); pattern repeat 9cm (8.5 in). Note the use of a coarse version of the Midlands point ground in addition to the picoted bar ground.
c. Depth 10cm (4in); pattern repeat 3.5cm (1.4in).
d. Depth 10.5cm (4.2in); pattern repeat 4.5cm (1.8in).

Plate 270:
a. Collar: late 19th-20th century. Depth of lace 7.5cm (3in); length of inner edge 34cm (13.5in).
Designs including this simple flowerhead with its point ground center, the pointed leaf and the edging of tiny, picoted scallops, called a '9-pin' edging, were in use for at least 50 years.
b. Fragment of an edging: 2nd half of the 19th century. Depth 6.5cm (2.6in); pattern repeat 3.5cm (1.4in).
This is worked in a finer thread than examples a, c, and d and is probably of earlier date.
c. Edging: 2nd half of the 19th century. Depth 6cm (2.4in); Pattern repeat 4cm (1.6in).
This has a ground of tallies arranged to form square meshes, known as 'plaited' ground.
d. Cuff: about 1870-90. Width 27cm (10.7in) Depth 12cm (4.8in).

Loose Ends

Hand-made Net Grounds

Collated here are only those grounds commonly associated with specific lace types. It must be remembered that other grounds were also used in the major laces; the characteristics listed in the foregoing chapters must therefore be used in association with the grounds before a lace can be identified.

Brussels point de gaze

Rows of buttonhole stitches each looped into a stitch in a previous row to form fine meshes, usually about 1 mm (0.02 in.) across and roughly hexagonal to the naked eye.

Found mainly in Brussels laces from the mid-19th to 20th centuries - in needlepoint, bobbin, and mixed bobbin and needlepoint laces.

Alençon

Rows of buttonhole stitches as above but with each row strengthened by an additional thread run back through the stitches. In good-quality, unrepaired work the meshes are roughly hexagonal to the naked eye and about 1/2 mm to 1 mm (0.01in-0.02in) across but repairs often pull the meshes into rectangles.

Found in French needlepoints from the mid-18th to 20th centuries and in some 19th-century Brussels bobbin laces, Honiton laces and tape laces (often on a larger scale).

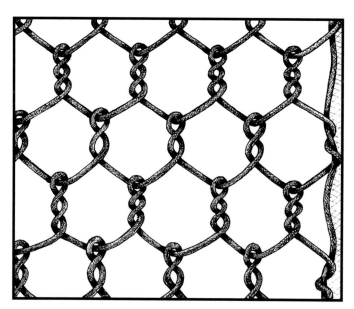

Plate 271: Brussels point de gaze

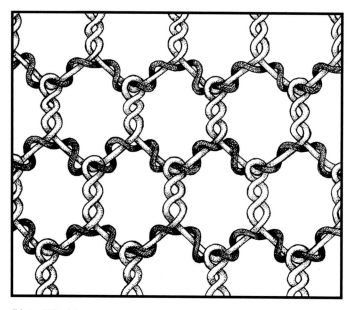

Plate 272: Alençon

Burano

Rows of buttonhole stitches strengthened with an additional thread but this is pulled taut and distorts the meshes into rectangles about 1/2 mm to 1 mm (0.01in-0.02in) across, giving a ladder-like appearance.

Found in Burano laces and in repaired Alençon laces.

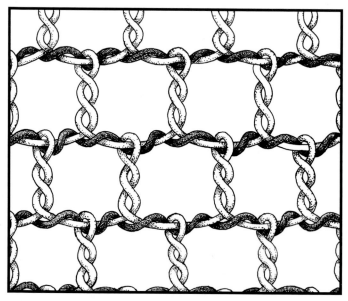

Plate 273: Burano

Argentan

Coarse hexagonal meshes about 2 mm (0.04in) across with closely worked buttonhole stitches along each side.

Found in French needlepoints from the early 18th century onwards but rare after 1780.

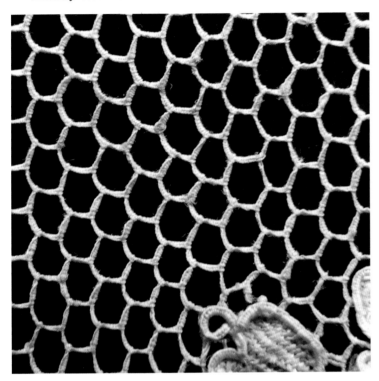

Plate 274: Argentan ground

Fond simple or point ground (also known as Lille ground or fond clair)

Meshes formed with four sides of two twisted threads and two sides of two threads crossed, and appearing hexagonal to the naked eye.

Found in Lille, East Midlands (Bucks) point, Chantilly, blonde, Tønder (Danish) and other bobbin laces from the late 18th century onwards. Many machine nets also have this form.

Plate 275: Lille, fond simple or point ground

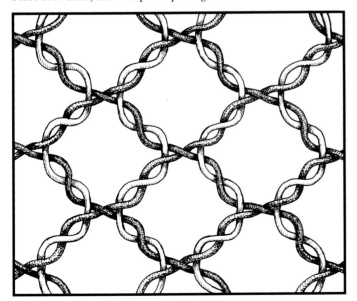

Tortillée

Hexagonal meshes with each side strengthened with widely spaced buttonhole stitches or a twisted thread: mesh size about 1mm (0.02in).

Found in French needlepoints from the late 18th century.

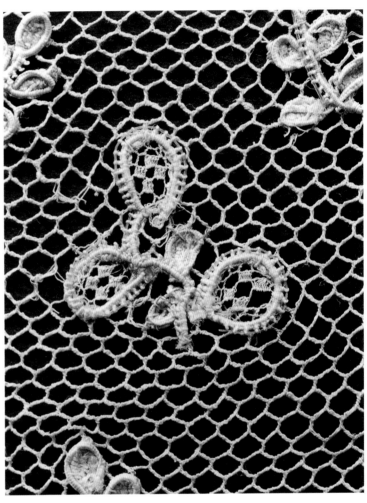

Plate 276: Tortillée ground

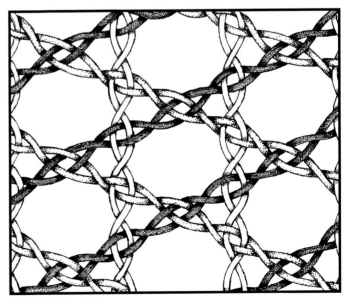

Plate 277: Point de Paris or kat stitch

231

Flemish round ground/ Valenciennes

This ground has several common variations but, in general, has hexagonal meshes with four threads plaited or crossed on all six sides. Mesh size in 'Flemish' laces-several mm (0.1in-0.2in).

Found in Flemish laces from the mid-17th century onwards. A very similar Italian ground is usually more tightly worked than the Flemish.

A fine version with a mesh size of about 1mm (0.02in) is found in 18th-century Valenciennes laces.

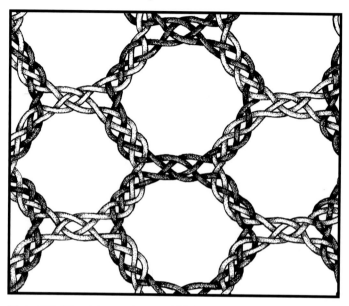

Plate 278: Flemish round ground/ Valenciennes

Valenciennes carrée, or diamond ground

Diamond-shaped mesh with four threads plaited on each side. The length of the sides varies considerably from about 1mm to 5mm (0.02 in.-0.2 in.).

Introduced into Valenciennes laces in the late 18th century and typical in the 19th century.

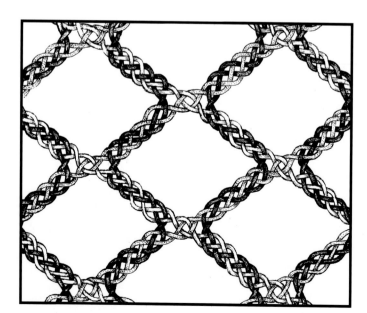

Plate 279: Valenciennes carrée or diamond ground

Mechlin 'eis' ground

Regular hexagonal meshes with four sides of two twisted or crossed threads and two sides of four plaited threads (shorter than vrai drochel).

Found in Mechlin laces from about the 1730s onwards.

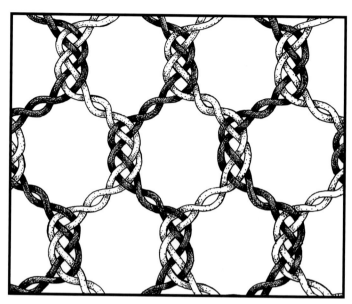

Plate 280: Mechlin 'eis' ground

Brussels vrai drochel

Slightly elongate hexagonal meshes formed with four sides of two twisted threads and two sides of four plaited threads.

Found in Brussels and Devon (Honiton) bobbin lace and as a ground for Brussels needlepoints from the early 18th century to the mid-19th century.

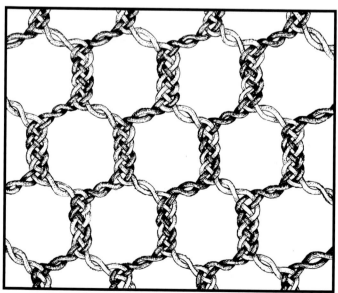

Plate 281: Brussels vrai drochel

232

Since the first machine-made nets were produced over 200 years ago, enormous quantities of lace have been produced on a wide variety of machines. Two examples have already been shown in **Plates** 35 and 175: here are just a few more examples to indicate some features to look for when sorting hand- from machine-made lace.

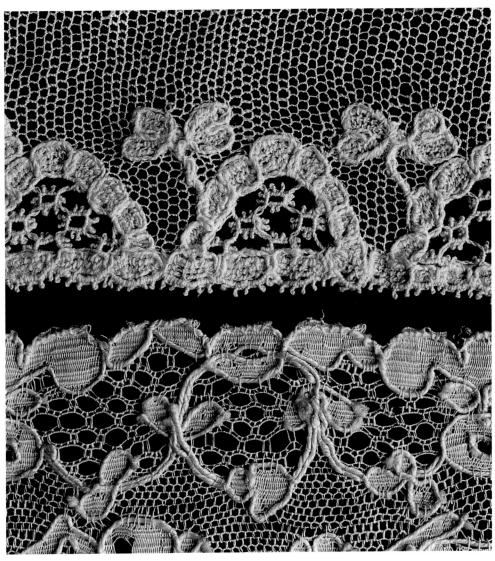

Plate 282:
a. (top) Burano needlepoint.
b. (bottom)Machine imitation of a needlepoint.
Early machine laces imitated hand laces as closely as possible. Although imitations improved generally in the 19th century, any one machine might be used to imitate various hand laces, with greater or lesser success. Here the well-defined raised outline on the right side of the lace suggests a needlepoint cordonnet but the ribbed appearance of the clothwork is totally different from the buttonholed clothwork of the needlepoint. No machine has ever successfully imitated the particular looped structure of needlepoint laces and in particular, the closely button-holed bars and cordonnets of some needlepoints although the looped structure of knitted laces might cause confusion initially.
This type of machine lace often imitates Mechlin laces but, in a straight bobbin lace, the gimp thread is normally incorporated within the thickness of the lace and is seen on both sides: it does not lie on one side as in this machine example. The exceptional Mechlin laces with a corded gimp (see **Plate** 216) are, perhaps, more likely to be mistaken but the ribbed clothwork of this machine example clearly distinguishes it.

Plate 283: Machine imitation of a 19th century bobbin guipure. This very effective imitation includes many features of the original: trails of clothwork; wheatears; a complex but regular ground of picoted bars; etc. The only immediate indication of its machine origin is the ribbed appearance of the clothwork. Close inspection of the grounds and edging also reveals a complex, twisted structure in which it is impossible to follow individual threads. To the naked eye this appears solely as a slight fuzziness but this and the ribbed clothwork are common features of machine laces.

Opposite page top:
Plate 284
East Midlands lace (left) with the kat stitch ground (right). Machine imitation: the ground, pattern areas and filling stitches, are, at first glance, very similar to those of the bobbin lace but the gimp thread passes in and out of the lace: it was not caught between the working threads as the lace was made but was run in by hand with a needle afterwards. When magnified, the lace structure is also seen to be confused.

Opposite page bottom:
Plate 285: A different machine imitation of a blonde bobbin lace. Here the imitation point ground to the right and left and the central filling stitch are extremely convincing but the finer threads in the imitation clothwork entangle the thicker threads in a totally different manner from those in true blonde (see **Plate** 243).

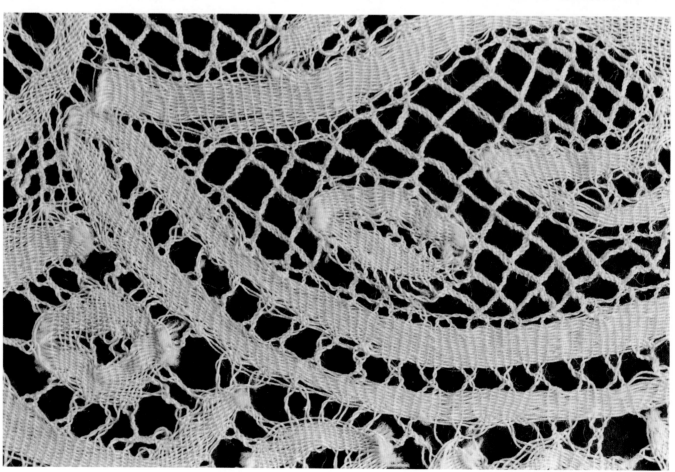

Opposite page, top:
Plate 286: Machine embroidered imitation of a Brussels point de gaze needlepoint (**Plate** 82). This type of machine embroidery, which can imitate even the raised petals of rose point de gaze, is effective only at a distance. Magnification clearly shows an almost woven structure in the clothwork and a net ground similar to a bobbin net, nothing like the looped structure of needle points. Also the tiny rings do not have the neat, ridged buttonholed surround.

Opposite page, bottom:
Plate 287: Machine imitation of 19th-century Valenciennes lace. This completely flat lace with its diamond-shaped ground immediately suggests a 19th-century Valenciennes lace but the ribbed clothwork indicates its machine origin. Cut ends at both ends of the clothwork are also found in hand-made examples so are not distinctive.
Close inspection of the ground shows a confused, twisted structure, not the neat plaits of the hand-made lace (see **Plate** 206).

Plate 288: A different machine imitation of 19th-century Valenciennes lace. The thick lines seen in this example on magnification distinguish it from Valenciennes, with its smooth texture. Also the ground consists of twisted rather than plaited threads.

Plate 289

a. (left). Hand-made Chantilly lace.

b. (right). Machine imitation of Chantilly lace.

This clever imitation has the half-stitch pattern, Lille ground and multi-stranded gimp of the Chantilly. The gimp even surrounds the pattern areas with few breaks but, in fact, it passes in and out of the lace - it is hand-run like the gimp in **Plate** 284 (bottom). In other close imitations of Chantilly, the gimp is incorporated in the fabric by the machine but has cut ends at each end of a motif.

Another clue to the machine origin is the stretched appearance of the half-stitch pattern - the hand-made half stitch is far more open and regular in appearance.

Plate 290: Machine imitation of a blonde bobbin lace. Again this machine lace has a hand-run outline but there are other give-aways: the visible threads in the clothwork pattern are twisted around each other rather than clearly interwoven with other threads at right angles; and there is a strong directional pull in the net ground.

Cleaning, Care, and Conservation

We are all used to handling fabrics in our everyday lives but expect to replace old clothes and furnishings after a limited lifetime. Lace, on the other hand, may already be over a hundred years old and much of it can never be replaced. It needs special treatment to preserve it for our own enjoyment and for future generations.

A detailed study of methods of conservation is beyond the scope of this book but I hope the following indication of dangers to avoid and the guide to washing and display will be of some help. For guidance on specific problems the reader should consult a book on textile conservation or a textile conservator.

Dangers

Air- Air contains oxygen which reacts with the fibers in the lace in a very slow 'burning', or ageing, process. This is what causes white or cream laces to turn yellow. Washing will remove the yellow color but weakens the lace since it removes the yellowed outer layers of the fibers, leaving the underlying fibers exposed.

Chemicals- Acids and alkalis eat into textile fibers and, if they are left in the lace, it will eventually fall apart. Bleaches are the most common source of acids in lace but many chemicals, from modern biological detergents to grandmother's special recipe, are potentially harmful.

Creases- Textile fibers break along creases if these are left for any length of time.

Cutting and rearranging- This destroys the aesthetic quality and historical value of a lace, whether a complete article or a flounce. It is often unnecessary, may not have the desired effect of producing a usable item and reduces its financial value.

Dirt- Dirt includes chemicals (see above) and also rough particles which abrade the fibers to break down their structure.

Handling- This includes thoughtless handling by those unused to dealing with old fabrics who pull a collar into shape or stroke firmly to get its 'feel' not realizing that the tension created, if not actually tearing the lace apart, is stretching some fibers, breaking others and generally weakening the lace. What is less often realized is that even gentle handling is harmful. The SWEAT transferred to the lace is acidic (see 'Chemicals', above).

Heat and light- Heat and light, particularly ultraviolet light, accelerate chemical reactions and quicken the degradation these cause.

Mending- A bad mend can do more harm than good. Needles and pins pushed through the lace fibers can break them. Threads used to catch torn edges together or to darn holes can pull even larger holes in a fragile fabric. It is often safer and less unsightly to ignore tears and holes.

If you still think mending might help, a book on textile conservation or your local textile conservator may suggest the best thread and methods to use.

Washing- Even washing can be harmful. The removal of yellow coloring has already been mentioned (see 'Air', above). The movement and handling of the lace during washing are obvious dangers; but there is yet another problem. Lace is usually composed of natural fibers which absorb water and swell when wet; this swelling can shatter old fibers and the lace may disintegrate. Chemicals in the lace may dissolve to form acids which will then degrade the lace.

Treatment

Washing- If lace has to be washed to remove dirt, then use a large, clean, shallow container with a plastic sheet in the bottom on which the lace can be spread as flat as possible.

Always remove the lace from the container by means of the sheet which thus supports its weight, especially when wet.

Use distilled or de-ionized water, if possible throughout the process but at least for the last one or two rinses.

Soak the lace in cold water before washing to loosen dirt and stains.

Use cold or lukewarm water for washing and cold water for rinsing.

For washing, use a dilute solution of a mild liquid detergent (products made for babies are usually the mildest on the market with the fewest modern additives). Allow the lace to soak in the solution for an hour. Brush discolored areas very gently or force liquid through by gentle pressure with a sponge. Do not rub!

After washing rinse at least three times and until there is no more sign of the detergent. For stubborn stains the washing may be repeated. Stains are often preferable to the holes left by bleaches and stain-removers but, if you should use them, remember it is safer to use very dilute solutions repeatedly than to use a strong solution. Wash and rinse very thoroughly afterwards.

NOTE: Stains are often less noticeable when the lace is dry.

Drying- Lift the lace, right side uppermost, out of its last rinsing water on the plastic sheet and place on a flat surface.
Add distilled water if necessary and gently float the lace out to its proper shape.
Soak up excess water with clean white fabric and leave to dry.

Ironing- Avoid whenever possible but, if necessary, use a cool setting and place raised laces upside-down on a towel so that you do not flatten the raised work. Gentle steaming with distilled water is often sufficient to remove creases.

Storage- Drawers and boxes should be lined with aluminum foil or polythene and acid-free tissue paper to prevent acidity from the wood or cardboard damaging the lace.

Conditions should be cool and dry with the lace kept as flat as possible between layers of acid-free tissue paper. White is preferable as colors may run from colored papers. If lace has to be folded, a roll of acid-free tissue paper in each fold will help prevent hard creases.

Long flounces and edgings are best rolled on tubes slightly longer than the width of the lace. Cardboard tubes should, ideally, first be covered with polythene, then acid-free tissue and tissue should be interleaved with the lace on the roll. Although not generally recommended by conservators for reasons explained above, I find that it is helpful to interleave black tissue paper with the outer end of each roll: this allows me to see the lace on each roll clearly so that I can easily pick out examples for talks etc. without disturbing other laces in a drawer.

Display

Lace should be sewn on to a fabric which has been washed to remove any excess dye and finishing chemicals and stretched on an acid-free support. The fabric should preferably be a single-fibre fabric such as pure cotton to minimise tensions within the fabric due to changes in temperature and humidity. All stitches should pass through holes in the lace; avoid making new holes!

On display, the backing should preferably be inclined rather than vertical to support the lace better. The lace should not be in contact with glass or plastic.

Lighting should be dim and/or the lace should be kept covered most of the time. I find that, if one keeps textiles covered much of the time, one enjoys them much more when they are unveiled.

Reading List

Bouvot, Claudette et Michel. *Dentelles Normandes: la Blonde de Caen*. Condé- sur-Noireau, France: Editions Charles Corlet, 1997. (French language)

Bruggeman, Martine. *L'Europe de la Dentelle*. Bruges, Belgium: Stichting Kunstboek, 1997. (French language)

Bruggeman, Martine. Lace and Costume. Bruges, Belgium: Bruges Municipal Museums.

Buck, Anne. *Thomas Lester, his Lace and the East Midlands Industry 1820-1905*. Carlton, Bedford: Ruth Bean, 1981.

Channer, Catherine C. and Buck, Anne. *In the Cause of English Lace*. Carlton, Bedford: Ruth Bean, 1991.

Channer, Catherine C. and Roberts, M. E., *Lace making in the East Midlands*. Luton.

De Chaves, Lila, *Greek Lace in the Victoria & Albert Museum*. Athens: Indiktos Publications, 1999.

De Lantsheere, A. Carlier. *Trésor de l'Art Dentellier*. Brussels and Paris: Librairie Nationale d'Art et d'Histoire, 1922. (French language)

Despierres, Mme. G., *Histoire du Point d'Alençon*, (English translation, *Alençon Lace*, by Roberta Morgan). Aberdeen, Aberdeen University Press, 1987.

Earnshaw, Patricia. *The Identification of Lace*. Princes Risborough, Bucks, U.K.: Shire, 1980.

Earnshaw, Patricia. *Lace Machines and Machine Laces*. London, Batsford, 1986.

Von Henneberg, F. A. *The Art and Craft of Old Lace*. London: Batsford, 1931.

Jourdain, M. *Old Lace: a handbook for collectors*. (Reprint of 1908 Edition).London: Batsford, 1988.

Kasparian, Alice Odian, *Armenian Needlelace and Embroidery*. McLean, Virginia: EPM Publications, 1983.

Kraatz, Anne, *Lace History and Fashion*. London: Thames and Hudson,1989. (English translation from French original *Dentelles*: Paris: Editions Adam Biro, 1988)

Levey, Santina M. *Lace, A History*. London: Victoria and Albert Museum/Maney & Son, 1983.

Levey, Santina M. & Payne, P. C. *Le Pompe, 1559: Patterns for Venetian Bobbin Lace*. Carlton, Bedford, U.K.: Ruth Bean, 1983.

Lewis, Fulvia. *Lace*. Florence, Italy: Edizione Remo Sandron, 1980.

Longfield, A., *Irish Lace*. Dublin: Eason & Son.

Mason, Sheila, A. Nottingham Lace. Ilkeston, Derbys, U.K.: Cluny Lace Co., 1994.

Malotet, A. *La Dentelles à Valenciennes* (Reprint of 1927 Edition). Marseille: Lafitte Reprints, 1983 (French language).

Montandon, Marie-Louise. *La Dentelle à Neûchatel*. Auvernier (NE), Suisse: Editions Le Roset, 1998. (French language)

Nevill Jackson, Mrs. F. *A History of Hand-made Lace*.(Reprint of 1900 Edition). New York: Dover, 1987.

Ó Cléirigh, Nellie. *Carrickmacross Lace*. Portlaoise, Ireland:Dolmen Press/ London: Dryad, 1985.

Palliser, Mrs. Bury. *A History of Lace*.(Reprint of the 1911 edition). New York: Dover, 1984.

Pollen, J. Hungerford. *Seven Centuries of Lace*. Heinemann & Macmillan, 1908.

Rutt, Richard. *A History of Hand Knitting*. London: Batsford, 1987.

Sharp, Mary, *Point and Pillow Lace*, London: John Murray, 1913.

Simeon, Margaret. *The History of Lace*. London: Stainer & Bell, 1979.

Staniland, Kay and Levey, Santina M. *Queen Victoria's Wedding Dress and Lace*. London: Museum of London.

Tomlinson, Margaret. *Three Generations in the Honiton Lace Trade*. Exeter: Devon Print Group, 1983.

Treadwin, Mrs., *Antique Point Honiton Lace*

Vinciolo, Federico. *Renaissance Patterns for Lace, Embroidery and Needlepoint*, (Reprint of 1587 Edition). New York: Dover, 1971

Voysey, Cynthia. *Needlelace in Photographs*. London: Batsford, 1987.

Voysey, Cynthia. *Bobbin lace in Photographs*. London: Batsford, 1987.

Wardle, Patricia. *Victorian Lace*. Carlton Bedford, U.K.: Ruth Bean, 1982

Wright, Thomas. *The Romance of the Lace Pillow*. (reprint) Chicheley, Bucks, U.K.: Paul P.B. Minet, 1971

Yallop, H. J. *The History of the Honiton Lace Industry*. Exeter, University of Exeter Press, 1992

Yefimova, L. & Belogorskaya, R. *Russian Embroidery and Lace*. London: Thames and Hudson

Price Guide

It is rare that one comes across a piece of antique, hand-made lace identical to one seen elsewhere. The following prices, therefore, relate to lace of a similar type and style to that shown in the illustrations, in good, but not pristine, condition. Lace in pristine condition does command a substantially higher price while, naturally, lace which is soiled or damaged should be very much cheaper than the prices indicated.

The prices given are those which one would expect to pay a knowledgeable dealer who can guarantee the authenticity of his/her identification. In practice, few dealers are able to describe their lace accurately by type and date: late 19th-early 20th century reproductions of earlier laces can easily be mistaken for the originals, while machine-made lace is frequently sold as hand-made, often through ignorance rather than a deliberate attempt to deceive. This is just as true of those who have been handling lace for thirty years or more as those who have recently become involved. The prices one is asked therefore fluctuate wildly and this is inevitably reflected in the wide price range given for some of the laces. It also means there are bargains out there: good hunting!

The prices given below are based on market values in Autumn, 2000. Prices are per item, or pair of items, in the case of articles such as collars, cuffs, sleeves, etc. and are per running foot in the case of edgings, flounces, and insertions.

NEEDLEPOINT LACES
Plate 12: Reticella sampler $2000-3000.

Plates 14-18: Cutworks, reticella, braid-based reticella, punto in aria and other early needleworks with geometric designs. $50-200, depending on depth and fineness (dress or furnishing quality.

Plate 15, bottom: Punto in aria and related needlepoints, late 19th-early 20th century copies $25-50.

Plates 20-23: Punto in aria and related needlepoints with figural or floral designs. $180-350.

Plate 24: Punto in aria and related needlepoints, collar $40-$60.

Plate 25: Venetian flatpoints $40-100 (examples of late 17th century simple designs are much cheaper than the earlier, more elaborate patterns).

Plates 27, 31, 32: Venetian rose points. $50-175, depending on fineness and complexity of raised work (examples which have been rearranged considerably at a later date should be much cheaper).

Plate 34: Venetian rose points. Late 19th-early 20th century copies $40-70; collar b: $30-50.

Plates 36, 39, 43: Point de France: flounce $100-160 (the example in **Plate** 36 is cut down and altered – deep, unaltered flounces can be upwards of $300).

Plate 45: Bertha $400-500.

Plate 47: Alençon sleeve ruffles $600-800.

Plate 55-58: Alençon/ Argentan edgings $20-80 (examples with the simple designs of around 1800 are generally cheaper than earlier and later examples)

Plate 61: Alençon lappets $250-400.

Plate 62-64: Mesh-grounded flatpoints $20-100 (early, complex designs are very much more expensive than later, simpler ones)

Plate 65: Burano edgings $30-50.

Plates 68, 72: Brussels needlepoints $70-150.

Plate 73: Brussels fichu $250-380 (Brussels needlepoints on drochel ground are comparatively rare)

Plate 24: Brussels bonnet veil $100-180.

Plate 77: Brussels fall cap $80-120.

Plate 81: Brussels flounce $80-150.

Plate 83: Brussels collar $120-180.

Plate 85: Hollie point bonnet $200-300 (earlier babies' clothes with hollie point can be upwards of $400).

Plate 86: Youghal plastron $150-220.

EMBROIDERIES AND MINOR TECHNIQUES
Plate 88: Tatting $30-50.

Plate 89: Macramé 19th century - $25-50; earlier $80-120.

Plates 90-96: Irish crochet small collars/ cuffs/ fall cap/ jabot $25-50; large collars $80-120.

Plate 98: Sol work collar $40-60.

Plate 100: Bibila tea cosy $60-100; shawl $80-100.

Plate 105: Tape lace shawl collar $250-320.

Plate 107: Tape lace edgings $8-15.

Plate 108: Tape lace flounce $30-50.

Plate 108: Tape lace collar $40-60.

Plates 112, 113: Filet flounce $40-70; edgings $8-12.

Plate 113, 114: Burato edging and flounce $75-100.

Plate 116: Tamboured net handkerchiefs (each) $60-90.

Plate 118: Needle-run net stole $200-300.

Plate 120: Carrickmacross collar $90-150; scarf $70-100.

Plate 123: Knitted bonnet $35-50.

BOBBIN LACES

Plate 125, 126: Torchon $3-10 for cotton or wool, $10 or more for metal thread.

Plates 127-130: Early bobbin in simple geometric or trail designs $40-100; late 19th-early 20th century examples: $2-10 for derivative designs in cotton, $20-30 for good copies in linen.

Plates 131, 136: Milanese flounces $100-180.

Plates 134, 137, 138, 140,141: Milanese flounces $40-80 (narrow flounces which are good examples of the 1660s-1680s baroque style are generally more sought after even than wide flounces in the later styles).

Plate 142, 149: Flemish: flounces $100-180.

Plates 146-148, 151, 153: Flemish: flounces $40-80.

Plate 154: Central and Eastern European: 18th century flounce $40-80.

Plate 155: 19th century edgings $10-40.

Plate 157: 'Russian' collar $50-80.

Plates 158, 163: Brussels lappets, per pair $500-700 for late 18th century - $1800-2500 for early 18th century (the price differential between early and late 18th century applies to all lappets; all single lappets cost less than half the price of a pair) edgings

Plates 162, 173a: Brussels $20-80 (b and c would be more expensive than a or d)

Plate 164: Brussels veil (drochel ground) $400-700.

Plate 166: Brussels veil (machine net ground) $300-500.

Plates 167, 168: Brussels 19th century edgings $16-30.

Plate 169, 176: Brussels flounces $45-130.

Plate 172: Brussels fan $450-600.

Plates 167, 173, 178: Brussels collars, tie and jabot $30-90.

Plate 177: Brussels bertha $70-90.

Plate 184: Honiton lappets $400-2000; flounce $60-100.

Plates 185, 187: Honiton edgings $20-60.

Plate 188: Honiton stole $240-300.

Plate 190: Honiton bertha of exceptional quality $200-300.

Plates 191, 192: Honiton collars, cuffs, mittens, tie, modesty $25-100.

Plates 195-197: Flemish edgings and flounces $40-180 (mid-17th century laces are particularly difficult to find).

Plate 198: Valenciennes/ Binche lappets $500-2500.

Plates 201, 204a-e: Valenciennes/ Binche 18th century edgings $40-80.

Plates 204e-205, 209: Valenciennes/ Binche later edgings $4-20.

Plate 208: Valenciennes/ Binche flounce $35-50.

Plate 210: Mechlin cap back $200-300.

Plate 213: Mechlin lappets $900-1500.

Plates 214-219: Mechlin edgings $12-60 (one would expect the edgings in **Plate** 218, which have the simplest designs, to be cheapest).

Plate 220: Point de Paris lappets $400-600; edgings and insertions $10-30.

Plate 224: Point de Paris mat $15-40.

Plate 225: Lille apron $500-1000.

Plates 228, 230, 238, 240: Lille and Buckinghamshire point edgings $50-100; bonnet veil $220-350.

Plate 231: Lille handkerchief $30-50.

Plate 233: Buckinghamshire point shawl collar $200-280.

Plate 237: Buckinghamshire point babies' bonnets $80-160.

Plate 239: Buckinghamshire point babies' bonnets $60-90.

Plate 241: Buckinghamshire point fall cap and bertha, each $100-180 (large items with interesting designs, such as the veil, apron and collars are exceptional).

Plates 242, 244: Blonde fichu and stole, each $130-180.

Plate 246: Blonde black shawls each $400-700; edgings $10-20.

Plates 247, 252: Chantilly bonnet veils each $150-250.

Plate 251: Blonde Chantilly fall cap $120-180.

Plate 253: Chantilly scarf $90-150.

Plate 254: Chantilly white bertha $140-200.

Plates 257, 260: Maltese collar, plastron, and fascinator $40-150.

Plate 259: Maltese black veil and scarf $40-75.

Plates 261, 264: Le Puy capes $70-180.

Plates 263, 265: Le Puy flounces $6-25.

Plate 267: East Midlands (Beds.) guipure collar $200-300 (this is of exceptional quality).

Plates 269, 270: East Midlands (Beds.) edgings $4-12.

Plate 270: East Midlands (Beds.) small collar and cuffs $20-30.

Glossary

The meanings of many technical terms have changed over the centuries and, even now, mean different things to different people. This glossary therefore gives the meanings which I attribute to technical terms appearing in this book in order to avoid confusion.

Further technical terms are explained in the introductory chapters on bobbin and needle laces, in the chapters on alternative lace-making techniques, or where they first occur in the text. This is particularly true of items of dress. All such explanations may be found through the index.

Applied/appliqué work Work in which motifs are attached, usually by sewing, to a base fabric such as a net to form a design.

Bar or Bride A cord worked with a needle or bobbins to connect adjacent edges of pattern motifs together.

Brode French name for the raised outline of a needlepoint lace, also sometimes called the 'cordonnet.'

Buttonhole stitch This is the basic stitch in needlepoint laces and comprises a single thread formed into a loop and twisted once on itself. Many variations are also used.

Buttonholed bar/bride A bar or bride covered with buttonhole stitches, often worked so close together that they touch.

Cloth stitch A stitch used in bobbin lace to form areas resembling woven material, or cloth. Also called whole stitch.

Clothwork An area resembling woven material. This term should strictly be reserved for bobbin laces where the clothwork is made by cloth stitch but it is also used for densely worked pattern areas in needlepoints.

Cordonnet Foundation threads within a needlepoint lace but also used for the raised outline on the right side of a needle lace. Also used for the outline of some bobbin laces.

Couching A technique in which a thread, or group of threads, is sewn on to a surface by a different thread.

Drawn-thread work An embroidery technique on a woven fabric in which the embroidery threads are used to draw the fabric threads apart and so create decorative openwork patterns of holes and stitching. Also known as pulled work but in this book I have used the term 'pulled work' for a different technique.

Filling (Filling stitch) A fancy stitch usually employed to fill a small area within a pattern to create a decorative effect. There is an enormous variety of such stitches. Also known by the French terms 'mode' and 'à jours'.

Footing A narrow tape provided along that edge of a lace which is to be attached to a garment or other article to take the strain of the sewing. It is sometimes worked integrally with the lace but is often sewn on so that it can be replaced when damaged.

Footside That edge of a lace intended to be attached to a garment or other article.

Gimp A bobbin-lace thread which is thicker than the majority of threads in a lace. This is an East Midlands term but is used throughout this book for similar threads.

Ground The linking part of a lace which connects the pattern motifs. It consists of a series of bars in a guipure lace, a network of fine meshes, or a machine-made net.

Guipure Any lace in which the pattern motifs are close together and linked either where they touch or by bars connecting adjacent edges and in which relatively large openings are left. Tape and geometric laces where connecting bars form part of the pattern are included.

Half stitch A bobbin-lace stitch used *inter alia* to create areas of grille-like structure. See **Plate** 4.

Headside The free edge of a lace opposite the footside.

Insertion A strip of lace with a footside along both edges which can be sewn between two lengths of fabric to form a decorative seam.

à Jours See Filling.

Leadwork A decorative bobbin-lace stitch in which one thread is woven back and forth between three others, usually forming a square or rectangular spot. This is the usual Honiton name for a stitch more commonly called a 'tally' or 'point d'esprit' in East Midlands laces. Other names include 'leaf' and 'wheatear' but I prefer to use these for spots with pointed ends.

Mode See Filling.

Needleweaving An embroidery technique in which a thread is darned back and forth through two or more other threads to create a woven structure. A similar effect can be created in bobbin laces.

Overcasting An embroidery technique in which a sewing thread is taken over and under a thread, or group of threads, repeatedly in a helix to strengthen the thread or bind threads together. Also known as 'whipping' or 'oversewing.'

Picot A decorative point or loop often used to decorate raised work, edges or bars. Also called 'purl' or 'pearl.'

Picoted bar/bride A bar, or bride, decorated with picots.

Point d'esprit See Leadwork.

Point de racroc A general name for a bobbin stitch used to join two panels of bobbin lace together invisibly. The stitch varies according to the type of lace being joined.

Pricking Term used for a lace pattern on which the work is carried out.

Pulled-thread work An embroidery technique on a woven fabric in which some threads are pulled out of the fabric to leave open areas crossed by other threads which are drawn together, strengthened and deco-rated by embroidery threads. Also known as drawn-thread work but in this book I have used the term drawn-thread work for an alternative technique.

Purl See 'picot.'

Purl bar The Devon name for a bar or bride decorated with picots.

Raised work Three-dimensional detail on the right side of a lace.

Sewing A stitch used to join a pair of bobbin-lace threads to an edge. One thread of the pair is pulled through the edge with a pin or hook to form a loop then the bobbin carrying the other thread is passed through the loop to link the two threads to the edge.

Tally See Leadwork.

Wheatear See Leadwork.

Whole stitch See Cloth stitch.

List of The Portraits and Fashion Plates

Index